THE FRAGRANT GARDEN

The Fragrant Garden

KAY N. SANECKI

Line drawings by Rosemary Wise

B.T. Batsford Ltd London

Horticultural Adviser: John Sales

First published 1981

ISBN 0 7134 2373 0

Typeset in Compugraphic Trump Medieval by
Graphicraft Typesetters, H. K.
Printed in Great Britain by Robert MacLehose & Co. Ltd
Renfrew, Scotland.

for the publishers, B.T. Batsford Ltd
4 Fitzhardinge Street, London W1H 0AH

Contents

Acknowledgements

THE BOOK in your hand would not have materialized without help from numerous sources. My gardening friends have 'sniffed' at and investigated fragrances, and tried to describe them for me, almost always registering recall of some other plant material. I have found that most contemporary available information falls into one of two categories; it is either a repetition of work of about 1900–1920, or contradicts it completely! Perhaps fragrance represents all things to all people.

I have tried to strike some intermediate note, adding my personal observations, and so the catalogue includes some less commonly cultivated plants as suggestions, and the lists yet further plants. If your favourite plant has been omitted, I can only apologize; it has not been possible to produce a definitive account.

My warm thanks are due to Rosemary Wise for enhancing the work with her delightful line illustrations and to Noël J. Prockter, for reading the Catalogue of Plants in manuscript and for several helpful suggestions and corrections. He gave so freely of his knowledge of fragrant plants. His help was most encouraging. For answering my questions at various stages, thanks to Graham S. Thomas and John Sales, and a special thankyou to Ken Lemmon. My gardening experience has been only south of Birmingham, although I know numerous gardens in the North. Ken Lemmon has advised me in the compilation of the list of fragrant plants hardy in the north of the country. I must express my appreciation of the work Elizabeth Walker, of Meadow Herbs, has done on *pot pourri* and its history, and my thanks go to her for allowing me to use her ideas freely. The time I spent in her sweet-smelling establishment stimulated my researches enormously. The Southern and Western Regional Association for the Blind readily answered my questions about gardens for the blind and disabled. I am grateful to Ruth Duthie and to Daphne Mitchell who typed the bulk of the manuscript with immense care and interest. Finally, a word of thanks to the Editors, for presenting the work.

Beyond that I can only acknowledge the encouragement I had in early childhood to derive sheer pleasure from plants, a pleasure which I only hope is conveyed, in some measure, among the ensuing pages.

Kay N. Sanecki
Dorset 1981

'. . . I know that if odour were visible, as color is,
I'd see the summer garden in rainbow clouds.'

Robert Bridges
Testament of Beauty

CHAPTER ONE

Fragrance and the Plant

'FRAGRANCE IS the voice of inanimate things' wrote Mary Webb, and because there is no scale of measurement, or vocabulary of precise description, each of us has a unique set of values in appreciating the scent of a plant. We can admit, only, that the emotions are stirred to heights of enjoyment, or cruel rejection, by the power a scent can have in searching us out. Between two breaths, it can catch us unaware and transport us to some other moment in time. It stimulates disused mental circuits to recall forgotten episodes, old loves, past states of mind, totally without warning.

Few people are anosmic, that is lacking in a sense of smell; yet comparatively few have educated themselves to recognize, and appreciate, any but the predominant perfumes of the garden. When Thomas Hill (writing under the pseudonym Dydymus Mountain) composed his dedicatory address in *The Gardener's Labyrinth* (1577) to his patron, William Cecil, Lord Burghley, the Lord High Treasurer of England, he wished '. . . that hee [God] would vouchsafe to graunte unto you the sweetes savour of his chiefe fragrante floures, that is his comfort to cleave faste to you, his mercy to keep you and his grace to guyde you nowe and evermore.'

Nothing is permanent in scent; the first impression fades to an appreciation of the more lingering overtones, or the olfactory nerves are stunned. This numbing effect happens at the first investigation of the violet's perfume, and almost immediately the flowers appear to be scentless. In fact the olfactory nerves have been virtually anaesthetized, or extremely fatigued, by the perfume. Perfumers have experimented for generations to stabilize a scent, and fixatives are still employed for this purpose. Science, ever accelerating, now claims that by atomic bombardment, a floral scent can be enhanced and preserved.

Discrimination is developed by practice in the appreciation of plant scent, just as a wine-taster may distinguish nuances of bouquet in a selection of wines. Once we begin to investigate plant scents, formerly imperceptible differences become apparent, and signal recognition and the enjoyment of plant material are enhanced. The olfactory system is so closely allied to that of taste where qualities of sweet, sour, bitter and salt can be distinguished, that a considerable amount of 'smelling' is done by the palate. Although the olfactory organs are lodged in two small areas of mucus membrane in the upper part of the nose, a flower fragrance can be registered by breathing in through the mouth, almost as if the flavour of the scent can be sensed.

It seems to be claimed generally that dark-haired people have a more sensitive sense of smell than the fair haired, and that the total albino is anosmic. But it is the emotional reaction to scent that we recognize in others and so have no confirmation that they are experiencing the same sensation or intensity of interpretation as we are ourselves. The non-smoker obviously has a heightened sensitivity to various scents; nicotine dulls the palate and olfactory system, and during the past 10–15 years as cigarette smoking has declined, it is remarkable that there has been an increase in interest in aromatic and fragrant plants.

Paeonia

Scent or fragrance is all things to all people, and a curious vocabulary has evolved for the description of it. One plant is often described as being scented of another: for example the catkins of *Salix triandra* are described as almond-scented and so is the foliage of *Filipendula ulmaria*; *Clematis vitalba* and *Lupinus arboreus* as vanilla-scented; *Iris reticulata* and *Acacia dealbata* as violet-scented; *Cytisus battandieri* as pineapple-scented. This does little but refer us to the almond, the vanilla, violet or pineapple . . . and how can we describe their aromas? We describe a scent as fulsome, ambrosial, pungent, heady, overpowering, smoky, refreshing, all of which are personal assessments of one fragrance in relation to others.

This is why one person will enjoy a fragrance and others almost dislike it, or one person find a plant to be richly scented and another consider it to devoid of any scent. Apparently, some people cannot discern any scent at all in freesias, while others consider them to be among the most strongly scented of plants. Try as I will, my personal 'flat spots' – plants in which I find no perfume – are alstroemerias and paeonies. During the preparation of material for this book, I have discussed plant fragrance with many people and most claim to find paeonies sweetly but faintly fragrant of a rose-like perfume. I admit only to finding the freshness of a sweet clean baby in the paeony flower, and a distinct rankness in stem and leaf. *Paeonia mlokosewitschii*, admittedly, is a supreme example of a plant whose appearance suggests the scent. For me, the heart of its citron-yellow flower resembles lemonade crystals and that scent can be detected also. It has been used by plant hybridizers to impart scent, and during the 19th century French breeders produced a range of scented paeonies, which came to be known as 'Paeony Roses', for the fragrance was reminscent of roses. Gertrude Jekyll did not name the varieties she planted in the scented garden at Barrington Court (see page 52) but as everything else in the garden was scented, her paeonies were obviously selected for this quality. Cultivars today are listed as scented, but alas, I cannot smell them: 'Edith Cavell', richly scented; 'Kelway's Glorious', 'scent of a rose'; 'Kelway's Rosemary', 'spicy perfume of the rosemary'; 'Sarah Bernhardt', 'powerfully scented'.

OPPOSITE
Honeysuckle growing over the gate to a cottage garden

Conversely there are flowers that one feels ought to be fragrant, flowers that look richly attractive, and yet upon inspection are quite scentless. The fuchsias and saintpaulias remain odourless.

Unpleasant scent

Linnaeus, working in the 18th century, grouped the plant odours into seven classes, only three of which were pleasant – aromatic, fragrant, ambrosial, which suggests that either the looked-for qualities in scent have changed, which seems unlikely, or greater attention was paid to the classification of the unpleasant plant odours. Most familiar are the flowers of the hawthorn (some of which have distinctly fishy overtones), the sorbus, cotoneaster, pyracantha, *Castanea sativa*, elder (to some people), *Viburnum opulus* with its distinct smell of perspiration, and *Arum maculatum*, which, if touched, contaminates the skin for hours and cannot be removed by washing. This aminoid scent group is characterized by the presence of trimethylamine and propylamine, present in the early stages of putrefaction, and for this reason attractive to dung and other flies. The heavy and slightly stale odours of this group become even more pronounced in the foetid odour of *Stapelia variegata*, dubbed Carrion Plant or Carrion Flower, and well named for its offensiveness. The constituent indol is responsible for the dreadful smell, to which bluebottles respond by the dozen. *Stapelia hirsuta* takes its unpleasantness even further; called the Hairy Toad plant, it seems to mimic rotting flesh, not only in odour, but in appearance also. Foetid smells are associated with dingy appearance and such plants are frequently blotched with purple. *Amorphophallus* species are said to resemble carrion-garlic-skunk in odour and some of the dark fritillarias are also pretty evil-smelling. *Fritillaria imperialis* carries this unpleasantness, described as 'foxy', especially in its bulb.

Some plants bear their warning labels in their names. *Helleborus foetidus*, *Iris foetidissima*, and *Viburnum foetidum* are examples, but they often beg a place in the garden for some other attribute, such as the glossy foliage and green flowers of the Stinking Hellebore, the tangerine beads of the tricorn seedhead of the Stinking Iris or Gladwin, and the luscious red autumn fruits of the viburnum.

Sweetness in a name

Far more frequently, the attractive aroma or pungency of foliage, or intense fragrance of flower, is revealed in the plant's name. *Osmanthus suavis*, the sweetly scented one; *Osmanthus fragrans*, the fragrant one; *Aloysia citriodora*, lemon-scented; *Centaurea moschata*, musk-scented; *Eleagnus pungens*, pungent; *Lonicera fragrantissima*, most fragrant; *Viburnum odoratissimum*, sweetest scented; *Laurelia aromatica*, aromatic and *Myrrhis odorata*, sweet-scented.

Not infrequently, within a range of associated scents it is possible to have varying degrees from distinctly unpleasant to truly delightful. Scent, as we shall see, emanates from the essential oils of a plant. Within a Natural Order the composition of these oils often bears some similarity; the ingredients are constant, but the ratios and combinations vary. Thus at one extreme with Rosaceae, there are the horrid smells of the sorbus and cotoneaster, through various permutations to the rich fruitiness of some roses at the other extreme.

It seems indisputable that flower scent, at least, acts to summon insects to their banquets, where, in return, they fertilize the flower. Ghostly calls often must ring, beyond our range of scent, as the call of a bat exceeds our hearing. This most refined of sense impressions, for human beings, may be but a section of the true range of scents, and only part of nature's largesse. Nature, it is said, spreads her sweets for the poor; perhaps the rose-scented sedum roots are for those that have no attar of roses! Further, fragrance is never the personal property of the gardener, for it is carried across to the neighbouring gardens, into the passing street, and whenever the breeze runs by we know where he has been!

Essential oils

The scent or aroma of all flowers and most leaves is due to an attar or essential oil, the former word usually relating to flower scent. The term 'essential oil' is rather misleading; far from being essential, the oil is a biproduct of the plant, and to consider it as a volatile oil would be more accurate.

Some plants seem totally inodorous until they are crushed by the hand, to rupture the containing cells and release the contents. Increased temperatures also will stimulate the escape of oils, so that on a warm day or in a warm room plant scent is usually better detected. The volatile oil liberated from the glands of *Dictamnus albus* on a sunny day can be demonstrated quite conclusively by igniting it. Flames will flutter about the plant – hence its name, Burning Bush.

Several theories exist and avenues of research are followed, but despite advanced understanding of plant physiology, the role of essential oils remains a minor mystery. Obviously, the scent of flowers bears a close relationship to pollination, attracting those insects for which the floral mechanism is adapted for fertilization. But the necessity for the aroma of leaves is less obvious. It has been suggested that it acts as a deterrent to browsing animals and as a protection against pests. But this raises the interesting point as to why the most vulnerable young fresh growth contains the least amount of essential oils – and the slugs love *Monarda didyma* and some mints! Certainly, such foliage is toxic to disease-causing bacteria and many oils act as an antiseptic. Common examples are oil of wintergreen from *Gaultheria procumbens* and a substance called thymol extracted from the oils of thyme, marjoram and mint.

The principal chemical compounds that combine to form essential oils all contain carbon and hydrogen: most contain oxygen, very few nitrogen and some of the offensive-smelling ones some sulphur. The rank smell of many crucifers is due to the presence of sulphur. The commonest compounds, are esters, formed by the combination of acids with alcohols, and the alcohols often provide the 'scent' which we recognize; eucalyptol, for example, is camphorous, and geraniol rose-scented. Also common are the terpenes, containing hydrogen and carbon and which are in themselves odourless, but there are innumerable permutations which lead us into the realms of organic chemistry. Even if we did understand the various formulae, our sense of smell would always respond in the same way. It seems to be an accepted fact that as human beings age this sense fades. The impact of perfumes perhaps remains the same, but their apparent intensity is reduced.

One major advantage for the botanist, now that the composition of essential oils can be analysed, has been the certainty with which related species can be identified. Mentha species, for example have been clarified, especially the hybrids.

If scent is dependent upon the composition of the essential oil, it is tempting to ask why within a genus of plants it can behave differently. Why, for instance is the air redolent around some species of lonicera, and yet there are almost scentless flowers in others? Why are some rhododendrons aromatic of leaf and the majority not? Why are a few ceanothus scented? Among the hypericums, there are the scentless species, such as *Hypericum calycinum*, Rose of Sharon, the distinctly appalling *H. hircinum*, dubbed Goat-smelling St John's Wort, and *H. androsaemum*, known as Sweet Amber, with its resinous scent. Sometimes a genus that is regarded as being characteristically scentless will produce an odd species that carries perfume, as *Hosta plantaginea* and both its forms *grandiflora* and 'Royal Standard'. Scent is a hereditary factor, so if one or both parents carry the gene for scent, the progeny may well do so; but it is impossible to have a hybrid carrying scent from two scentless parent plants.

Scent and cultivation

Why is scent lost, so often, in cultivation? As for example in the common bluebell, *Endymion non-scriptus*; its scent comes balsamic in spring in a sunlit wood. Gerarde called it 'a strong sweet smell, somewhat stuffing the head'. But in the cultivated forms, sunshine or no, the scent is lacking. Plant breeders have concentrated upon the production of size and colour, remontant qualities, and disease resistance, and the forgotten genes for fragrance have gone astray. Modern varieties of, say, sweet peas can be virtually scentless.

It may be safe to say that as colour is bred into a flower, scent is often lost. A collection of 17th-century plants, most of them scented and aromatic, can be seen in the Queen's Garden, Royal Botanic Garden, Kew, where the lack of bold colour is noticeable, suggesting almost that in modern plants colour has been substituted for scent. *Clematis montana* in the popular *rubens* lacks fragrance, but the form itself, and the white-flowered 'Alexander' and *wilsonii* are fragrant. Of the extensive array of large-flowered clematis only the white-flowered 'Duchess of Edinburgh' carries any degree of perfume. Research has proved that the order of incidence of strength of perfume in flowers related to their colour is: white, blush white, pale pink, mauve pink, pale yellow, yellow, purple, blue, orange, brown, red. (Here is one of the fields in which published work differs widely – other lists put red after pink.)

Roses presumably are mainly included in the pinks, and of the red flowers with fragrance many are from the warmer regions of the world. The possible well-known exception is *Monarda didyma*, and the scent is faint. The richly honey-scented *Embothrium coccineum* is a rare treasure indeed. The almost honeysuckle-like fragrance fills conservatories where it is cultivated, but as an eye-catcher, set against the white boles of eucalypts at the head of the Gully Garden at Mapperton, Dorset, it is a masterpiece in planting. On a warm damp early June day, the scent from this particular 'fire bush' is memorable.

It follows, therefore, that a white garden – a popular feature of modern garden design – can virtually be a scented garden, so wide is the selection of plants.

Some scented plants to grow in a white garden

Alyssum maritimum
Anthemis nobilis
Artemisia 'Lambrook Silver'
Buddleia auriculata
Buddleia davidii alba
Choisya ternata
Clematis flammula
Clematis 'Duchess of Edinburgh'
Clethra alnifolia
Convallaria majalis
Deutzia gracilis
Deutzia × *maliflora* 'Avalanche'
Dianthus 'Mrs Sinkins'
'Her Majesty'
Dictamnus albus
Eucryphia × *nymansensis* 'Nymansay'
Fragaria vesca
Fraxinus ornus
Galtonia candicans
Helichrysum serotinum
Hosta plantaginea grandiflora
Hesperis matronalis alba
Jasminum officinalis
Lilium candidum
Lonicera japonica 'Halliana'
Magnolia spp
Malva moschata alba
Myrtus communis
Narcissus poeticus
Olearia avicenniifolia 'White Confusion'
Olearia ilicifolia
Olearia macrodonta
Osmanthus delavayi
Osmaronia cerasiformis
Pieris floribunda
Philadelphus coronarius
Philadelphus incanus
Phlox paniculata 'Mai Ruys'
'White Admiral'
Populus × *candicans* 'Aurora'
Prunus × *yedoensis* 'Ivensii'
Pterostyrax hispida
Rhododendron 'Angelo'
Rhododendron auriculatum
Rhododendron canescens (white form)
Rhododendron 'Midsummer Snow'
Rhododendron 'Polar Bear'
Rhododendron 'Solent Swan'
Rosa banksiae alba-plena
'Blanche Moreau' (Moss)
'Bobbie James' (Wich)
filipes 'Kiftsgate' (Cl)
'Iceberg' (Flori)
laevigata (Cl)
'La Perle' (Ramb)
longicuspis (Cl)
'Shailer's White' (Moss)
Rubus deliciosus
Rubus 'Tridel'
Skimmia japonica 'Fragrans'
Smilacina racemosa
Syringa 'Monique Lemoine'
Syringa 'Vestale'
Thymus nitidus albus
Thymus serpyllum albus
Trachelospermum jasminoides
Yucca spp

Scent and bees

There are comparatively few fragrant blue-purple flowers, and it is always a happy discovery to find one. Muscari, scilla, nepeta and viola spring to mind, but other blue-flowered plants for the fragrant collection fall into the category of aromatic foliage: hyssop, caryopteris, and salvia.

Oddly enough many of the blue flowers are good bee plants; perhaps scent is less important to bees than to most other flower-visiting insects.

Simple archway pergola covered with a Clematis montana

Curiously though, they can impregnate honey with flower perfume. Honey from holly flowers is quite strongly perfumed, although the nectar is secreted deeply at the base of the petals and the scent of the flower is difficult to detect. Lavender honey is white and perfumed, although the flowers themselves are scentless (the fragrance lies in the scent glands of the calyx). Melilot produces a perfumed white honey too, and the flower is often described as 'honey-scented'. Honey from lime flowers is greenish, thick and distinctly perfumed.

Variation in fragrance

Several factors, in addition to pigment, influence both fragrance of flower and aroma of foliage. Obviously, the period of the year, or flowering-period over-rules all other factors for fragrant flowers, and often the aromatic foliage of plants with scentless flowers is at its best at the point at which the flowers just attain maturity – or, as the herbalists would say, 'just before maturity'. At this point in the plant's cycle, essential oils are of superior quality, strength and effectiveness. Leaves of the mint family, commonly used in the making of mint sauce, are more refined in flavour prior to flowering, and at their strongest as the flower spikes begin to open. Autumn mint leaves, other than the new shoots, are far more stale in scent.

Are there some plants that are scented only at a particular time of year? For me *Polygonatum campanulatum* is totally scentless from the moment it begins to flower in late June or early July and remains so until the days shorten in late August or early September. Then, it takes on a rich almond-vanilla fragrance, which lasts until the first frost turns the flowers slimy. Of some plants, it is the young growth that is scented. Balsam poplar is an obvious example. Of others, the dying leaves emit a sweetness they have not offered before, like those of the strawberry, especially the Wood Strawberry, and *Cercidiphyllum japonicum*, with its toffee-like smell. Other plants, such as viburnums, lose their scent entirely when cut.

Atmospheric quality has some relevance to the intensity of fragrant odours. During hot dry periods much flower fragrance is lost, but the aroma of foliage is enhanced, especially when it is crushed. This is because the volatization of the essential oils is increased. Gardeners therefore create sheltered corners for their aromatic and fragrant plants, utilizing reflected heat from walls and paving to lift temperature. A fine spray washed over plants for a few minutes during dull warm weather is often sufficient to release scent – a factor most noticeable after the damping-down operation in a greenhouse. After a shower of rain, flower fragrance resumes a dominance and foliage scents recede. Wallflowers after rain become almost over-powering as does the scent of the young growth of the sweetbrier. A saturated atmosphere seems to hold more perfume. Could there be some trigger mechanism in the plant's metabolism, so that, refreshed after rain, it begins to advertise its presence again? Similar mechanisms must play a part in those plants that increase their perfume after being cut. *Jasminum nudiflorum*, *Galtonia candicans*, and tulips, come to mind. Some flowers, fading for need of water, both out of doors and when cut, will strengthen their scent, as a cry for help. Again, some are enhanced by drying, such as *Asperula odorata*, *Acanthus mollis* and a few grasses, especially Sweet Vernal Grass, *Anthoxanthum odoratum*, strongly impregnated with coumarin which gives the scent to new-mown hay.

Undoubtedly there is an arc of fragrance, resembling a spectrum for habitually several plants change their perfume along the way. They perhaps start life smelling of violets, and change to something richer nearer to banana, or assume vanilla-like overtones – all controlled by the subtle change in chemical composition of the essential oils. Others appear to be fragrant at certain times of day, the evening being the richest period. Dames Violet, *Hesperis matronalis*, can pervade the air over a considerable range with its sweet scent in the evening, but during the day, it is almost undetectable even upon close inspection. Popularly the Evening Primrose and tobacco plants are scented only in the evening, but present-day cultivars have, to a considerable extent, overcome this defect simply because the flowers can now be persuaded to remain open during higher light intensity. Bonus perfume follows.

Classification of plant fragrance

Scent, therefore, is the oxidization of the essential oils of a plant, and the composition of it varies according to the component ingredients of the oil, rendering one perfume different from another. Of these components, the most frequent are esters, resulting from the combination of acid with an alcohol. They seldom occur singly, but almost invariably in closely related groups, and are most prevalent in the more sweetly scented plants. Esters, however, are absent in those flowers that are rose- or violet-scented. Alcohols predominate in the rose group. The essential oil geraniol is here combined with fruity-scented substances, honey-scented substances or even spicy-scented substances, together with some intermediate indeterminate components. A range of fragrances, immediately recognizable as 'rose' is produced, but described variously as raspberry-like, lemony, tea-scented, tarry or spicy. The tarry overtones are recognized most readily in the Hybrid Tea scent, the fruity scent in the sweetbriers, and the honey scent is best identified in the Hybrid Musk roses.

Conversely, some pelargonium leaves, and the roots of *Sedum rhodiola*, are described as rose-scented, simply because geraniol is the dominant constituent of the essential oil. The Rose-leaved Perlargonium when in leaf bud smells more of lemon, changing only to rose tones on opening; the scent matures as does the leaf. A close relationship exists between lemon freshness and rose sweetness, the former produced by the presence of citral which is the first product of geraniol as it oxidizes. The two scents are therefore often found together in a range of combinations, giving very subtle variations of virtually the same perfume. Few flower scents, then, are really built up around one tone, but can better be likened to a musical chord. Just like a musical chord, the tone can seem to vary, or may be interpreted differently by several listeners, so the overall perfume varies from one moment to the next and from one person's interpretation to that of another. Some dominant theme will assert its character, or linger to reduce the sensation of another tone, altering the impact.

A mixture of scent

The *pot pourri*-maker experiments with a whole range of plant perfumes, all of them emanating from essential oils, exploiting the dominant tones, blending, waiting to test the result. There are scents which the perfumer and *pot pourri*-maker term 'accords'; they are, as the word suggests, compatible and lend enhancement to each other by their association. It is interesting to note that frequently such accords are from the closely related essential oil groups, so that often a basic rose-scent plant will be combined with a basic lemon one, or a basic clove scent with a basic camphorous one. Further, two spicy pungent aromatics can be persuaded together to mingle happily, when combined by rose and the closely related lemon, or camphor and the close clove.

Elizabeth Walker of Meadow Herbs, explains this mysterious variation in perfumes, relating to *pot pourri* in her book *Pot Pourri* (1978). Using the metaphor of the musical chord again, she classifies some scents as top notes, some as bass notes, and other as heart notes. Top notes are such plants as bergamot, coriander, fennel, lavender, lemon, lime, marjoram, orange and tangerine. Curiously, these are the very scents that are referred to as 'overtones' in descriptions of flower scent because these are the ones which evaporate quickly. The bass notes which she lists are all perfume fixatives, the rich and the subtle, only coming into their own when combined with other scents – calamus, cinnamon, clary, orris, patchouli, sandalwood, Tonquin bean, vanilla and vetiver. Such fixatives preserve a perfume of lasting quality, or hold it, as the sustaining-pedal of the piano can hold the chord.

Heart notes – Elizabeth Walker's admirable term – are those that form the melody without dominating. These are the deep scents which persist and are not lost at the first sniff: basil, clove, geranium, honeysuckle, pine, rose, rosemary, tansy, thyme, verbena and wallflower.

Thus by explaining the way in which the product *pot pourri* can be manipulated using the essential oils themselves, it can be shown how the composition of the perfume of a flower can be so closely allied to that of another or even vary from time to time.

Lavendula angustifolia

Leaf scent

Invariably, the essential oils of leaves are simpler than those of a flower, and may even be formed of a single active substance, often with a number of scentless terpenes. Where the scent of the leaf resembles that of the flower, the latter is normally the sweeter or 'more flowery'. It is possible to have fragrant foliage on a plant with scentless flowers. Further, the meadow-sweet, *Filipendula ulmaria*, has differing fragrances in flower and leaf.

Leaf scents are more generally described as aromatic or pungent, because some of the rougher-smelling components are not contained in the flowers and 'flowery' scents. For example the refreshing crisp scent of pine is that of borneol acetate, not found in flower essential oils, and camphor and eucalyptus are absent from flower essential oils.

Leaf scent groups

Various combinations of these two oils, camphor and eucalyptol, are commonly present, sometimes one predominating, sometimes the other. They can be detected by handling the foliage of such plants as: *Santolina virens*, the camphor plant (*Balsamita vulgaris*), catmint (*Nepeta* spp), Carolina Allspice (*Calycanthus floridus*), and bay (*Laurus nobilis*).

Resulting from these closely and subtly combined essential oils of foliage much conjecture as to composition seems to have been inaccurate in the past. The object here is not to analyse the components of each leaf scent, but to identify some general groups of related aromas. Many of these secret treasures of the plants are still obscure for the general reader.

Camphor and eucalytus

These scents are detectable in the foliage of sage, chamomile, tansy, thyme, artemisias, *Perovskia atriplicifolia*, and lavender – where they are sweetened by geraniol; in rosemary – where they are spiced; and in the eucalypts themselves where they vary in intensity and sweetness. In *Cedronella triphylla*, the scent groups are bridged, as it combines with lemon.

Lemon

Crisply lemon scent is detectable in *Aloysia citriodora*, *Thymus citriodora*, *Pelargonium crispum*, *P. citriodorum* and *Melissa officinalis*.

Pine

The resinous fresh scent of pine, in addition to being present in many of the *Pinus* species, is commonly found in *Pelargonium fragrans*.

Fruit

Between the lemon and the fruit group, the foliage of *Acorus calamus* needs to be included, enhanced on drying to become more fruity. The foliage of *Juniperus communis* and *Pelargonium odoratissimum* is scented of apple, as is that of *Rosa rubiginosa: Thymus azoricus* resembles tangerine, *Salvia rutilans* pineapple. The thuyas are fruity, far less resinous than, say, the pines.

Flower

Flowery scents are rare in foliage, but *Hebe cupressoides* is sweetly reminiscent of violets, and several pelargoniums of rose. *Pelargonium graveolens* is called the Rose-scented Geranium; it is the parent of many rose-scented varieties and has even been used in the distillation of perfumes for its nearness to the flower scent.

Fragrant

By 'fragrance' in describing foliage, a muskiness is usually indicated, suggesting something more aromatic than 'flowery'. Such fragrance is evident in *Olearia* spp, especially *moschata*, *Monarda didyma*, and *Salvia sclarea*.

Mint
Perhaps it is debatable whether mint aroma is nearer to camphorous ones than to aromatic ones, but apart from the *Mentha* spp themselves, which vary quite dramatically, some pelargoniums are distinctly minty. *Pelargonium tomentosum* in particular is strongly mint-like.

Aromatic
By far the greater number of scented foliage plants fall into this group, ranging from *Chrysanthemum* spp, and the nutmeg-like *Pelargonium fragrans*, to the sweet balsamic scent of *Populus* × *candicans* and *P. balsamifera*. Hyssop, myrtle, marjoram, and *Chimonanthus fragrans* may all be variously described as aromatic, and yet the incense-like scent of *Humea elegans* and the curry-like aroma of *Helichrysum serotinum* belongs here also.

Hysoppus officinalis

Flower scent

The chemical composition of the essential oils of flowers is highly complex, and no wholly satisfactory classification of fragrance has ever been produced. It is amusing to build up some sort of classification in a subjective approach. Whereas the number of odorous substances, although extensive, is limited, the same scent wherever it occurs is due to the presence of given components. There may be subtle nuances distinguishing one fragrance from another, which identify individual plants. Some general classification along the following lines appears to be universally accepted.

The aminoid group
The general quality of scent is stale and sickly-sweet, sometimes even distinctly fishy, and for this reason alone, some flowers which ought to be included are widely considered to be odorous and even offensive. Examples are pyracantha, sorbus, cotoneaster, some *Pyrus* spp, sweet chestnut and some spiraeas. Elderflowers for many people fall into this nauseous category but, happily, upon distilling they assume the delicacy of muscat, and so are used extensively in home-winemaking to produce elderflower champagne.

Musk and honey group
A similar fishy or animal scent often accompanies the sweet musky odour, especially in full-blown flowers of this group. Sweet Sultan and *Buddleia alternifolia* are sweetly musky but fade to emit a rather more 'smelly' overtone. Edging towards a lighter honey scent are flowers such as *Olearia macrodonta*, *Buddleia* species in general, dipeltas, *Erica arborea*, weigelas, and the evening-scented *Abronia umbellata*.

Fruit group
For some people, flowers at the lower end of this group of scents remain fur-like or animal in their associations, and yet to others, the same plants can be distinctly pleasant. The flower of the gorse spans this particular bridge, 'coconutty' and fruity to some people and 'clean dog's bed' to others. The

odour that dog hair causes in a domestic vacuum cleaner is reminiscent of gorse on the breeze to some people – but 'something to be dealt with' to others!

Further up the scale of this group are the apricot scent of agrimony, now rescued from the wild and brought into the herb gardens, the pineapple scent of *Cytisus battandieri*, and the orange-blossom scent of the *Philadephus* species; among the roses, the raspberry scent of 'Madame Isaac Pereire' and 'Golden Fleece', and the rich fruitiness of 'Mme Alfred Carrière'. Rose scent frequently nudges towards lemon, as in 'Leverkusen'. To describe a scent as 'pineapple' or 'apricot' is merely a recognition of the fact that the component substances are those of the essences of the particular individual fruits.

Lemon group

Elusive in many flowers, lemon is a scent more easily detected in foliage than in flower, primarily because it is very closely associated with that of the rose, and its freshness is snatched away at the first investigation, the fuller rose scent persisting. But the flowers of the water lily (*Nymphaea odorata*) and some magnolias, notably *M. wilsonii*, suggest lemon. Sharpening up, lemonade crystals, clean and cheap, seem to emanate from the yellow paeony *Paeonia mlokosewitschii*.

The freshness of violets falls within the same group, although there may be no hint of lemon. A reasonably pure violet scent is in the perfume known as orris, especially in the roots of *Iris florentina*, from which orris itself is made. It is detectable also in the flowers of *I. reticulata*, especially when gathered from the winter garden and taken indoors to a warm atmosphere. *Rosa banksiae*, in both the white-flowered and the pale-yellow-flowered forms is violet-scented.

Aromatic group

Most flower scents are included in this group, merely because the composition of essential oil is complex, the fragrance as variable as that of *pot pourri*. These are considered to be the most refined or sophisticated of flower scents, most of them containing distinct tones and not dependent upon a dominant essence. All the flower perfumes display the same pleasing quality and an exquisite richness not encountered in the other floral groups. There is the warm, rich, spicy clove scent of some of the pinks and stocks, the sweetness of anise found in some of the primulas, the balsamic fragrance of the broad bean flower and nicotianas, the vanilla of *Clematis flammula* and the rather solid almond scent of *Prunus yedoensis*, *P. laurocerasus* and *Corylopsis pauciflora*.

A rough spiciness, devoid of pungency, comes in the flowers of the Mexican Orange, *Choisya ternata*, and the coppery tassels of Carolina Allspice, *Calycanthus floridus*.

Heavy group

Moving along the scale, there remain only the strong heady scents, caused mainly by the presence of indole in the essential oil, but combined with refreshing substances to retain sweet overtones. Perfumes described as

Aromatic plants in a cold greenhouse: scented-leaved pelargoniums, heliotropes, eucalypts and myrtle

exotic belong here; the tuberose, the jonquil, lilac, some ligustrums, lily-of-the-valley, hyacinth and stephanotis.

Fragrance of plant fabric

Most trees with fragrant wood come from sub-tropical climates and yield commercial products such as camphor from *Cinnamomum camphora*. But several trees and shrubs habitually cultivated in temperate regions may be grown for their scented wood and bark. The resinous barks of conifers are well known, the clear fresh turpentine-pine fragrance resting on the air in warm sunshine. *Drimys winteri* first aroused interest by its fragrant bark, *D. aromatica* is strongly fragrant too. The barks of *Magnolia* × *soulangiana*, crisply lemon, and *Davidia involucrata*, balsamic, are, like most scented woods strongest when the tree is mature, and remain fragrant upon drying. All parts of *Calycanthus floridus*, wood, bark and roots, are fragrant.

Roots often hold the fragrance of the plant, after the plant has died down as in the mints, or after lifting as in *Iris florentina*, *I. pallida*, *Acorus calamus* and *Sedum rhodiola* (Syn. *Rhodiola rosea*) – the so-called Rose Root of the cottagers, not to be confused with *S. spurium* 'Roseum', the roots of which are quite scentless. The roots of *Inula helenium* are fragrant of banana, lightening to a violet-like aroma with age. *Eryngium maritimum* used to be commonly candied as a sweetmeat, and even the dried root is sweet to the taste, but lacks any fragrance – one of the examples of the absence of scent where it is justifiably expected.

Few seeds are aromatic; those that are, are employed as culinary flavouring. Anise and caraway are the most popular, but those of alexanders (*Smyrnium olusatrum*) are distinctly incense-like in aroma. The seed of coriander is an ingredient of chypre, a perfume formerly much in demand.

Fruit

Much of the enjoyment of edible fruits is in the aroma enjoyed before the taste. Luscious sweetness, almost intoxicating in its wine-like quality, comes with a ripe peach, a restrained fragrance with the nectarine, and a deeply satisfying warmth of fragrance with a sun-warmed fig. The scent of the quince always belies its cross-grained flesh, that of *Chaenomeles japonica* of our gardens is almost rose-like. Plums, dusky and ripe, need to have the skins ruptured before the scent is enjoyed. How well the wasp knows this! Greengages are perhaps the best of all, refined and full of perfume.

The scent of the apricot is best when the velvety fruit has been sun-warmed; strawberries and raspberries on the other hand, are at their best when cool. The sweet-scented fragrance of the little conical fruits of *fraise de bois* (*Fragaria vesca*) is more flower-like than fruity, delicate and quite indescribable, and distinctly different from the musky sweetness of its foliage in maturity.

Pears, so juicy that one needs to sit in a bath to eat them, are always most lusciously fragrant. Apples vary enormously in aroma. The entire house can smell of apples in the early autumn when they are first stored or 'saved' indoors. The old cool domestic fruit store of former days acted only to maintain a low temperature to retard the chemical processes of ripening, and full aroma. Perhaps more than any other fruit, the domestic apple changes its scent thoughout its climacteric from harvest to decay. If the fruit is kept too long it turns 'woolly' and loses sweetness and fragrance. Apple scent also varies considerably from one variety to another, always sweeter or 'fruitier' in dessert varieties than in cooking varieties. Slightly fruity-aromatic is the blackberry's scent, which always sweetens on cooking, and the same scent is held in the foliage and flowers as the summer progresses.

Vines, especially those cultivated under glass, have an evocative scent, best enjoyed once the skin of the grape has been removed, and the variations in variety resolve to give the bouquet of wine. The flowers themselves are described as 'one of the precious perfumes of the year' and yet so much a part of the vine itself that one hardly dreams of seeking them out to examine. There is no need, for they pervade the air with their almost violet-like fragrance.

CHAPTER TWO

The Love of Scent

It is highly probable that man has appreciated the fragrance of plants since prehistoric times, but the earliest records of perfumery, as such, are those of the ancient Egyptians. Sweet-smelling oils and lotions and flower waters were prepared from plants, and there are records of 'recipes' for perfumes and primitive deodorants, dating from 1500 BC. Fragrant plants abounded in the Middle East and it was from there that later civilizations carried them to more distant parts of Europe, almost as souvenirs are taken home today.

To the Greeks, scent was of divine origin; the Gods were believed to have the exclusive right to the sweet odours that were considered part of their aura – the ambrosia of the Gods. Writing in the 4th century BC Theophrastus of Eresus in a treatise entitled *Concerning Odours* distinguishes between simple and more complex perfumes and suggests appropriate ways of blending them. He said: 'Perfumes are compounded from various parts of the plant, flowers, leaves, twigs, root, wood, fruit and gum.' He knew the rose, the gillyflower, lilies, mints, saffron, jonquil, cyclamen, myrtle, meadowsweet, iris, rosemary, lavender, lilac and many others as well as the Eastern spices.

The ancient paradise gardens of the East seem to have been resorts decorated with scented flowers, shaded by perfumed trees, abundant with luscious fruits and set about with the aromatic plants we now consider herbs. Milton's imagined Paradise was:

> . . . a place
> Chosen by the sovereign Planter, when he framed
> All things to man's delightful use . . .
> Laurel and Myrtle . . . of fragrant leaf, on either side
> Acanthus and each odorous bushy shrub,
> Fenced up the verdant wall; each beauteous flower,
> Iris all hues, Roses, and Jessamine
> Reared high, their flourished heads between, and wrought
> Mosaic; underfoot the Violet,
> Crocus, and Hyacinth.

Fabulous tales have been handed down of scented festivals and rituals, some quite extravagantly exaggerated. Whether we elect to believe them or not, there is no escape from the fact that all plants seem to have blossomed at the same time, or even perpetually: . . . never retiring for their resting period as in the cooler, temperate regions. Herein lies the key to the different, less exotic fragrance of numerous plants when cultivated in our gardens. A warm day, a warm moist evening, even a sunny spot in the garden, can enhance the perfume of a plant almost beyond recognition.

On the other hand, there are some of the scented oils which became far more refined in cooler climates, producing more exquisitely balanced perfume. The most famous example of this phenomenon is the coveted English oil of lavender, that, early in the present century, was considered to be the finest in the world – far superior in fragrance to that cultivated in the Grasse area of southern France. The surrounding air there is permeated by an almost overwhelming, dull lavender scent, but in England, the sharp refreshing scent of lavender fields is far more elusive. Peppermint, also, when grown in the cooler climates of northern Europe produces a refined oil with clean sharp fragrance. The same may be said of the rose; its fragrance is wearied in warmer climates, especially at low elevations, and lacks the clarity that it displays in Britain.

Roses were grown commercially for their perfume extracts certainly by the first century AD in the Middle East, and over the following centuries the extracted scent became a valuable commodity and highly prized. Dues and taxes have been paid in rose water, and fortunes accumulated from the sale of attar. Today in Bulgaria 10,000 acres are devoted to the cultivation of the Damask Rose, *Rose damascena*, for the production of rose water and attar of rose. It is of interest to note that the main centre for the industry is in a moderate climate in the cool foot-hills of the Balkans, and not, as one may be forgiven for supposing, in the windswept sun-baked plains of the exotic east.

Rosaries, or rose gardens, are known to have existed in the country around London in the early 16th century, and were probably designed for the production of the scented petals. One such garden was near Tottenham Marsh, on land in the possession of George Chapman and his wife Susan as custodian tenants. The holding was known as Asplins 'with a Barne Stable Cowhouse garden and backside to the same belonging and also one Crofte of land called Hencrofts, now converted into a garden of Roses.' Other tenants nearby owned the Little Fielde 'with a small garden of roses at the east end thereof' and '. . . one Close of pasture with a little Garden of Roses at ye west end thereof . . . .'

Later there was rose cultivation on quite an extensive scale in Oxfordshire and Derbyshire, but the main commercial enterprise was in the Mitcham district of Surrey, famous for its lavender farms. There, early in the 19th century the Potter and Moore concern had 'seven acres of damasks', which was, in all probability *Rosa gallica officinalis*, three acres of Provence and other smaller holdings nearby where roses were cultivated commercially for their fragrant petals.

The entire flower was used for the distillation of rose oil or attar. The resultant oil was considered superior if the calyx of the flower was removed; obviously, a labour-intensive task: women and children were employed '. . . twice a day in order to secure the buds before they are too expanded.' Up to 2000 flower buds made up to 100lb of fresh flowers and 10lb of dried. The buds were dried rapidly to retain the colour, by stove heat, and marketed as dried flowers. Those destined for use in conserves were

A hedge of the Apothecary's Rose, *Rosa gallica officinalis*

marketed fresh and one has only to research the household encyclopaedias and recipe books of the period to find delightful suggestions for rose-petal jam and rose-petal sandwiches. The conserve is rather like the pink Turkish delight, the fragrance more enjoyable than the flavour itself.

The London centre for the marketing of aromatics by the 16th century was Bucklesbury Market at Cheapside. In Shakespeare's *Merry Wives of Windsor*, Falstaff alludes to the perfumed dandies as 'smelling as sweet as Bucklesbury in spring time'. Most of the Mediterranean herbs and sweet-scented plants were grown in 'small holdings' in the countryside surrounding the city, or gathered from the wild, and many were sold fresh. The possession of a mint still represented considerable wealth and a means of income, through distilling for the less well-equipped growers.

Aromatics had been first brought to Britain by the returning Crusaders, whose home-coming gifts were costly toiletries, and from that time the use of perfumes gained in popularity. Toilet-waters made by extracting the scented oils from plants by distillation with spirit of wine (alcohol) rather than by water first appear in Europe in the 14th century. *Eau de toilette* then was a distillation of fresh flowers such as rosemary, marjoram, lavender and rose.

Professional perfumers and housewives alike bought from markets such as Bucklesbury, and those in the provinces patronized either itinerant pedlars of aromatics, or purchased from the apothecaries' main centres of distribution, which were York, Chester, Norwich and Bristol. The wealth of fragrant material was extended considerably during the 15th, 16th and 17th centuries by the introduction of so many new plants into England. Botanical knowledge of the Renaissance period resulted in a whole range of plants being newly cultivated in England as 'exoticks'. The word truly means 'stranger', or 'something from afar' and it by this association with a new and richer range of scent that 'exotic' so often describes an unfamiliar and emotive fragrance.

Tudor gardens

Decorative gardening as we know it today had its origins in Tudor times. Many plants were cultivated for garden delight and perfume rather than as an economic requirement such as had been the order previously in mediaeval and monastic herb or still-room gardens. Colloquially, the word 'herb' has come to signify a plant employed for its fragrance or flavour or medicinal quality, but the 'herber' of the early gardens was synonymous with 'arbour', denoting a flowery, elaborately sheltered plot, set about with all manner of sweet-smelling plants. Reflecting the rich, detailed designs in general of the Tudor period, intricate knots were laid out in gardens, sometimes highly complex in concept and 'so knotted it cannot be expres't'. Geometrically designed, and always upon a level site, the outlines and divisions were formed in fragrant plants, usually clipped close to the ground. Rosemary, lavender, box, santolina, hyssop and germander were used in this way – all of them fragrant. Pebbles, shale, shells, or coloured earth were used to cover the ground in the spaces emphasizing the pattern, and forming what was known as an open knot. Sometimes, in the even more elaborately arranged 'closed knots' marigolds, violets, gillyflowers (pinks), double daisies, bugle and pennyroyal would be set out to fill the spaces of the pattern and provide seasonal colour. Here then, is one of the first firm examples of scented plants being cultivated decoratively in Britain.

Strewing herbs

Previously, for generations, aromatic plants had been used – and indeed they continued to be used – for medicine and for the flavouring of food; every household had little else but plant material for these purposes. Wild plants were known for their virtues, and several were maintained for their property of retaining fragrance after drying. These were used for strewing: Sweet Woodruff (*Asperula odorata*), Sweet Rush (*Acorus calamus*), mints (*Mentha* spp), thymes (*Thymus* spp), hyssop (*Hyssopus officinalis*), germander (*Teucrium chamaedrys*), costmary (*Balsamita major*) and chamomile (*Anthemis* spp), all of which are plants which, being crushed and trodden upon, release their captive aroma. They also served to deter fleas, vermin, lice and frogs, and were raked up and renewed from time to time. Queen Elizabeth I retained a woman in her household with a fixed salary to provide an adequate supply of suitable plants and flowers for strewing the floors. Cardinal Wolsey is reputed to have indulged in the extravagance of ordering the strewing herbs to be used plenteously and renewed frequently.

Gerarde wrote that 'The leaves and flowers [of the meadowsweet] far excell all other strewing herbes to deck up houses, to strew in chambers, halls and banqueting houses in summer time, for the smell thereof makes the heart merry and joyful, and delighteth the senses.' Bridewort was then a common name for the meadowsweet, from the old custom of strewing houses with it for wedding festivals, but whether the festivities proved too much, or the scent of the plant too overpowering, it came to be associated with sleep and death.

Houses and chambers were scented also by burning aromatic plants like artemisias, especially southernwood (*Artemisia abrotanum*), spikenard (*Inula conyza*) and sage (*Salvia officinalis*) to release the sweetly pungent odour in smoke. Aromatic seeds of wild plants such as angelica (*Angelica sylvestris*) were fired in this way, burning them on a chafing dish or griddle. Nosegays and other sweet-scented conceits were carried, given and hung about in rooms and privies, certainly in Tudor times, to freshen the atomsphere. Rosemary and lavender were both used in this way, and Sir Hugh Plat, in *Delights for Ladies* (1594) suggested 'in summer, the chimney fireplace be trimmed with a bank of fresh moss and at either end have a rosemary pot'.

Pot pourri

Some of the richest *pot pourri* recipes are derived from the necessity to strew aromatic plants and dispose scented conceits about the dwellings for antiseptic and deodorant reasons. They originated in Elizabethan days as natural developments of the fashionable scented garden, and whereas wands of aromatic plants had been strewn, now the flowers were amassed into jars and pouncet boxes, small containers with a perforated lid.

Moist *pot pourri*

This French term *pot pourri* literally translated means 'rotten pot', and in the early days of *pot pourri*-making the flowers were virtually pickled and kept moist. Brandy or some other spirit was added to the mixture from time to time, to maintain the moist condition, and the jars were opened only when a room was to be perfumed. Thus the 'preserve', richly pervasive and pungent, remained effective over extensive periods.

In the modern versions of moist *pot pourri*, petals are partially dried to a leathery texture, stored in an earthenware vessel, and added to as the season progresses, so that daphnes and wallflowers will blend with roses and pinks and late summer privets and viburnums. Each layer of petals is covered by a salt mixture and stored until further petals and leaves are added. (Bay salt is always recommended, but in modern parlance this is sea salt.) Cover the mixture carefully, pressing it down by the weight of a plate or chopping board, and when more semi-dried plant material is to be added, remove the weight, mix the existing materials, add the layer of latest material, scatter more salt and cover again.

The mass that forms will resemble the garden compost heap in consistency, – damp, fermenting, tangy – and it may even froth. None of this denotes anything other than success. By pouring off the excess liquid, and keeping the squelchy mass covered and in a cool place, the season can progress. By September or October the whole cake can be flaked, a spice mixture added, some crushed dried citrus peel or zest of lemon, and once the entire ingredients are thoroughly and evenly blended (this is best achieved by the hands) a drop or two of oil may be included according to individual taste, though often it is unnecessary for moist *pot pourri*.

Once mixed, it is put into a covered jar, pressed down handful by handful, and left for about 6–8 weeks to 'ripen'. Moist *pot pourri* is usually only uncovered when required to perfume a room, and can reasonably be expected to remain deliciously effective for many years. If and when the mixture becomes too dry and seems to withhold its aroma except upon close inspection, add a few drops of brandy. A moist *pot pourri* will last far longer than a dry one, and is worth all the time and effort required for its formulation. On the other hand it is less attractive visually than the dry one and is not intended to be disposed about the house in open bowls nor used in scented sachets or pillows.

Lavenders used to edge a scented border

Recipes are almost impossible to formulate exactly, but if the flower-leaf cake is measured in gallons, the following quantities of spices are *approximately* what will be required for each gallon, and can be manipulated to individual taste.

ground clove	1oz
orris root	½oz
nutmeg	½oz
powdered mace	½oz
gum benzoin	2oz

Dry *pot pourri*

The most satisfactory results are assured from dry *pot pourri* when dried flowers, petals and leaves are blended with fixatives and spices. Provided that the plant material is carefully and completely dried previously and the mixing utensils are 'crock' – non-metal and non-plastic – little can go amiss. Restraint in adding spices or an oil needs to be exercised, and it is always advisable to 'make haste slowly', often leaving the mixture aside for a week or so to ascertain the development of the blend, before adding more, and certainly before adding spices. These can be milled in a pepper-mill or coffee-blender, so that a mere pinch can be made available, as required.

The art of *port pourri*-making has developed and changed with time and as new fragrant plants have been introduced into northern gardens, no doubt their blossoms have been experimented with as possible *pot pourri* ingredients. Victorian recipes, probably for this reason, appear to be a free-for-all, and every housewife seems to have had her own favourite recipe. That many new ideas have been put forward does not detract from the fact that the scented plants and aromatic leaves used today in *pot pourri* are the same, rich in essential oil, and retain their perfume on drying. Modern recipes can be controlled or contrived to be sweet, herby, spicy, aromatic, seasonal, but as always achieving an acceptable fragrance in the final mixture depends upon the blending in of the fixatives, oils and spices. Restraint with them is the key, and naturally, avoidance of a mixture overloaded with any one sort of flower or leaf.

Ingredients to use include: dried petals or flower heads of roses (always the fragrant ones – *Rosa gallica officinalis* and *R. centifolia* are the ones to select *par excellence*!) mock orange, stocks, wallflowers, carnations and pinks, jasmine, lavender, chamomile, bergamot, lilac, calamint, lily-of-the-valley, heliotrope, sweet pea, mignonette and marigold. Leaves to include could be rosemary, lavender, thyme, marjoram, artemisias, lemon balm, lemon verbena, scented-leaved pelargoniums and santolina. Or be adventurous and experiment with apple mint, the young foliage of balsam poplar and sweetbrier, peach blossom, mimosa, wisteria, yucca, broom; these are not encountered in published recipes, but have a contribution to make to the final composition.

Sweet-jar

A modern, less meticulous version of moist *pot pourri* is the so-called sweet-jar. For this, partially dried rose petals are mixed in the ratio of about 6:1 with petals of lilac, rosemary, lavender and pinks, together with about

½oz of ground calamus root, inula root, and ½ a grated nutmeg, a good pinch of cinnamon, two crushed bay leaves and the skin of an orange dried in a very low oven, then ground. Put this mixture into an earthenware jar, in alternate layers with a few fingerfuls of sea salt, moisten with a thimbleful or two of brandy. Seal the jar and leave it to mature for about two months. Then after turning well with a wooden spoon, it can be used in the manner of a moist *pot pourri*.

Old recipes

An 18th-century recipe for *pot pourri*:

> Take Orange Flowers, a pound; common roses picked without yellow Pedicles a pound: Clove-july flowers picked with the white end of their leaves cut off, half a pound; Marjoram, and Myrtle leaves picked, of each half a pound: Musk roses, Thyme, Lavender, Rosemary, Sage, Chamomile, Melilot, Hyssop, Sweet Basil, and Balm of each two ounces; fifteen or twenty Bay leaves, two or three handfuls of Jasmine, as many little green oranges and a half pound of Salt. Put them in a proper vessel, and leave them together a whole month, carefully observing to stir the mixture well twice a day with a wooden spatula or spoon. At the month's end, add twelve ounces of Florentine Orrice-root in fine powder, and the same quantity of powdered Benjamin; of Cloves and Cinnamon finely powdered, each two ounces; Mace, Storax, Calamus Aromaticus, all in fine powder, and Cypress- powder, of each an ounce; Yellow Sanders and Cyperus or Sweet Flag, of each three quarters of an ounce. Mix the whole thoroughly by stirring and you will have a very fragrant perfume.
>
> *The Toilet of Flora* (1771)

A Victorian recipe:

> Gather and dry as many as can be had of the following, until they fill a large bowl – roses and rosebuds, thyme, rosemary, lavender, mignonette, southernwood, lemon verbena, sweet marjoram, sweet basil, leaves of sweet bay. Stir well with two ounces of crushed cloves, powdered orris root and powdered all-spice mixed together, and one ounce of crushed dried lemon peel. Add a few drops of oil of musk.

Snuff was scented in a very similar way; an 18th-century recipe reads:

> The Flowers that most readily communicated their flavour to Snuff are Orange Flowers, Muck Roses [moss rose?] Jasmine and Tuberoses. You must procure a box lined with dry white paper; in this strow your Snuff on the bottom about the thickness of an inch, over which place a thin layer of flowers, then another layer of Snuff, and continue to lay your Flowers and Snuff alternately in this manner, until the box is full. After they have lain together four and twenty hours, sift your Snuff through a sieve to separate it from the Flowers, which are to be thrown away, and fresh ones applied in their room in the former method. Continue to do this till the Snuff is sufficiently scented; then put it into a canister, which keep close stoppered.'
>
> *The Country Lady's Directory* (1732)

Tussie-mussies

Little posies of sweet smelling plants were habitually given in Tudor days to visitors, to those setting out on a journey, and as tokens of love and friendship. Plants combined to convey a message – the language of flowers – and so came to be gathered especially for weddings, St Valentine's Day, funerals, betrothals and reunions. John Parkinson gave us the name in 1629. Small tightly arranged bunches were later formed of dried flowers, so that the fragrance was slight, and needed to be sought by the nose, but the token was not disposable and represented a lasting sentiment.

A tussie-mussie was given to Queen Elizabeth II as she entered Westminster Abbey on the occasion of her Coronation in 1953. We are not told the message of the plants! More recently, in 1979 when she distributed Maundy Money at Winchester Cathedral, the tussie-mussie presented to her contained twenty-one fragrant plants. The modern versions, usually have a rose bud at the heart surrounded by chamomile, artemisias, marjoram, pinks and marigolds, all previously dried in silica gel. The accompanying scent is so faint that for a special gift the ribbons are scented appropriately and dried before trimming the nosegay . . . or the posy is sprinkled wth a few drops of a proprietary *pot pourri* reviver . . . cheating!

Scent extraction

Scent glands can be found in many different parts, according to the plant: deep in the heart of a flower, as in sweet peas, heliotrope, wallflowers, hyacinth, clove pinks, and lilac; in the calyx, as in lavender and the moss rose where the glands are extended to form the 'moss'; in bark, as in *Calycanthus floridus*, *Drimys winteri* and cedars; in the roots, as in elecampane, angelica and rose root, or the rhizomes of *Iris florentina*, *I. pallida* and *Acorus calamus*; or in the seed of anise, cumin, and fennel or the fruits of citruses. Wood, also, can be scented, for example apple, cedar and calycanthus, which sometimes exude resins.

However, the scent glands of leaves, some of them almost visible, when they are near the surface as in rosemary, are the ones most familiar. Everyone knows that aromatic leaves such as bay, mint, thyme, sage, and rosemary can be dried and will loose much of their weight – 90 per cent to be precise – and retain their aroma, for use as culinary flavouring or as an ingredient of *pot pourri*. Dried flowers can also retain their perfume (see *Pot pourri*, page 33).

The extraction of the oil is more complicated. There are several old methods, still quite effective, but commercially today fragrant plant material is laid on perforated metal plates and some volatile solvent (e.g. petroleum ether) is passed over them. Once the solvent is rich in essential oils a further process of separation is carried out to give what are known as floral absolutes. They are considered to be the purest extracts and to represent the flower scents most accurately.

Distillation

When aromatic material is held in steam, the oils will evaporate and mix with the steam. Once the steam condenses, the essential oil will separate out and float on the water surface. Because many plant oils are, to a greater or lesser degree, water-soluble, the distillate is skimmed off and redistilled to render it a higher quality. Redistillation removes the odourless adulterant terpenes. Modern distillation methods contrive to pass steam through the plant material, and carry the evaporated oils through a series of water-cooled pipes. The oils are then collected into special receiving vessels.

Maceration and *enfleurage*

By soaking fragrant plant material, usually petals and flower heads, in warm oil, the scent glands can be made to rupture and release their contents. These dissolve in the oil, and as petals are removed and replaced with fresh ones daily, the oil becomes increasingly strong in scent. The now-outmoded and long-winded process known as *enfleurage* was very closely allied to maceration in that warm oil was used to soak freshly gathered petals in the same way. The oil or grease was spread on glass sheets supported on wooden frames and the petals spread over the grease. Once the perfume was absorbed into the fat the petals were changed for fresh ones. The resultant saturated fat was then known as a pomade – and sometimes sold as such.

CHAPTER THREE

The Search for Scent

THE ENGLISH GARDENS of the late 16th and early 17th centuries were an attempt to realise a fantasy, which was only achieved in reality by those of the princely estates and palaces, and in the modest plots where private collectors amassed their plants. It is only possible to sketch in part of the story, and that part but a compromise, relating only to fragrant plants and fragrant gardens since that time.

Remarkably, a great number of the plants then known and cultivated were scented ones. Over the later centuries some have fallen out of cultivation, others have been 'improved' and new ones have been introduced, sometimes, as in the case of roses and lilac for example, producing a whole new race of highly fragrant plants.

Before 1600 an influx of exotic flowers had given enthusiasts a glimpse of some of the floral treasures of the world, and influenced their whole attitude to gardens. Previous generations had had the native plants and those introduced by the Romans, Normans and returning Crusaders. But the improvements in seafaring and the extension of the trade routes brought seemingly strange and wondrous plants to our shores, along with numerous new ideas.

Native plants

We can turn to lists of plants of the 14th and 15th centuries compiled by Gardener, Turner, Lyte and Gerarde and to the medieval and Elizabethan poets and playwrights; many of whom describe the plants and the uses to which they were put, in quaintly succinct terms. Let us look briefly, then, at some of the scented plants available at that time (using the present-day names for clarity).

Among the indigenous fragrant plants there were the highly aromatic ones known for their flavouring and medicinal qualities: Wild Thyme (*Thymus serpyllum*), Common Calamint (*Calamintha ascendens*) Lesser Calamint (*Calamintha nepeta*), Catmint (*Nepeta cataria*), Basil Thyme (*Acinos arvensis*), Wild Basil (*Clinopodium vulgare*), Wild Angelica (*Angelica sylvestris*) which, being raised to garden status, became *Angelica archangelica*. Of the mints, certainly Pennyroyal (*Mentha pulegium*), Spearmint (*M. spicata*), Common Mint (*M. arvensis*), and Water Mint (*M. aquatica*) were grown, often in ditches or moats. Peppermint (*M.* x *piperita*) a natural hybrid between spearmint and water mint, was also cultivated.

Then we have the Sweet-Scented Violet (*Viola odorata*), two daphnes – Mezereon (*Daphne mezereum*) and the Spurge Laurel (*D. laureola*), the sweetly fragrant White Campion (*Melandrium album*) which the poet Drayton says was employed for *pot pourri* with the Sweet Woodruff (*Asperula odorata*). The Elizabethans cultivated double-flowered forms of this campion, and of its close relative the Ragged Robin (*Lychnis floscuculi*) and the Red Campion of the hedgerows (*Melandrium rubrum*) – the two latter lacking the scent of *M. album*.

Other natives were marjoram (*Origanum vulgare*) the aromatic meadow clary (*Salvia pratensis*) and wild clary (*S. horminoides*), less aromatic, but one that has attracted more attention over the years, yarrow (*Achillea millefolium*) and the Scentless Mayweed (*Matricaria chamomilla*), whose slightly oily growth emits an apple-chamomile scent when handled. The true chamomile (*Anthemis nobilis*) is one of the natives cultivated certainly in the 13th and 14th centuries, not for its medicinal properties, but for banking to form seats, and for walks and lawns. The trimmings, we are told, were mingled with the strewing herbs. For strewing, great quantities of meadowsweet (*Filipendula ulmaria*) were cut from the ditches, as was also Sweet Rush (*Acorus calamus*). Insufficient was available from the Fens to meet the demand, so cut sheaths of this rush were imported from the Low Countries, where it abounded. The sweetly scented Solomon's Seal (*Polygonatum multiflorum*) was brought into cultivation early and called 'scalacely'. By the 18th and 19th centuries double-flowered sweetly scented forms with pink and purplish stems had been obtained.

The musky scent of the box (*Buxus sempervirens*) and the honey perfume of the privet (*Ligustrum vulgare*) perhaps did not grace the Jacobean gardens for both plants were tortured by clipping and prevented from flowering – both are indigenous. The box to this day retains its favour as a plant for clipping but the Common Privet has been superseded by the late-19th-century introduction *Ligustrum ovalifolium*, from Japan.

The flowers of the Common Honeysuckle or Woodbine (*Lonicera periclymenum*) were described by Gerarde as '. . . long white, sweet of smell . . . with threads growing out of the middle . . .' and its night-scenting characteristic was noted by several poets: Thomas Moore spoke of its evening perfume and Ben Johnson of its 'odoriferous shade'.

Several roses are indigenous. Gerarde called the Burnet Rose (*Rosa spinosissima*) the Pimpinell Rose, and the progeny formed a group of roses very popular before the middle of the 19th century, raised especially by Scottish nurserymen. The Sweetbrier or Eglantine (*R. rubiginosa*) is to this day one of the plants most fragrant of foliage, the leaves and young growth scenting the air with its fruity ripe-apple fragrance. The Small-leaved Brier (*R. micrantha*) was known also, and the Dog Rose (*R. canina*) whose sweet scent is held in the stamens. One of the truly ancestral roses, for it was united with the Damask Rose, it provided the Alba Roses with most of their good characteristics, including a delightfully sweet fragrance.

Plants in cultivation

Cottage gardens profuse with flowers and smothered in roses did not exist in this period; the simplest gardens contained a few vegetables and maybe a fruit tree, and about the doorway some healing herbs brought in from the countryside for convenience. But many of the plants that were known and cultivated then have come to be called 'cottage garden flowers'. Several were well established, like the clove- or nutmeg-scented gillyflower, *Dianthus caryophyllus*, believed to have arrived with the Normans, and the stock gillyflower, *Mattiola incana*, so called for the resemblance of its rich perfume to that of the dianthus. It was distinguished from the dianthus by its 'stock' or woody stem, part of the name retained today. Wallflowers, *Cheiranthus cheiri*, also of ancient cultivation, were known by a string of names: Bee-Flower, Yellow Stock Gillyflower, Cheiry or Keiry. Sometimes they were even known as Sweet William, or as the 'hand flowers' of generations predating the Elizabethans. Posies of wallflowers were carried at festivals for their sweet, strong scent alone, and were cultivated for the same reason, because the herbalists failed to ascribe to them any medicinal properties. A white wallflower seems to have been grown for many years but has fallen out of cultivation. The yellow-flowered 'Harpur Crewe' cv is certainly old of cultivation, thought not necessarily under that name. It is a small plant which was resuscitated by the Rev. Henry Harpur Crewe, a rector botanist of Drayton Beauchamp, near Tring in Hertfordshire, in about the 1870s . . . so this is a scented plant that spans the centuries.

Another favourite Tudor flower was the Queen's Gillyflower or Dame's Violet (*Hesperis matronalis*), strongly perfumed in the evening. There was a striped form, and a double-flowered one that arrived with the Huguenots, *H. tristris*, and whose dingy appearance gained it the name of Melancholy Gentleman – though he cheered up in the evening to give a rich and delicious clove-like perfume.

Feverfew (*Chrysanthemum parthenium*) in a double-flowered form was another favourite, as was lavender. The two sorts grown were *Lavandula spica* and *L. vera* probably introduced by the Romans who scented their baths with it. In 1568 Turner wrote that it could be 'quilted in a cappe and daylye worne for all diseases of the head that come of a cold cause and comfort the brayne very well'. There is little doubt that it was grown for use rather than for decoration. The French Lavender (*L. stoechas*) was described by Parkinson in 1629 and was probably used, in the same way, for its more camphorous scent, and not cultivated so widely over the years for this reason, in addition to its less robust attitude to the English winter. Lavender Cotton (*Santolina chamaecyparissus*) was newly introduced in the second half of the 16th century and gained popularity quickly, at first erroneously called French Abrotanum. The true Abrotanum is Southernwood (*Artemisia abrotanum*), cultivated before the mid-15th century, and was planted 'by the outside of flower gardens for the improvement of nosegays'. Its sweet refreshing foliage and its tolerance of adverse positions recommended it in the 18th century for 'training about a foot high with rounded bushy heads for which there is a ready sale in Covent Garden and Newgate markets; the inhabitants buying them to place in their courtyards, balconies and windows in assemblance with other hardy plants that bear the smoke' (Abercrombie 1778). The native Field Southernwood (*Artemisia campestris*) and Wormwood (*A. absinthium*) were also grown or collected, but evidence is sparse. Tarragon (*A. dracunculus*), the French or true tarragon, was grown during the 16th century and is certainly recorded in the Royal gardens, and Gerarde had some in his garden at Holborn.

Soapwort, or Bouncing Bet (*Saponaria officinalis*), whose double-flowered form is a true cottage-garden plant, is one of the native/naturalized plants that smudge the garden fence for the botanist, as do the artemisias, convallarias, *Stachys*, *Mentha*, and other common aromatic plants.

The auricula had arrived in the 16th century with the Huguenots, while the Sweet William (*Dianthus barbatus*), thought to have been introduced by the Carthusian monks in the 12th century, was commonly grown and was formerly called Velvet William, London Tufts, and Bloomy-downs, suggestive of its softness. Speckled and splashed forms were known, and early attempts at hybridization were made with this plant. The Madonna Lily, (*Lilium candidum*) was well known, as were verbena (*Verbena officinalis*), Sweet Cicely (*Myrrhis odorata*), savories (*Satureja spp*), lily-of-the-valley (*Convallaria majalis*) in double-flowered and pink forms, and Caraway (*Carum carvi*). Some narcissus species were being grown, some of them double-flowered, and others called narcissus but obviously wrongly classified. The exquisitely scented jonquil was a new arrival from Spain; Bear's Breeches (*Acanthus mollis*) which scents the air as it fades and dries, especially after cutting, arrived from Italy in the middle of the 16th century at about the same time as the African Marigold (*Tagetes erecta*) and the heliotrope (*Heliotropium arborescens*) The laburnum (*L. anagyroides*), shedding its golden scent in less robust tassels, came before the turn of the century from central and eastern Europe, the nasturtium (*Tropaeolum minus*) from South America. Via Turkey came some of the dominant gems of the fragrant garden: the hyacinth about 1580, the tulip a year or two before, *Lilium chalcedonicum* and saffron (*Crocus sativus*), Summer Jasmine (*Jasminum officinalis*) and Sweet Sultan (*Centaurea moschata*). Presumably along the silk route from China the Day Lily (*Hemerocallis fulva*) arrived.

Shrubs already known were less exciting, and of course, were not used as they are today, but were overpowered by clipped yews and privets. Most of them were relegated to the orchard and grown among other woody plants. Examples are *Viburnum tinus* and *V. opulus*, and the Cherry Laurel (*Prunus laurocerasus*), which had arrived from Turkey, as had lilac (*Syringa vulgaris*), and *S.* × *persica*, and the Mock Orange (*Philadelphus coronarius*).

The Mock Orange, inevitably confused with the ture lilac (*Syringa*), arrived from the same place at about the same time, and seems to have made little impact in spite of its heady perfume. By 1629 Parkinson was referring to them both as 'pipe trees' on account of the white removable pith; he called them the 'blue pipe tree' (*S. vulgaris*) and the 'white pipe tree' (*Philadelphus coronarius*).

Of the introduced roses, *Rosa damascena*, brought back by the Crusaders, was already here as were both single- and double-flowered forms of the Cinnamon Rose (*R. cinnamomea*) and the later-flowering *R. moschata*, with its musk-like scent. The myrtle was a newish plant, Spanish Broom (*Spartium junceum*) was known and certainly one or two of the cistus, such as *Cistus ladanifer*, which were then called Holly Roses.

Seventeenth-century uncertainty

Constant reference to the scent of a flower by those who wrote about gardens bears witness to the awareness and importance of fragrant plants. While some, like Bacon, fantasized on the ideal garden, there is every indication that the decorative fragrant garden presented some sort of problem as time passed and little attempt was made to display these plants. Gervase Markham was one of the first to give advice on the planning of gardens, and he differentiated between the kitchen garden and the pleasure garden, the latter divided again into the herb garden and the nosegay garden. His nosegay plants included gillyflowers, lilies, daffodils, violets and 'such strange flowers as hyacinths, dulopps [tulips] and narcissus'; the herb garden was for rosemary, southernwood, hyssop, lavender, basil, rue, tansy, pennyroyal and mint. Markham had a deep interest in scented and aromatic plants which resulted in his preparation of a skin lotion which gained enormous popularity, distilled from fennel, violets, rosemary, feverfew and nettles.

Francis Bacon was fantasizing in his much quoted essay *Of Gardens* (1625) and had a princely outlook into the bargain, but the ideal was a garden in which

> . . . the breath of flowers is far sweeter in the air (whence it comes and goes, like the warbling of music), than in the hand, therefore nothing is more fit for delight, than to know what be the flowers and plants that do best perfume the air. Roses, damask and red, are fast flowers of their smells; so that you may walk by a whole row of them, and find nothing of their sweetness; yea though it be in a morning's dew . . . . That which, above all others yields the sweetest smell in the air, is the violet, especially the white double violet, which comes twice a year . . . . Next to that is the musk-rose; then the strawberry leaves dying . . . then sweet-brier, then wallflowers . . . pinks, gilliflowers . . . the lime trees, honeysuckles. But those which perfume the air most delightfully . . . being trodden upon and crushed are . . . burnet, wild thyme and water-mints; therefore, you are to set whole alleys of them, to have the pleasure when you walk or tread.

Many of the fragrant plants known to the 17th-century writers, and gardeners, are assembled in The Queen's Garden at The Royal Botanic Garden, Kew.

Dominated by rigidity and artificiality, the 17th-century gardens, large and small, were encased in and contained by hedges, alleys, walks and formal water. Flower gardens – a thing apart – were confined to repetitive rectangular plots, pathways between, each small bed planted with one kind of plant, in the manner of former physic gardens. Many plants, especially the newly acquired ones, were grown in pots.

An affirmation of these rigid ideas came from the great French designers, and at the time of the Restoration English estates extended across the countryside, avenue upon straight line, bosket upon formal *parterre*. The flower garden remained apart, safely enclosed in the walled confines of the kitchen garden area. Brave ideas of a flowering mead, fragrant and country-like, were promulgated from time to time. John Evelyn tried to persuade the King, Charles II, that during the rebuilding of London, following the Great Fire, extensive areas, 30 acres in extent, ought to be maintained in a 'green belt' fashion, with 'such shrubs as yield the most fragrant and odiferous flowers, and are aptist to tinge the air upon every gentle emission at a great distance.' Flower beds were to be filled with 'pinks, stocks, gillyflowers, primroses, avunculas, violets ....'

At the end of the century a posthumous publication of Timothy Nourse's on the *Benefits and Improvements of Husbandry* (1700) still showed a preoccupation with fragrant plants, almost as though amid the strenuous planning there was no exact place for them. He suggested that in the boskets there should be 'up and down ... little Banks or Hillocks planted with wild Thyme, Violets, Primroses, Cowslips, Daffadille, Lillies of the Valley, Blew-Bottles [cornflowers] Daisies, with all kinds of Flowers which grow wild in the Fields and Woods; as also amongst the Shades Strawberries, and up and down the Green-Walks let there be good store of Camomile, Water-Mint, Organy and the like; for these being trod upon yield a pleasant Smell ....' Richly scented and tender plants he amassed in the greenhouse (at that time roofed over, the plants cultivated in pots and taken out of doors on to the terraces to be enjoyed during the summer months). Here he suggested should be grown 'Orange and Lemon-Trees, Myrtles, of which the small leav'd Myrtle is more difficult to be preservéd: *Tuberosus's*, which will hold their Flowers in Winter, *Jessamins* of all sorts, as the Spanish or *Jessamine* of *Catalonia*, the *double-blossom'd Jessamine* ... as likewise *Mavyn, Syriacum*, which tho a little Shrub, or a sort of *Mastick Thyme*, is much to be valued for its rich Balsamick Smell: the Pomegranate-Tree, the Oleander or Rose-Lawrel.'

Lavender adorned alleys and walks as an edging plant, but was kept trimmed for conformity, and even in the 18th century Miss Reid in *The Scots Gardener* (1766) wrote, 'But for the sake of the flowers which are often used, we must have a plantation of it [lavender] apart.' By the mid-19th century it was considered to be 'worthy of being rescued from the bye-corners into which it is generally thrown' and grown alongside herbaceous plants. Sometimes, especially in Ireland, it was block-planted and very close-clipped, used as a lawn, in much the same way that chamomile and thyme were for pathways and walks in the 17th and 18th centuries.

New plants

Scented and aromatic introductions of the century included the chrysanthemum in 1629, the striped Rosa Mundi, *Liriodendron tulipifera* in *c* 1663, and *Robinia pseudoacacia* in 1640, although none of them outstandingly enhanced the fragrant assembly. The horse chestnut and laburnum were already firm favourites, though neither was grown particularly for its fragrance.

Small town gardens, privy gardens, and manorial plots about which so little has been written were less affected by the stalking avenues, and they must have been corners in which the flowering treasures were nurtured. Every contrived, reticulated, diapered or formal marking that could be stamped upon the petals of a polyanthus, auricula, gillyflower or pink was treasured, and as the plants hybridized easily fragrance persisted, if not improved, to enhance the newest seedling. Tulips also, less scented, and the hyacinth received the same passionate attention, the flowers flaked and striped and dappled. Tradescant's 1656 list included 30 named forms of tulip. Artificiality was admired so much, and it may be that these dainty humble plants owed their continued existence to their happy knack of surprise, as if controlled by the flick of the illusionist's wrist.

Thus a picture emerges of a period in which scented plants were not really catered for in the prevailing fashion. Humbler plots, unchanged by the passing years harboured the old plants, while the new introductions were cultivated mainly in the botanical collections, and in the kitchen garden areas of mansions, and by the rising generations of nurserymen.

CHAPTER FOUR

The Centuries of Growth

The eighteenth century

It would not be appropriate here to enlarge upon garden design, for on the greater canvas of the 'landskip' of the 18th century, scented plants had no place. Garden 'decoration' meant follies and temples, grottos, fountains, cascades and statuary.

Aromatics for both the pot and the medicine cupboard were firmly established in the kitchen garden, grown in rows in the manner of vegetables. Flowers obviously continued to be harboured there and in the more modest gardens also. Flowering shrubs were scattered in the orchard, planted singly like fruit trees. Herbs for physic were sometimes assembled in a physic garden and there escaped the attentions of the hybridist (and, indeed were to continue upon their appointed course to the present day). That the known scented plants were grown in various haphazard ways is beyond doubt, and throughout the 18th and 19th centuries many were overlooked in the excitement of new horticultural practices.

Florists' delights

Little wonder that the fecund primulas, dianthus and gillyflowers in general became the darlings of those who had but a modicum of garden space. Even then, they were grown in pots.

The Tudor and Stuart gardeners had been the first to admire curiousness and artificiality of form in flowering plants, and where simple crosses for varying forms of indigenous plants occurred, they were nurtured and brought into the garden. The ensuing, almost implicit obedience of the plants represented the early beginnings of plant breeding and hybridization. Perhaps more than any other plants, the variants of the primula and the pink epitomized Tudor flower gardens. Freaks, both sports and natural hybrids, of cowslip (*Primula veris*) were grown, called Galligaskins, Jackanapes-on Horseback and Hose-in-Hose (double-tiered). *Primula vulgaris*, the primrose, native of wooded banks and grassy hollows, was cultivated in double-flowered forms, and the natural marriage of the cowslip and primrose in both the wild state and in gardens engendered the oxlip. It was only following the introduction of what Parkinson called 'Tradescant's Purple Primrose' from Turkey in about 1640 that coloured primroses were known. At first it was grown only in collections and botanic gardens, but soon, because of its willingness to breed, introduced colour strains, and provided enthusiasts for generations with curiously elusive plants. The mutant, *Primula* x *variabilis*, the polyanthus, was a vital step in the enrichment of the scented garden.

Its birthdate is obscure – probably some time about the 1660s or '70s. Shortly, it captured the imagination of the fanciers, with its 'un-numbered' eyes of various colour and its willingness to break into patterned variants. Early in the 18th century it was widely grown, but by the middle of the century had become the darling of the florists. Early in the 19th century, the weavers and miners of Lancashire, Cheshire and the Falkirk area of Scotland lavished excessive affection on these little plants. Gold-laced Polyanthus, or Exhibition Gold-laced, became immensely popular, reaching a climax in the 1840s and '50s.

Bunch Primroses, as they were first called, were deliciously scented, and have been faithfully cultivated over three and a half centuries. Considered to be a truly British plant, it is still known on the European continent as the English Primula. The present-day colour range has sacrificed something in fragrance, and there is a prim sadness about the little caricature faces of some modern polyanthus.

Throughout the 18th century new and interesting spice flavours imported from the Far East, the rise of the pharmaceutical industry in the 19th, and the cosmetic industry of the 20th with the synthetic perfumes of the 1920s, combined to reduce the important of many aromantic and fragrant plants in cultivation and for garden decoration.

New plants

Meanwhile, some of the scented introductions of the 18th century were plants that were eventually to revolutionize gardens. Neither space, nor the confines of the subject allows all of them to be catalogued, but they included Evening Primroses (*Oenothera* spp) and bergamot (*Monarda didyma*) from the Americas, and Virginian Stock – a misnomer if ever there was one, for it is *Matthiola maritima* of the Mediterranean islands and was first called Dwarf Annual Stock, on arrival in 1713, for its resemblance in scent and flower to the gillyflowers. The stock or gillyflower itself (*M. incana*), known since the Middle Ages, was developed in the Brompton Nurseries, to the west of London, as a biennial form and called the Brompton Stock. The annual form was known by 1730 to be capable of producing flowers within 10 weeks, hence its 18th-century name of Ten-week Stock, which has remained.

The middle of the century brought the Tree Lupin, (*Lupinus arboreus*), and the Sweet Mignonette (*Reseda odorata*), the latter to assume enormous importance as a pot plant until the beginning of the present century. The sweet vanilla fragrance was prized, so it was used as a 'window plant' and in conservatories and parlours – a fashion said to have been instigated by the Empress Joséphine at Malmaison. An unheralded arrival early in the century

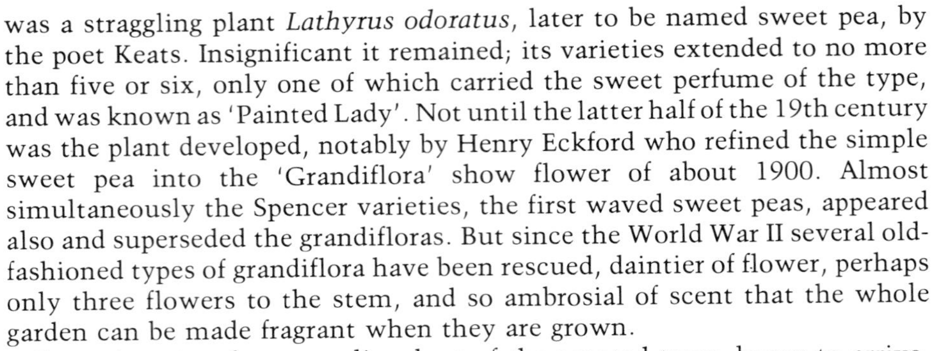

was a straggling plant *Lathyrus odoratus*, later to be named sweet pea, by the poet Keats. Insignificant it remained; its varieties extended to no more than five or six, only one of which carried the sweet perfume of the type, and was known as 'Painted Lady'. Not until the latter half of the 19th century was the plant developed, notably by Henry Eckford who refined the simple sweet pea into the 'Grandiflora' show flower of about 1900. Almost simultaneously the Spencer varieties, the first waved sweet peas, appeared also and superseded the grandifloras. But since the World War II several old-fashioned types of grandiflora have been rescued, daintier of flower, perhaps only three flowers to the stem, and so ambrosial of scent that the whole garden can be made fragrant when they are grown.

From America the magnolias, best of the scented trees, began to arrive. *Magnolia grandiflora* was one of the first, about 1736. By the end of the 18th century they were being used quite decoratively, planted in the so-called American gardens – flower and shrub gardens, in which were assembled plants from the north American continent. Magnolias from the Far East are comparative newcomers, arriving in our gardens only about the turn of this century through the expeditions of Delavay and Wilson.

This oversimplified account of the scented plants formerly to hand belies the growing lists of the nurserymen of the time; obviously potential gardening customers must have existed. Numberless plants have dropped by the wayside, swamped out of cultivation by the demands of fashion, or by fungus, while simultaneously many popular garden flowers were being created. There were others also that attracted little or no attention. *Phlox paniculata* is one of these, grown now for its excessive sweetness in the evening. It was introduced from America in the 1730s and not developed until a century later, mainly on the European continent, and in England by Capt. Symons-Jeune only this century.

Lilies, many of them deliciously scented, had always reveled in a reputation for being difficult to grow, keeping them aloof. *Lilium speciosum*, one of Siebold's introductions in 1832 had been loved for its studded beauty and fragrance, but the arrival of *L. regale* from the border-land of China and Tibet very early this century had a considerable impact. Its influence upon lily growing in general was far reaching, and its rise to popularity rapid.

Lathyrus odoratus

The rose

Many new forms of rose originated during the 18th and 19th centuries, not simply for the love of the varied flowers, but without doubt for their scent. Late in the 18th century, the China Rose (*Rosa sinensis*) arrived, known for a thousand years in the gardens of China, and displaying some remontant characteristic not previously known here in the genus. Some were tea-scented; 'Hume's Bush', 'Tea-Scented China' and the 'Yellow Tea-Scented China' were both brought home from China in the early years of the following century, introducing the tarry tea scent that has dominated the breeding of the Hybrid Teas of this century. Some of the early remontant roses were the parents of the deliciously perfumed Noisettes and Bourbons, and the incestuous family history provided Hybrid Perpetuals, and finally

Hybrid Teas with their conical tall bud and typical fragrance. The first surviving Hybrid Tea rose is 'La France', introduced in 1867, with silver lilac-pink flowers of rich fragrance. Without doubt, these various bush roses revolutionized the garden style, needing beds where they could be displayed, and it was when the Hybrid Polyanthas were first produced, in 1900-1905, that the use of roses as bedding plants was firmly established. The rose has persisted as the plant most extensively employed in this way.

In turn, the Polyanthas were crossed with the Hybrid Teas in the 1920s to give the race known as Floribundas. Late in the last century, the yellow single flowered Austrian Briar (*R. foetida*) was used with Hybrid Teas, infusing a colour range in roses not previously known. *Rosa foetida* itself had been crossed previously with other species roses; *R. harisonii* for instance was one of its progeny (1830). The specific *foetida* denotes an unpleasant smell, and it is interesting that this scent is ameliorated by warm sunshine, and that it has been inherited in many instances.

Poets have written with enthusiasm and emotion about roses, especially during the Victorian era, and the Moss Rose was almost adopted as an emblem of that time. It was produced early in the 18th century as a form of *Rosa centifolia* in which the scent glands of the stem and calyx are extended into moss-like growth. The fragrance lasts very well after cutting, so it became a favourite corsage decoration, especially for the Victorians.

An article in *The Rose Annual* (1980) reflects the continued interest in

Scented climbing roses can be trailed across the top of a dividing fence or railings in a suburban garden

scented roses. An assessment of fragrance made over a period, allocating a points system from 'scent just detectable' to 'supreme scent', shows that in this respect some of the older named forms hold their own with modern invaders. Those gaining the highest points are: 'René d'Anjou' (Moss), 'Lilian Lobb' (Moss), 'Mme Pierre Oger' (Bournon), 'Blanc double de Coubert' (Rugosa), 'Comtesse du Cayla' (China), 'George Dixson' (HT), 'Buff Beauty' (H Musk), 'Yvonne Rabier' (Polyantha) 'Eden Rose' (HT), 'Prima Ballerina' (HT), 'Papa Meilland' (HT), 'Blue Moon' (HT), 'Apricot Nectar' (Floribunda), 'Michelle' (Floribunda), and 'Elizabeth of Glamis' (Floribunda).

A listing of aromatic and scented plants introduced from the American continent during the 19th century would be cumbersome, but notable are some of the plants discovered by David Douglas.

For example, the American currants (*Ribes* spp), add to the fragrance of the garden early in the year; we should also mention his fir (*Pseudotsuga menziesii*), some *Abies* specis, lupins, Evening Primroses and *Mimulus* species of which the famous Monkey Musk (*M. moschatus*) was one. Probably more has been written about the loss of scent of this plant than of any other, and yet it seems totally comprehensible when Douglas himself wrote, 'the musk odour is apparently not characteristic in plants at the coast.' He was collecting then in Colombia, and this would suggest that some strains carried the musk scented glands in the foliage, and others did not. *The Morning Post* of 8 January 1924 seems to offer the most acceptable answer. A new hybrid scentless musk (*M. moschatus harrisonii*) was introduced in 1877 by Harrison & Sons of Leicester – a cross between *M. moschatus* (scented) and *M. moschatus* (unscented). So wide was the popularity of this plant that many people grew it believing it to be the introduction, and were puzzled by the loss of scent. In *Sweet Scented Flowers and Fragrant Leaves* (1893) Donald McDonald says of *Mimulus moschatus*, 'Mimulus Harrisoni is a large flowering variety.' Is it not probable that as a popular pot plant this showy scentless form was preferable?

Lilacs

To day, lilac provides one of the most floriferous and fragrant groups of plants; some of the species were introduced from China about the turn of the century, others cultivated in Britain for many years previously. *Syringa* × *persica* is thought to have been here before 1640. It is the cultivars that enhance gardens today, raised over a long period extending from the 1870s to the 1920s and '30s by Lemoine father and son at Nancy, France. More recently, the range has been extended by Clarke of California. Synonymous with the 'syringa' is Mock Orange (*Philadelphus* spp) and Lemoine is a name closely associated also with some of the best hybrids of these plants. *Philadelphus* × *lemoinei* raised in 1884 provides a series of fragrant plants now, such as 'Avalanche' and 'Innocence'.

Scent from China

In The Far East, China especially revealed a wealth of plants throughout the last century, particularly during the second half, through the expeditions of Maries, Fortune, Forrest, Wilson and Delavay. Some plants were fragrant gems, and whilst the frenzied search for rhododendrons led to the undervaluing of some other plants, many of our treasured scented shrubs came from this source. Examples are *Buddleia alternifolia, B. davidii, B. fallowiana, Cercidiphyllum japonicum, C. sinense, Clethra delavayi, Deutzia* spp, *Dipelta floribunda, Eleagnus* spp, *Hamamelis mollis, Hemerocallis* spp, *Jasminum nudiflorum, Lilium regale, Lonicera fragrantissima, Mahonia japonica, Magnolia delavayi, M. wilsonii, Osmanthus* spp, *Pieris formosus forrestii, Primula* spp, *Prunus* spp, especially the double-flowered Japanese Cherries, *Spiraea arborea*, and *Viburnum farreri*.

Earlier in the 19th century China had provided the fragrant *Wisteria sinensis, Matricaria* spp, *Rosa banksiae* and *R. filipes*, and above all *Chrysanthemum morifolium* (*sinense*) which is the florists' chrysanthemum, the univesal flower of garden and greenhouse for both amateur and professional alike. Many people find the scent too blunt and rough, and would not describe it as fragrant, but rather odorous. It is contained in all parts of the plant but especially in the crushed flower bud. Beverley Nichols referred to it as 'the rough male scent of the chrysanthemum'.

The Asiatic primulas vary considerably in their degree of fragrance; some are quite fulsome, others less so. Among the sweetest introduced are probably *Primula alpicola, P. chionantha, P. florindae, P. involucrata, P. malacoides* and *P. nutans*. Just prior to World War II one of Frank Kingdon-Ward's introductions was *Primula hyacinthina*, which, as the name reveals, is intensely sweet-scented like the hyacinth.

Nineteenth-century plant-hunting enthusiasm was directed into a somewhat feverish search for rhododendrons. Some scented ones came from China, noteably *Rhododendron decorum*, sent home by David as one of his last introductions. The richly scented *R. auriculatum* arrived about the same time and was introduced by E. H. Wilson, although it had been found and recorded earlier by Augustine Henry. Wilson is also credited with the late-flowering *R. discolor* from Szechwan, parent of many useful hybrids. One of the first fragrant species was named *R. fortunei* after Robert Fortune during the 1850s and one of the latest, an aromatic plant, was *R. tsangpoense*, brought home by Kingdon-Ward in the 1930s.

South America and the orchids

Several warmly exotic fragrant plants have originated from the South American continent. In the 18th century the Golden Ball Tree, *Buddleia globosa*, so unusual in form, must have been an appealing curio. *Aloysia citriodora* (*triphylla*) and later *Azara macrophylla, Laurelia serrata* (the Chilean Laurel) and *Eucryphia glutinosa* arrived. During the present century this latter plant climbed to stardom as *E.* 'Nymansay'. A further delightful introduction was *Drimys winteri*, which came as a living plant in 1827 but had been known beforehand for its fragrant bark, a piece of which had been brought to England by a Captain Winter, from one of Drake's ships.

Of all the 19th-century arrivals from this continent, none plucked at both heart and purse strings quite like the orchids. A Czech, Roezl, explored the rain forests of South America for these plants, later Hooker found some orchids in Sikkim, and others have arrived from Malaysia.

A number of garden periodicals (a new idea in the 19th century) allocated considerable weekly space to the cultivation of orchids and other greenhouse exotics – some of which were really hardy plants, but on first sight thought to be tender because they had arrived from a foreign land. Orchids became an expensive craze and today are plants of the higher echelons of horticulture, the international aristocrats of the plant world. Many of them are fragrant: *Cattleya citrina*, sweet and mellow of scent like that of the limes, *Cattleya intermedia*, *Coelogyne barbata*, scented of musk, *C. custata* with a banana-coconut scent, *C. massangeana*, rather sweeter, and *C. speciosa*, again musky. *Cymbidium simulans* from the Sikkim is sweetly scented, *C. eburneum* strongly fragrant, and *C. ensifolium* also fragrant. *Dendrobium aggregatum* is honey-scented, *D. chrysotoxum*, *D. devonianum*, and *D. moschatum* musky. *D. nobile* is said to change its perfume through the day, reminiscent of sweet new-mown hay or honey in the evening but strengthening to primrose in the morning. The enthusiasm of earlier writers for orchids, credits *Epidendrum fragrans* with the various scents of stephanotis, syringa, carnation and anise. Similarly they eulogize on the scent of the *Lycaste* species, comparing them with a whole hedge of hawthorn, or with strong vanilla or almonds. The scent is rich and heavy, but clearly lemony in *Lycaste aromatica*; *Odontoglossum pendulum* is rose-scented, and *P. pulchellum* exudes the rich sweetness of the lily-of-the-valley. The *Vanda cristata* and *V. tricolor* are both fragrant, but *V. suavis*, true to its name, is redolent of gillyflowers.

Hoya vella, introduced from India early in the nineteenth century

CHAPTER FIVE

The Fragrant Garden Emerges

THE YEARS at the beginning of this century are now sufficiently in perspective, for it to be confirmed that some selection and order was achieved, to calm down the garishness of Victorian abundance, while simultaneously admitting a freedom of garden style. From the ponderous over-abundance of gaudy flowering plants used in greenhouses and bedding on the one hand and ferns and sombre shrubs on the other came the influences that were to lighten and decorate our present gardens. Pages have been written already about the general ideas of William Robinson and Gertrude Jekyll and their peers – their haloes must rest somewhat heavily at times – but from their work a 20th-century garden style has emerged.

Shafts of light were thrown upon the use of plant material, allowing its form and quality to determine garden planning, in much the same way that the impressionist painters had thrown light on their subjects. Pillars and pergolas for support of climbing roses and other scented scrambling plants were popularized, adapted from the shaded terraces of Italian gardens and harking back to the trellised arbours of Renaissance gardens in England. Piers, swags and arches added to the floriferous exuberance of Edwardian formal gardens. Meanwhile, the flowering shrubs culled from the plant-hunting expeditions and the European plant breeders of the past fifty years, gave a permanence to flower borders not previously achieved. Woodland areas evolved from old parkland, and were integrated into the garden proper, and the added impetus of rhododendron planting led to the deliberate formation of wild or woodland gardens.

In addition there were armies of professional gardeners in private service, with eagerness and all the facilities for cultivating a plethora of plants. Gardening was not, as it is today, a weekend and evening hobby. Over all this reigned the Royal Horticultural Society. The unique rôle played by the Society in the first half of this century as co-ordinator of the gardening public and the nursery trade is often overlooked. Through the system of trials (from which the Awards emanate), floral committees and shows, the trade and private gardener alike have been able to promote new and interesting plant material.

When the discerning influences began to take effect, two kinds of garden emerged: firstly flowering and semi-formal, and secondly woodland, where the rhododendrons, lilies, and bulbous plants could merge with nature. In retrospect, the alternating rigidity and freedom of style of preceding eras had offered no place where fragrant plants could be assembled. The Victorians for example, embraced the new, carelessly enjoying the brilliance of colour, to the almost total exclusion of the simple plants older in cultivation. Perhaps only in some cottage gardens and provincial country areas were they still treasured, remnants of former tenants. Miss Jekyll's delight in compartmented gardens has provided a style which has allowed the formal scented garden to be established. Fragrant shrubs, invariably with some accompanying attraction, have found a home in the fluid lines of the shrub borders, but the lowly aromatics and pervasively fragrant flowering plants are now established in the 'scented garden'.

The fragrant garden

A phase in the evolution of the fragrant garden was the rise of a formal herb garden. It is vain to search among Victorian writing for references to herb gardens, for the plants, where they were grown, were denizens of the kitchen garden. The decorative herb garden emerges as an area bordering a lawn where aromatic plants were undertrodden, the idea echoing Bacon's ideal of 1625. Research further suggests that some of the gardens described never existed. An example is at Broughton Castle, near Banbury, Oxfordshire. No herb garden existed according to the family memories and yet there is a delightful description of one there, purporting to be a faithful copy of a past garden, where plants offered themselves to be trodden upon. The garden was heralded by letters clipped in santolina and reading 'Ye Herbe Garden' . . . such were the fantasies.

The clipping of herbs to form texts, ribbons or patterns echoed the former knot garden ideas, and by 1900 the only manifestation was, perhaps, as border edging, or as concentric rings around a central sundial. In hindsight, it is hardly surprising that when Gertrude Jekyll came to plan herb gardens, she visualized them within a 'plat' or level area of formal shape (as the Tudor's had done), and she usually enclosed them, to enhance the aroma and prevent it being snatched by the breeze. The watershed came in the first decade of the 20th century; writing in *Home and Garden* (1900) she included herbs in the chapter on Kitchen Gardens, but, in practice, six or seven years later, she was planning formal herb gardens and allowing these simple plants the bold formality they require to set them off. Interestingly, not all her plans for small plots were executed. In 1907, she designed a herb garden for Knebworth Park, Hertfordshire which was never carried out, but is, at present, being included in the restoration of the garden. Her plan for this little herb plot was based on an existing Victorian feature, *near* the kitchen garden; perhaps just the first step out of it!

By the time she was designing for Barrington Court, Somerset in 1923 her ideas for a rose and paeony garden comprised a formal treatment with central pool, the seven-foot walls decorated with escallonias, Macartney Roses, laurustinus, (trained) honeysuckles, and roses 'Climbing Aimée

OPPOSITE
Wisteria clothes a house wall in a particularly decorative way

Vibert', 'The Garland', and 'Zephirine Drouhin'. The beds were to be planted with paeonies and roses; the former were not named, but the roses she selected were 'Caroline Testout', 'General McArthur', 'Hugh Dickson', 'Radiance', and 'Mrs Edward Powell'. Here assembled and enclosed was a garden of scented plants.

Miss Jekyll's *pot pourri*

A profusion of flowers abounded in the Edwardian flower garden and Miss Jekyll used many of these to make *pot pourri*. She tells how when she first embarked upon *pot pourri*-making it could be

> mixed in a large red-ware pan; as I grew more ambitious the mixing was done in a hip-bath, in later years in a roomy wooden tub; but now the bulk is so considerable that it can only be dealt with on a clear floor space. The heap rises, and from time to time has to be flattened, as the jolly party all round throw on their handfuls. . . . The heap grows like one of the big ant-hills in the wood, until at last all the jars are empty and everyone's hands are either sticky with salt or powdery with sweet spices. Now the head Pot-pourri maker takes a shovel, and turns the heap over from left to right and then from right to left, and backwards and forwards several times till all is duly mixed. Then the store cask is brought forwards, a strong iron-hooped oak cask with a capacity of fifteen gallons. It looks as if the fragrant heap could never be got into it, but in it goes shovelful by shovelful, and . . . it must weigh a hundredweight and three-quarters, possibly more. If the mixture stays some weeks or even months in the cask before any is taken out, by remaining untouched for a while it seems to acquire a richer and more mellow scent.
>
> The studio floor is left in a shocking state of mess. A wide space in front of the ingle shows a dark patch of briny moisture; footmarks of the same are thick in the neighbourhood of the site of the heap, and some small tracks further afield show where little feet have made more distant excursions; . . . and there will be a half-day's work for the char-woman tomorrow.

The fullblown fragrance of the garden was thus captured!

Bringing the aromatics together

Writers who were mindful of fragrance in the early years of the 20th century included Gertrude Jekyll (she even suggested that the children should have a 'herb patch' in their gardens), Donald McDonald, Ellen Wilmott, E. A. Bowles, and F. A. Hampton; but for early reference to the making of scented gardens, as such, we must turn to Frances A. Bardswell's *The Herb Garden* (1911). First she writes, 'Very often a piece of the kitchen garden is portioned off to make the Herb Garden. If possible, this plot should come between the flower garden and the kitchen garden, where it will be a sort of debateable land between the purely useful and the purely ornamental.' Here is a suggestion as to where the fragrant plants might be assembled, though a declaration of uncertainty as to their rightful place. She continues: 'Here, too, we may enjoy such old fashioned Roses as were valued for their sweetness and are banished these days, when, owing a good deal to the demands of Flower-shows, size, form and colour are put before fragrance.'

Horticulture gained in exuberance once World War I was over and herb gardens became accepted, often created, still within the confines of or at best very close to the kitchen garden; but sometimes deference was made to the flower garden by assembling them in an arrangement of the herbaceous border type. A large border of this kind was made by Lady Margaret Watney in the nut garden at Cornbury, Oxfordshire, which had once been the home of Lord Danby, first benefactor of the Oxford Botanic Garden in 1621. Lady Margaret wrote a little book (1922) about the garden, quoting from the old and contemporary writers something of the virtues of each plant she included in her garden. In her preface she said that in making her garden she

Low-growing fragrant plants including thymes dotted about the steps and the centre of the path. To the left are rosemary and roses; to the right Jasminum officinale *grown in a container raised so that the fragrance can be enjoyed in passing*

went straight to the old herbalists and found to her delight that '. . . they include most of our beautiful flowers, Roses, Lilies, Hollyhocks, and there is no need to have the dingy border we are apt to associate with the words "Herb Garden" . . .'

What appears to have been a halting start to the renewal of interest in growing these green aromatics in gardens for themselves gained momentum during the 1930s when Eleanour Sinclair Rohde was designing herb gardens. She designed one to be purely ornamental at Lullingstone Castle, Kent, reviving the chequerboard design of mediaeval gardens. Her work and writings were principally concerned with herbs, but she wrote also *The Scented Garden* (1931).

The formal scented garden

The first formal scented garden that I have been able to trace was begun by Vita Sackville West at Sissinghurst Castle, Kent, in 1938 when the enfolding hedge was planted to provide shelter. Not until World War II was over did she did she plant the garden, as a herb garden, in 1947, set out on very formal simple lines – a central bowl and cruciform grass paths. Subsequently (1968) the National Trust paved the paths to allow for the extra trafficking.

Herbs, as such, represent only a part of the story, and to digress and record the valuable contributions made by Lady Rosalind Northcote, Margaret Grieve, Dorothy Hewer, Mrs C. F. Leyel, and again Eleanour Sinclair Rohde is very tempting. Margaret Brownlow did an enormous amount of work with both herbs and fragrant plants, farming and designing gardens. Her book *Herbs and the Fragrant Garden* first published in 1957, and very recently in a handsome new edition, has become a classic even among a profusion of present-day herbals. She designed the ornamental herb garden at Knole, Kent, which is being restored at present. Since her untimely death in the early 1960s the impulse has strengthened to grow herbs in a decorative way, usually in the formal way which sets off these humble plants so well. Quite apart from the revival of interest in natural products which began in the early 1960s and has gained momentum during the last decade, gardeners are now growing herbs alongside other scented plants and cottage garden flowers. That formal herb gardens reached their apogee in the 1970s there is little doubt. The forward movement is to make scented, or nosegay gardens. Gardeners, at last, after 400 years, have found a place for these scented, fragrant – call them what you will – gorgeous plants.

Modern scented gardens

Several excellent scented gardens exist now, where what we call today herbs and cottage-garden plants grow side by side with fragrant plants from many corners of the world, together with some products of more modern horticultural techniques. The herbs are cloaked in folklore, which merely proves their ancient cultivation, trailing their superstitions through the centuries; the garden originals are there by dint of dedicated plantsmen, but all of them were culled and cultured by generations of gardeners.

On the ancient site of the Privy Garden, now prosaically the Lower West Garden at Hatfield House, Hertfordshire, the Marquess of Salisbury has created what is undoubtedly the most ambitious scented garden in England. There have been gardens at Hatfield since the 17th century, for when the mansion was first built John Evelyn the diarist (and gardener) visited it on 11 March 1643 and afterwards wrote, 'I went to see My Lord Salisbury's Palace at Hatfield, where the most conciderable rarity, besides the House, were the garden and vinyard, rarely well watered and planted.'

The present scented garden is extensive and has an enclosed herb garden at its centre encircled by a clipped hedge of fragrant sweetbrier. Paths are clothed in chamomile and aromatic thymes, and laid out on the simplest of formal lines, with a sundial at the centre. Low-growing aromatic plants form pools of ground cover, splashed about with pinks, variegated mints and violas. And there also are Painted Sage, Purple Sage, Golden Sage, Variegated Rue, Variegated Lemon Balm and in the surrounding garden proper, raised on two sides, grow Gallica, Damask and Bourbon roses, lavenders, Scented-leaved Pelargoniums and a host of scented plants like Dame's Violet, lily-of-the-valley, irises, tulips and fragrant flowering shrubs such as lilacs, Mock Orange, *Cytisus battandieri* and the even more tender *C.* 'Porlock'. The enfolding walls are curtained with scented roses and *Clematis recta*, *C. rehderana*, *C. flammula*, and *Jasminum officinalis*; wisteria, magnolias, pear blossom give up their perfume in the spring.

Lady Salisbury's other garden is at Cranborne Manor in Dorset, where a masterly herb garden has acquired something of the air of a scented garden during the past few years. A formal rectangular plot is encompassed by high yew hedge on three sides and a brick rendered wall on the fourth to form a sheltered microclimate in which aromatic plants may best be enjoyed and appreciated. Fragrant roses scale the wall, Lemon Verbena sprawls happily and honeysuckles and clematis entwine. Grass paths separate eight formal beds, geometric in concept, each edged by clipped santolina. Tulips, alliums and irises add splashes of colour in the early part of the year and a long narrow bed of lily-of-the-valley that extends the length of the garden on one side scents the air in early May, and later makes an attention-attracting groundwork colour when the vermilion berries ripen. Every herb and aromatic plant is there. This is a marvellous garden in which to learn, or even test one's knowledge, and several treasures are to be found. As dot plants, standard honeysuckles lend height, sweetening the air in mid-summer. How short is the season for all these favourite plants! Other gardens where fragrance may be enjoyed are the small scented garden at Arley Hall, (Cheshire), Sissinghurst Castle (Kent), particularly in June when the old garden roses are at their best, The Royal National Rose Society's Display Garden, at St Albans (Hertfordshire) and Mottisfont Abbey, Hampshire. It is here, in the old walled garden that the National Trust has assembled its own collection of old garden roses, and rose species, the scent of which is quite indescribable. A more recent collection of roses, where fragrance is of paramount interest is at Castle Howard, Yorkshire. A delightfully decorative fragrant garden is at Horsted Place (East Sussex) where in addition to great swags and baskets of roses, there is a whole area designed around the use of scented plants, all at ground level. One of the series of gardens at Mannington Hall, (Norfolk) is a scented one and there is a well designed perfumed garden as an integral part of the Pavilion Gardens at Buxton (Derbyshire).

The recent interest in herbs manifests itself in the numerous herb gardens, or collections of aromatic plants that have been formed during the past fifteen years or so. Several good ones are maintained by the National Trust, namely at Hardwick Hall (Derbyshire) where a large herb garden contains kitchen and economic plant; at Little Moreton Hall (Cheshire), at Charlecote Park (Warwickshire) where the collection is formed of plants that Shakespeare mentioned, at Sissinghurst Castle (Kent), Bateman's (Sussex), Felbrigg Hall (Norfolk), Castle Drogo (Devon), Scotney Castle (Kent) where the recently formed garden is called a Nosegay Garden, and at Gunby Hall (Lincolnshire) where there is an emphasis on fragrant plants. Other good herb collections are at Elvaston Castle (Nottinghamshire), Liverpool University Botanic Garden (Ness, Wirral), Gauldon Manor (Somerset), Longstock Park (Hants), Hall Place, (Bexley, Greater London), Wye College (Kent), Hever Castle (Kent), Denman College, Women's Institute Education Centre (Berkshire), Claverton Manor (Avon), Fulham Palace (London), and those that have already been described in some detail. Many of the nurseries, and herb centres are now specializing in fragrant plants in addition to the accepted aromatics that belong in the herb garden.

Scented gardens for the blind

'Gardens for the Blind' has become a somewhat ill-considered name for gardens intended to afford some special enjoyment and relaxation for the blind and partially sighted people. Such disabled persons do not need to visit these gardens alone, for sighted people can enjoy fragrance of flowers and newly mown grass and the deep smell of earth after rain every bit as much. Also, the blind derive great pleasure from the company of their sighted friends; indeed, they may be dependent upon them to reach the gardens, and really do not want a 'hard to find' braille label when they get there. Many local authorities have made special corners where plants can be examined by hand for leaf texture, or where the beds are raised to bring plants nearer to nose level, or where perhaps a handrail is provided. Others, alas, have a forlorn corner of permanent aromatic planting, which looks decidedly abandoned, with perhaps one or two seats.

By regarding such gardens more broadly as 'Gardens for the Disabled', far more attractive results can be achieved. Raised beds, enabling wheelchair visitors and arthritic people to enjoy the plants at close range, will at the same time provide a guiding wall for the blind or partially sighted person. Wide level paths, where the lame can be relieved of troublesome steps, and where they can be easily accompanied by a stronger companion, also provide easy access for wheel chairs, as well as uncluttered ground for the blind. Seats aplenty can be recessed for safety, where the scents and sounds of the garden may be enjoyed. Water, perhaps as a fountain, or in a pool raised for safety, where pleasure can be derived from trailing the hands in the water, adds movement and sound. Such a raised pool is at the Royal Horticultural Society's Garden at Wisley, Surrey in the garden for the disabled.

A permanent garden for the blind and disabled has been opened at the Royal Agricultural Showground, at Stoneleigh, Warwickshire, to encourage the disabled to attempt and to enjoy gardening. It is maintained by the Warwickshire Association for the Blind, but, unfortunately because of its distance from the road, the disabled are finding it somewhat inaccessible. Other scented gardens, of particular interest to the partially sighted and disabled, where sound, touch and smell are of primary consideration are at: Weston Park (Staffordshire), Jephson Gardens, Leamington Spa (Warwickshire) Queen's Park Gardens, Harborne, Birmingham and Abington Park, Northampton. Special guided tours can be arranged at the Royal Botanic Garden, Kew, and at Wallington Hall, Northumberland, a braille leaflet is available to help in the enjoyment of the lovely flower garden there.

Most helpful of all, apparently, is the provision of a recorded tape, relating to numbered beds; the numbers should be large and embossed. An altenative suggestion is an embossed map of the garden at the entrance, based on a simple plan that may be memorized, and individual plant labels either on the raised bed edge, on the hand rail, or on posts to make them easy to find.

A list of plants to include has been prepared by the Royal Horticultural Society and tallies, in general, with the catalogue later in this book. Of special interest are the plants with textured foliage and flowers, such as *Phlomis fruticosa* with its dry stiff foliage and stems and hooked sturdy flower heads; *Buxus sempervirens*, for its small tough evergreen leaves contrasting so well with, say, the soft leaves of Lad's Love, *Artemisia abrotanum*, feathery and sweetly camphorous in scent, or the silky flannel texture of *Stachys lanata*; the tufted flowers of pinks and Sweet William, compared with the soft rounded flower heads of phlox or velvety wallflowers. The resilient spikes of lavender contrast with the coral-like growth of santolina, the cold smooth foliage of *Choisya ternata* with the lobed soft leaf of the flowering currant. The tacky growth of *Cystus* species is foiled by the smooth sickle-like leaf of some of the eucalypts. All play a part in the enjoyment of plant appreciation, quite apart from and in addition to their fragrances. Such plants afford a selection of sufficient diversity to be used in creative planting schemes that will prove of interest and satisfaction also to sighted visitors.

Scented plants fall into two categories. There are fragrant flowering shrubs and plants that breathe their perfume into the air, such as daphnes, jasmines, pinks, wallflowers, and phlox. Then there are those that need to be inspected to reveal their fragence, like rosemary, lavenders, mints, bergamot, and thymes. Thus, in planning a garden *to be inspected* in this way, it is a considered practice to put those plants which waft their fragrance away from the path, and those that need to be handled near to the edge.

At home, where the garden is designed for the enjoyment of the frail and elderly, a little consideration to the planning of easy access to a patio or summerhouse, where tubs or decorative raised containers can be moved about and replaced, will afford continuous pleasure throughout the summer.

CHAPTER SIX

Gardening with Fragrant Plants

A GARDEN may be likened to a mobile; delicately balanced, multi-dimensional, never static, and supremely individual. The art of planting and creating one, more than any other art, requires practice, loving patience and a keenly observant eye. Visiting other gardens, and arranging successful or personally satisfying planting schemes are the best schools, and above all, a careful appraisal of plants themselves.

In planning a fragrant garden, a little more care and a little extra observation of plants are required. The general rules for planning, or even renovating, are followed, but in addition the introduction of plants selected primarily for their fragrance of flower or leaf has to be considered. A garden as a whole may be planned using only scented plants, or part of a larger garden set aside for fragrant treasures. Perhaps merely the establishment of an odd sheltered corner would be enough, where perhaps a seat or summer-house could be placed, surrounded by fragrant planting. On the other hand, a small secluded part of the garden could be devoted to such plants. However the idea is considered, the words 'secluded', 'sheltered', 'corner' seem to arise, striking the keynote to the enjoyment of a scented plot. Protection. Protection from prevailing winds affords the creation of a micro-climate within the garden, where plants flourish more happily without the disturbance of strong air currents. On an enfolded site, such plants as lilac, philadelphus, sweet brier, phlox and wallflowers that give their fragrance freely on to the air, do then not flower in vain, to have their fragrance snatched and whisked away by the wind. Other plants that need to be brushed or rubbed to release their scent will be far more fulsome of aroma for the protection.

So, it follows that the last place to make a fragrant garden is high on a windswept mountain – and the next-to-last place, on a new bare plot amid housing development. Alas, many of us have to tackle this sort of plot, where patience and some knowledge are of paramount importance. Temporary shelter is often provided by fencing, by using walls of the house, by retaining walls, even by plastic screening, but the creation of some form of canopy is a major consideration. Trees take time to establish, but there is no better a shelter for the fragrant garden, ultimately, than the semi-shade and semi-blanket cover provided by trees. Fragrance diffuses across a garden in trails and can only be held captive by enfolding hedges and shrubs, fences and walls, and only enjoyed fully where some light overhead screen – such as tree branches – keeps the evening temperatures reasonably equable by reducing the effect of radiation. Two or three trees in a reasonably small garden can act, also, as a baffle against passing traffic and other noise. The planting and selection of trees is dealt with later in more detail (page 136).

Shrubs, especially evergreen, usually provide better shelter than a fence or wall, because they sift the breezes, reducing the strength of the currents. Walls often form eddies of air so that a corner, perhaps chosen for sitting out, proves to be rough even on a warm day. For this reason alone a hedge, although it takes time to establish, provides the best shelter, best of all if it be evergreen (but slower growing). Hedges themselves can be scented, and need not necessarily be boundary hedges . . . lower internal hedges planted, for example, in the form of a horseshoe, allow for protected areas on both sides, forming sun and shade and a variety of minute micro-climates, as does a natural winding hedgerow. At the same time they add an element of surprise or even secrecy to the general outlook from the house, and create a more interesting garden tour. Impenetrable hedges as boundaries, where space and scale allow, can be of crataegus or sweet brier, strong ones of elder or roses, evergreen of escallonia, box, viburnums, *Olearia ilicifolia*, and of bay or rosemary in maritime areas.

To break up a large sloping windswept site, I planted a hedge of lilac in my

Azalea narcissiflorum

garden some years ago, which has developed into a perfect screen in summer and a flowering backdrop to look down upon in May. The idea came from Mr Secrett's farm in Surrey, where, to provide shelter for the salad crops, he planted lilac hedges and aligned them with the irrigation supply pipes – and, as a good businessman, he marketed the lilac crop in addition. Lilac hedges can of course, be pleached and trimmed, if required.

A selection of plants for fragrant hedges and screens

Buxus sempervirens (E)
Chamaecyparis lawsoniana
'Allumii' (E)
'Fletcheri' (E)
'Green Hedger'
Crataegus spp
Cupressus macrocarpa and some forms (E)
Escallonia cvs (E)
Eucalyptus gunnii (for milder counties)
Laurus nobilis (E) (for milder counties)
Lavendula angustifolia (E) (short lived)
Ligustrum ovalifolium (semi E)
'Aureum' (semi E)
Lupinus arboreus (E) (from seed, quick, temporary)
Mahonia aquifolium (E)
'Winter Sun' (E)
Olearia × *haastii* (E)
ilicifolia (E)
macrodonta (E) (especially maritime areas)
× *Osmarea burkwoodii* (E)
Philadelphus coronarius
Prunus laurocerasus (E)
lusitanica (E)
Ribes sanguineum 'Pulborough Scarlet'
Rosa centifolia
gallica and forms
rubiginosa
Rose: Floribundas,
Hybrid Musks
Rosmarinus officinalis (E) (not for cold exposed places)
Ruta graveolens (E)
Sambucus nigra
racemosa 'Plumosa Aurea'
Santolina chamaecyparissus (E) (ragged in winter, short lived)
virens (E)
Spartium junceum
Syringa vulgaris cvs
chinensis
× *Thuya occidentalis* (E)
plicata (E)
Viburnum tinus (E)

Planning for fragrance

It is the plants themselves that form the material of the integral design. Serious consideration has to be given to suitability of the plants to site scale, soil, altitude, and aspect as well as the general location. It is to advantage to work with all the salient features of the site, such as entrances and slope, and to accept any limitations imposed by soil, or existing large trees or water.

The mere selection of fragrant plant material and its disposal about the garden following any general rules of planting is not quite enough, where perfume is the primary consideration in the enjoyment of the garden.

A variety of 'tricks' can be devised to enhance fragrance, or to render it more accessible. Where the garden is enjoyed mainly in the evening, by those who are away at work during the day, evening-scented plants will prove most rewarding – in addition to the others. Where warm walls exist, and these will be the south, south-west and west-facing ones, absorbing heat during the day and radiating it during the evening, a scented climber can not only be enhanced in its effect by the warmth but can be persuaded to remain supremely fragrant in the evening. The violet-scented *Rosa banksiae* responds well, as does *Mandevilla suaveolens* when planted like this. A recessed seat beneath an established plant makes a warm spot to sit in until quite late on a warm summer evening. Other scented climbers that would be enriched by warm wall planting are *Clematis* × *triternata* 'Rubromarginata' and the cowslip-scented *C. rehderana* may be used in the same way. Where there is sufficient height, the rose could be used to outstrip the clematis, the former scented in June, the clematis in August and September. It is tempting where wall shrubs are planted to group smaller plants about their feet and knees, often obscuring lanky basal growth, but regard needs to be given to the combined effects of the perfumes. At Powis Castle, on a warm terrace wall, a treasured *Trachelospermum asiaticum* made plaintive appeal with *Helichrysum serotinum* at its base. Curry dinner filled the surrounding air!

Loniceras immediately spring to mind as evening-scented climbers; they advertise their presence most emphatically at dusk when the long-tongued moths are on the wing. While their sweet perfume compensates, fluttering moths around a peaceful seat will distract some people. When loniceras are grown on house walls, open bedroom windows can prove inviting to moths.

Scent for the evening

Here is a short list of plants that are particularly scented in the evening, indeed they have been called 'Vesper Flowers'!

Abronia umbellata
Cestrum parqui (night)
Daphne laureola (night)
Datura suaveolens
Hesperis matronalis
Lonicera spp especially × *heckrotii*
Matthiola bicornis
Mirabilis jalapa
Nicotiana alata 'Grandiflora'
Oenothera spp
Pelargonium gibbosum (leaves unpleasant, but flowers fragrant at night)
P. triste
Phlox paniculata
Reseda odorata
Saponaria officinalis

Hold fragrance aloft

Climbers and wall shrubs with fragrant flowers, however, gentle of scent, provide marvellous fragrant garden decoration. Where space and labour allow, a pergola displays plants to great advantage allowing the fragrance either to pervade the air, as with wisteria, roses, clematis, and sweet peas, or to be easily inspected. At Mapperton, Dorset, a rectangular area has been covered by a pergola upon which scented plants scramble – loniceras, vitis, actinidias and roses – and can be enjoyed at close range. From a pergola to a 'canopy' (a car-port type of structure, formed of cross-bars) is but a step, and quite effective canopies can be made by a garden handyman. Beware the drips in the English climate from this type of structure; its location needs some thought. I have seen trellis Nettlon-style used to form a 'tent' or canopy extended from the back of a garage, where *Passiflora caerulea* grew very happily. A more weigthy plant in such a position could present problems. Another delightful idea, using Nettlon, is to form an arched surround to a standard wisteria. It will take some years to look established,

A wooden structure such as this can be used to support fragrant plants. Here Wisteria sinensis *is lifted to form a scented canopy*

but the drooping racemes when in flower embellish it gracefully and make a filmy, floaty garden ornament. Laburnum can be used in this way too; the fragrance is at face level.

Pretty fibreglass and plastic arbours and arches can be purchased, stark in themselves, but purposeful when decked with roses, clematis, wisteria and honeysuckles. With patience, laburnums can be persuaded to trace the contours of such structures, and they are among the best plants from which to form a scented arcade, as at Barnsley House, Gloucestershire, and Bodnan, Tal-y-Cafn, N. Wales.

The domed frames used to display small-flowered standard roses make first-rate supports for standard honeysuckles. The stems are entwined to form a mushroom-like shape, which becomes a very pretty fragrant 'umbrella' when in bloom. Standard honeysuckles do not necessarily need this kind of support; they make good dot plants, resembling aerial bunches of flowers, as at Cranborne Manor, Dorset. However, when a frame is used, more growth can be supported. Standard roses, themselves, are a prim detail in the enthusiast's garden nowadays, and are not seen as often as they used to be; no doubt because they require careful staking and maintenance, the first winter gale can play havoc with them, and the stems are not sufficiently supple.

All manner of posts and tripods can be used, either as a repetitive feature to line the edge of a drive, or to dot about in a flower border to add height and visaul impact. Roses, clematis and loniceras, again, are the most successful plants to festoon about such structures, but sweet peas, and jasmine love this selective attention also. Wooden posts in groups of three driven into the ground and joined at waist or chest level with struts form 'vases' for support of shrubs. Roses particularly look well grown in this way. But, try them for shrubs that really do not need such support, and the effect of lifting the side branches creates more space and light for under-planting and changes the bulk and outline of the shrubs.

Selective pruning may be needed, so this idea is inadvisable for a shrub being grown for its delicacy of form, but scented decorative shrubs such as philadelphus, *Buddleia davidii* and *B. alternifolia*, *Lupinus arboreus*, bush roses, and deutzias, lend themselves to this decorative treatment.

Using the breeze

Obvious supports for scrambling plants are old trees, tree stumps or gate posts, or shed roofs over which they may fling themselves. The more vigorous climbers such as *Rosa filipes* may be whipped into a tree, where swags may be allowed to hang; this is a delightful way to show them off. The trick is to plant them on the windward side of the tree, so that the stems can be lashed through the arms of the host by the prevailing breeze.

Those plants that give freely of their scent are best positioned so that the prevailing breeze will float the fragrance towards the house or patio. In borders, these are the plants to put at the back or in the middle position, leaving the edges for fragrance to be searched out in foliage that needs to be crushed for enjoyment.

Raised beds

Another way of bringing plants nearer to nose level, is to cultivate them in raised beds, or 'table gardens' as they are sometimes called. Ideally, smaller and spreading plants give the most pleasing results; taller ones look quite out of place and should be left to the borders. Construction of raised beds in either stone or brick is costly and quite laborious, and they remain a permanent feature of the garden, but the proportions can be reduced merely to form a 'raised wall' as an edge to a patio or as a surround to a seat. Or, by constructing a retaining wall to a bank, and levelling the bank, perhaps a raised bed could be more simply formed. Smudge the edges by planting smaller plants such as primroses, polyanthus, pinks, achilleas, marjoram, thymes, savory, hypericums, and nepeta. General planting rules appertain to raised beds in particular because they resemble a framed picture; the composition and colour contours have to be right. Form bold clumps of plants (always putting an odd number of plants into a group) rather than a disintegrated dotted effect. And, for preference select only a few differing plants, that will give a succession of fragrant appeal. Use flat-growing or lax evergreen shrubs in such locations: *Juniperus horizontalis* 'Douglasii' or *J. h.* 'Montana' or *Juniperus communis* 'Hornbrookii', *Rosmarinus lavan-*

dulaceus, *Gaultheria procumbens* and *Helichrysum plicatum* and *H. serotinum*.

Raised beds are of special value in small town gardens, where the remainder of the area is paved to allow for sitting out. Further, where the elderly and infirm garden, such a raised working area makes the difference between being able to garden and not being able to do so.

Planting for interest

The key to successful planting is not simply the choice of the right plants to thrive in any particular spot and give some fragrance in season, but also consideration of the plant in relation to others and the role it plays in all-the-year-round interest. Devoid of balance or form, the garden will lack integration. Often in the period while trees and shrubs are growing in a new garden, proportions are awry, and it is advantageous to have some short-term planting schemes to overcome the sense of emptiness and lack of form. If young plants are packed fairly closely together in the larger spaces, some, or all, can be eliminated or planted elsewhere, later. Such overplanting encourages plants to grow, because they all love companions, and at the same time allows the gardener an opportunity to assess total effects before it is too late. Above all, it obviates much of the weeding. Transplanting later need not cause too much apprehension; some plants will have outlived their usefulness, and can be given away, and provided that a plant is never moved when it is dry, the move ought to be successful. Maybe it needs to be said that stout-rooted or brittle-rooted plants are better left alone, and so should be given their permanent quarters at the outset.

Many fragrant or aromatic plants have foliage that qualifies them for a winter garden; some evergreens have spring- or summer-scented flowers. Interest can be extended in this way. Few fragrant plants need be included unless they have some accompanying attribute. For example, the new leaves of *Pieris formosa forrestii* emerge bright red in spring, probably even more striking than their lily-of-the-valley-like flowers in April. Fresh foliage of *Photina serrulata* are shining red in spring and summer adding good colour to the April and May effect. The glossy foliage of *Choisya ternata* reflects light all the year round; *Eleagnus* species, especially *E. angustifolia* with its glistening silver leaves and the evergreen *E.* × *ebbingei* also catch the light – the latter providing the most elegant shelter in a very short time. The golden foliage of *E. pungens* 'Maculata' in winter sunshine can look almost flower-like across the garden and is far more useful for effect than a yellow-flowering winter shrub such as the scented *Stachyurus praecox*.

Many roses, the species in particular, provide dramatic heps in late summer and autumn. The period of interest, then, is longer than when they are in flower, and where some thought is given to companion planting, for late summer effect, the results can be striking. Grey-foliaged plants set off these coral and scarlet heps to great advantage, especially when the great arching branches of heps are allowed to sprawl over their neighbours. Many roses contribute great charm to garden colour early in the season, with their bronze-pink young growth and smoky-pink stems.

Passiflora cearulea in good seasons provides entertaining egg-like golden-yellow fruits, magnolias upstanding cone-like fruits, clematis silken sparklers, and *Ptelia trifoliata* curiously hop-like little dangling blobs. Even the elder, a gross grower really, when planted in the form *Sambucus racemosa* 'Plumosa Aurea' provides, in addition to fragrant flowers, decorative golden deeply cut foliage in summer and luscious red fruits.

Leaf texture, size and colour can be used to pierce the winter gloom. Large leaves, such as those of *Magnolia grandiflora*, the aromatic felted leaves of *Rhododendron rubiginosum* or the large handsome foliage of *R. auriculatum*, often play happy tricks with perspective, suggesting a nearness to the eye. Bright and reflective leaves like those of *Choisya ternata* always seem to be nearer than the pale, duller tones of, say, olearias, eucalyptus, perovskia, phlomis and santolina. An important point to bear in mind is that the evergreens themselves will form the winter scene. Winter flowers, as such – hellebores, *Jasminum nudiflorum*, crocuses, witch hazel, and daphnes – contribute very little to the winter effect unless they are in almost disproportionate quantity, or planted by the house or drive, where they are noticed daily as a jewel of the coming spring.

Prolong the season

Flowering seasons can sometimes be prolonged, by a selection of species of the same plant. For example, *Philadelphus delavayi* opens the season in May, coming with the lilacs; the gorgeous *P.* 'Avalanche' follows with *P.* 'Belle Etoile' (here is a deciduous shrub with changing winter bark of rich red-brown and beige). Later to flower is *P. incanus*, silky-leaved and misty. By careful selection this long season can accompany the roses. If ever two plants were 'made for each other' these must surely be the ones.

Lavenders, also, vary in their flowering time, and are an example of a plant which, used as an individual, forms a spiked large hummock, but when used *en bloc* adds a rigid architectural form to any area. Further, planted in a line, as a hedge, it makes a sinuous, caterpillar-like form that can crawl round corners or over banks. Earliest to flower are 'Munstead', 'Twickel' and 'Hidcote', the first probably starting late in June in early districts, the others in July. 'Hidcote Giant' is darker and later by about a week than 'Hidcote' itself and 'Grappenhall' is perhaps the latest, not coming into flower until the end of July. The white and pink-flowered forms are nothing like as fragrant as the true lavender flowered forms.

Containers

Plants grown in containers can almost be said to provide the technical 'props' of the garden. Moved about season by season, eliminated, grouped in different ways or at varying levels, they can draw the eye to (and consequently away from) any part of the garden. Perhaps most frequently employed as terrace and entrance ornament, they can be better used when lighting up a dark corner, emphasizing an otherwise dreary flight of steps, to lift the eye; arranged on shelving or staging they form an area divider. Endless possibilities present themselves and it is amusing to collect interesting containers of various form and size, over the years. Many are best used for summer effect, temporarily, or may be taken in for protection during the worst of the year. But in town areas, courtyards, and on balconies, they can be invaluable, and the only warning to be sounded is on the question of hardiness. Innumerable plants can be cultivated this way in cold greenhouses or plant rooms, and if when their fragrance is most prolific they are brought on to the patio, or even indoors where a house-bound invalid may enjoy them, the cultivation is well justified.

An outstanding advantage of container cultivation is that demands of light and compost can be met for a plant that it might otherwise be hard to grow in a particular garden. Large pots can be easily sunk into the border for the flowering period, to add garden effect – this is quite commonly practised with pot-grown lilies. Those lilies that flower late in the season, among them *Lilium speciosum*, *L. auratum* and *L. henryi*, are spoiled by September winds, or an early frost and if they are in pots, they can be rescued and brought into the protection of a porch or loggia. The lime-haters too benefit from pot cultivation, but remember that lilies grown in pots will not be quite as tall and will not increase as quickly as those grown in the open border.

The true 'Treasure Chest' is the trough or sink garden, where gems and miniature plants that hold a fascination all their own, can be grown and brought to a level at which they can be enjoyed.

Fragrant plants to grow in troughs

Asperula suberosa
Crocus spp
Cyclamen spp
Dianthus gratianopolitanus forms
Erodium petraeum glandulosum
Iris histrioides
Mentha requienii
Muscari spp
Onosma spp
Petrocallis pyrenaica
Primula auricula forms
  chionantha
Sagina pilifera
Saxifrage cotyledon
Thymus spp
Valeriana supina
Viola cornuta
  cornuta minor

Fragrant plants to grow in pans or troughs
where a leaf mould-peaty compost is provided and the container kept in some shade

Cyclamen spp
Epigaea asiatica
  repens
Linnaea borealis
Primula chionantha
Pyrola rotundifolia
Viola odorata

Fragrant plants to grow in containers and window boxes

Alyssum maritimum
Anthemis nobilis
Artemisia spp
Bergenia spp
Borago officinalis
Buxus sempervirens 'Suffruticosa'
Cheiranthus mutabilis
  cheiri
Convallaria majalis
Cyclamen spp (hardy)
Dianthus spp (pinks)
  Dianthus barbatus
Erysimum alpinum
Gaultheria procumbens

Hebe cupressoides
Helichrysum plicatum
Heliotropum abrotanum
Hyacinthus orientalis
Hyssopus officinalis
Iberis amara
Iris bakeriana
  danfordiae
  histrioides
  reticulata
Laurus nobilis
Lavandula stoechas
Lilium auratum
  speciosum
Matthiola forms
Miniature conifers
Muscari spp
Pelargonium spp and cvs (scented leaved types)
Primula polyantha
  veris
  vulgaris
Reseda odorata
Rhododendron saluenense
Rosmarinus officinalis
Ruta graveolens
Salvia rutilans
Santolina virens
Satureja montana
Scilla spp
Teucrium chamaedrys
  polium
Thymus spp
Viola odorata

Many of the larger plants can be included in containers as rooted cuttings; rosemary for instance is best used like this, and the shape and proportion maintained. Once their useful life is over they can be replaced and the larger plant put out into the garden. Decorative mints can also be included, but it is wise to contain their roots within a black plastic bag before putting them into the container.

Fragrant paths

Several aromatic plants expel their fragrance when crushed or trodden upon, and offer themselves as delightful material with which to embellish a pathway. Some, like the thymes, seem not to suffer too much even if a car is driven over them occasionally.

On driveways, paths and paved areas such as patios or swimming pool surrounds, small plants can be tucked between paving stones and will thrive quite happily. Others need to be allotted space at the edge of the area in a narrow border, where they can gradually flow over the outer edges of the path. Sometimes, it is better to remove a paving stone in order to plant something in the tiny soil area.

Thymes are most popularly used in this way. They are evergreen and look after themselves, requiring only a clipping back in the spring. Take care to select the form required for a particular spot. *Thymus vulgaris* and its forms make good hummocks of growth, while *T. serpyllum* is carpet rooting. The former is the best culinary thyme, hardy and happy almost anywhere, whereas *T. serpyllum* needs to have some soil over which to flow. It and the caraway-scented thyme, *T. herba-barona*, are for the drier areas, the latter never very long lived, as it hates winter sogginess.

Small dianthus such as *Dianthus gratianopolitanus* the Cheddar pink, and *D. deltoides* 'Bowles Variety', and some of the Alwoodii alpinus hybrids can spangle a pathway with their flights of pink flowers. They give their fragrance freely, especaily against sun-baked stones. Chamomile, *Anthemis nobilis* (choose the non-flowering form, otherwise there will be a certain raggedness) will love being undertrodden and in the evening, the warmth of the pathway after a sunny day encourages the scent of the foliage to diffuse.

Chamomile

Pathways have been formed of chamomile for centuries, and lawns fashioned from it present a pale-green knotted sward, fragrant, springy, and in warmer areas, considerably less demanding than one of grasses. After rain, or on a warm moist evening, the scent carries well and it is reputed that a headache can be cleared by sitting out on a chamomile lawn! There are two well established ones in front of the Queen's House at the Royal Botanic Garden, Kew. (Use the non-flowering form 'Treneague' for lawn-making, pushing in the roots at about 4in apart square, after the site has been cleared and levelled.) Pathways are carpeted with chamomile in the scented garden at Hatfield House, Hertfordshire, and make a relaxing pale green footway between conventional lawns. Paving stones set in stepping-stone fashion may be surrounded by chamomile, and once established it will present a path far easier to maintain than stepping stones set in grass.

Medieval gardens were simple rectangular plots, with a raised bank around, usually turved to form a seat. Chamomile was used sometimes for this turfing, as a fragrant seat. Find a simpler form in the Queen's Garden at Kew, where a chamomile bank enfolds a wooden seat. This idea of a recess in a bank, the face and surface of the bank being planted with some spreading aromatic plant, is very easy to introduce into any garden. Thyme and pennyroyal (*Mentha requienii*) may be used in this way in addition to chamomile.

Some scented and aromatic plants to use in conjunction with paving or gravel, on paths and patios:

Alyssum maritimum (sow seed in situ)
Asperula suberosa
Anthemis nobilis 'Treneague'
Calamintha glabella
Dianthus spp
Mentha requienii
Oxalis enneaphylla
Sagina pilifera
Satureia rupestris
Thymus fragrantissimus
serphyllum
vulgaris 'Silver Posie'

Renovation

When trying to reorganise an old or neglected garden, or to accommodate more fragrant plants, there is a great tendency to clear away too many plants in the first enthusiasm for the project. All that is really needed is some thinning out of the plants to be eliminated, replacing them with fragrant ones. Established plants will always encourage new ones to make good progress, providing both shade and shelter.

Thinning is best done in annual stages, over two or three years, depending upon the amount of unwanted plant material. Too frequently a wholesale felling is embarked upon, robbing the garden of all character. Perhaps unwanted tree branches can be lopped to give more light, or neglected shrubs chopped right back. This will mean sacrificing flowers for a year maybe, but the fresh growth is more easily controlled. Often, 'clearing out the garden' results in clearing out the old evergreens, and many of these give the plan its character and protection and so ought always to be embarked upon judiciously.

Overplanting of the areas cleared helps to furnish the garden well, or some quick growing scented plant such as *Lupinus arboreus*, which can be raised from seed can be grown. *Genista aetnensis* is quick to establish. Seasonal effect is easily and quickly gained from wallflowers, sweet peas, stocks, Sweet William, nicotiana, alyssum and heliotrope. Bulbs establish quickly and give good results. All these plants can be put into groups, and the effect does not need to be permanent, so that if mistakes are made, the loss is but a season of time. Containers come into their own in such a situation and can be moved about and refilled season by season to add interest or colour where it is otherwise lacking.

Fragrant plants for heavy soils

Abelia chinensis
triflora
Aesculus spp
Berberis sargentiana
vulgaris
Chamaecyparis spp
Choisya ternata
Crataegus spp
Cytisus spp
Deutzia spp and cvs
Eucalyptus spp
Fraxinus ornus
Hamamelis spp
Laburnum spp
Ligustrum ovalifolia
Magnolia spp
Mahonia spp
Malus spp
Osmanthus delavayi
× fortunei
suavis
Philadelphus spp and cvs
Populus spp
Prunus spp
Rhododendron hybrids
Ribes spp
Roses (all)
Skimmia japonica 'Fragrans'
Thuya spp
Tilia spp
Viburnum spp

Skimmia japonica

Fragrant plants for chalky and shallow soil over chalk

Acanthus mollis
Aesculus spp
Alyssum maritimum
Bergenia spp
Buddleia alternifolia
davidii and cvs
globosa
Buxus sempervirens
Ceanothus 'Gloire de Versailles'
Cheiranthus cheiri
Crambe maritima
Dianthus spp and forms
Dipelta floribunda
Erysimum spp
Fraxinus ornus
Hemerocallis spp and cvs
Hesperis matronalis
Iberis amara
Inula spp
Juniperus communis and cvs
Laurus nobilis
Lavandula angustifolia
stoechas
Lilium brownii
duchartrei
regale
Ligustrum spp
Lonicera spp
Magnolia grandiflora
wilsonii
Malva moschata
Malus spp
Melissa officinalis
Nepeta spp
Oenothera spp
Olearia spp
Philadelphus spp and cvs
Populus spp

Romneya × *coulteri*
Roses (many)
Salvia spp
Sambucus spp
Sarcococca spp
Spartium junceum
Syringa spp and cvs
Thuja occidentalis
plicata

Fragrant plants that will tolerate shade and overcast surroundings

Anthriscus cerefolium
Bergenia spp
Buxus sempervirens
Convallaria majalis
Daphne laureola
pontica
Eleagnus spp
Gaultheria procumbens
Gaultheria shallon
Hemerocallis spp and cvs
Hypericum perforatum
Ligustrum sinense
Osmanthus heterophyllus and cvs
Phillyrea decora
Primula vulgaris
Prunus laurocerasus
Rhododendon spp and hybrids
Rubus spp
Sarcococca spp
Smilacena racemosa

Fragrant plants that grow happily in towns

Aesculus spp
Alyssum maritimum
Bergenia spp
Buddleia spp and cvs
Buxus sempervirens
Calendula officinalis forms
Cheiranthus cheiri
Clethra alnifolia
Convallaria majalis
Crataegus spp
Crocus spp
Daphne mezereum
Davidia involucrata
Deutzia spp
Dianthus spp and cvs
Eleagnus spp
Escallonia spp
Filipendula ulmaria
Fraxinus ornus
Genista hispanica
Gleditsia tricanthos
Hemerocallis spp and cvs
Hesperis matronalis
Laburnum spp
Ligustrum spp
Liriodendron tulipifera
Lonicera spp
Lupinus arboreus
Magnolia denudata
kobus
× *soulangeana*
stellata
Malus spp
Narcissus spp
Nepeta spp
Olearia × *haastii*
Osmanthus spp
Paeonia spp and cvs
Philadelphus spp
Primula × *polyantha*
Prunus spp
Rhododendron Hardy Hybrids
Robinia pseudoacacia
Roses (all)
Rosmarinus officinalis
Sambucus spp
Sarcococca spp
Syringa spp and cvs
Tilia spp
Tulipa spp and forms
Viburnum spp (most)

Fragrant plants for maritime regions

(Those marked * are for the warmer sheltered maritime positions.)

* *Acacia dealbata*
Aloysia citriodora
* *Azara microphylla*
Buddleia alternifolia
davidii and cvs
* *fallowiana*
globosa

Callistemon citrinus
Caryopteris × clandonensis
Ceanothus 'Gloire de Versailles'
'Trewithen Blue'
Choisya ternata
Clematis flammula
* *Coronilla valentina*
Crataegus spp
Daphne mezereum
odora
Dianthus spp and forms
Eleagnus × ebbingei
macrophylla
pungens and cvs
* *Embothrium coccineum*
Escallonia hybrids
Eucalyptus gunnii
pauciflora
Genista spp
Iberis amara
Jasminum officinalis
polyanthum
Juniperus spp and cvs
* *Laurus azorica*
nobilis
Lavandula angustifolia
stoechas
Lupinus arboreus
Magnolia spp
* *Myrtus* spp
Nepeta spp
Oenothera spp
* *Olearia albida*
capillaris
× scilloniensis
Paulownia tomentosa
Phillyrea angustifolia
Phlomis fruticosa
* *Rhododendron auriculatum*
canascens
ciliatum
crassum
griffithianum
Roses (most)
Rosmarinus officinalis
lavandulaceus
Sambucus racemosa 'Plumosa Aurea'
Santolina spp
Spartium junceum
* *Teucrium fruticans*
Ulex spp
Viburnum spp (Evergreen)

Fragrant plants for dry soils

Acanthus mollis
spinosus
Alyssum maritimum
Buddleia spp
Clerodendron spp
Cytisus battandieri
Deutzia spp
Eleagnus angustifolia
Genista spp
Gleditsia triacanthos
Hebe cupressoides
Hypericum frondosum
perforatum
Hyssopus officinalis
Lonicera spp
Lupinus arboreus
Olearia spp
Robinia pseudoacacia
Rosa pimpinellifolia and cvs
Rosmarinus officinalis and forms
lavandulaceus
Salvia spp
Ulex spp

Fragrant climbers and wall shrubs

Abeliophyllum distichum
Acacea dealbata
rhetinoides
Actinidia chinensis
'Aurea-variegata'
polygama
Ceanothus 'Gloire de Versailles'
Clematis armandii
× aromatica
flammula
montana
paniculata
rehderana
× *triternata* 'Rubromarginata'
Coronilla valentina
Cytisus battandieri
Decumaria sinensis

Jasminum beesianum
officinalis
polyanthum
× *stephanense*
Lathyrus odoratus
Lonicera × *americana*
caprifolium and cvs
× *heckrottii*
japonica
periclymenum and cvs
Passiflora caerulea
Plumbago capensis
Rosa banksiae alba plena
banskiae lutea
filipes 'Kiftsgate'
laevigata
Roses, climbing, such as
'Aimée Vibert'
'Aloha'
'Compassion'
'Gloire de Dijon'
'Lady Hillingdon'
'Paul's Lemon Pillar'
'Souvenir de Claudius Denoyal'
'Zepherine Drouhin'
Schisandra chinensis
Stauntonia hexaphylla
Trachelospermum spp
Vitis riparia
Wisteria spp

Fragrant plants hardy in the north of Britain

I am indebted to Mr Ken Lemmon, for help in compiling the following list, and for many useful observations.

Abelia chinensis
Needs wall protection
triflora
Needs wall protection
Abeliophyllum distichum
Needs wall protection; at great risk, because of its early flowering
Acorus calamus
gramineus
Actinidia arguta
chinensis
Need wall protection
kolomikta
Thrives at Harlow Car
Aesculus hippocastanum
californica
× *carnea*
Allium moly
rosenbachium
Alstromeria ligtu
Angelica archangelica
Anthriscus cerefolium
Anthemis nobilis
May not always survive the winter and dampness; keep a supply of cuttings
Artemisia abrotanum
arborescens
absinthium
chamaemelifolia
dracunculoides
dracunculus
maritima
pontica
schmidtiana
tridentata
Keep a supply of cuttings, especially in heavy soil areas
Azara microphylla
petiolaris
Only in sheltered walled gardens. Bean's comment in *Trees & Shrubs Hardy in the British Isles* states that these plants are best suited to the south-east.
Balsamita major
Bergenia cordifolia
crassifolia
× *schmidtii*
× *smithii* and cvs
Buddleia alternifolia
davidii
fallowiana
Appreciates wall protection or much accompanying shrub planting; maritime areas
globosa
Buxus sempervirens
Calamintha grandiflora
Calendula officinalis
Calycanthus fertilis
floridus
Carum carvi
Caryopteris × *clandonensis*
Needs a sheltered 'pocket'
incana

Ceanothus arboreus 'Trewithen Blue'
(As wall shrubs)
× *delinianus* 'Gloire de Versailles'
Centaurea moschata
Cheiranthus cheiri
mutabilis
Chimonanthus praecox
Needs full sunshine the remainder of the year, and some shelter
Choisya ternata
Cladrastis lutea
Clematis flammula
heracleifolia davidiana
montana
recta
Clethra alnifolia
Would be worth trying perhaps with tree canopy
Colletia armata
With shelter
cruciata
Convallaria majalis
Coriandrum sativum
Corylopsis glabrescens
Suspected to be tender at Harlow Car
pauciflora
spicata
Crataegus spp
Crocus chrysanthus and forms
longiflorus
sativus
versicolor
Cyclamen africanum
cyprium
europaeum
libanoticum
neopolitanum
repandum
Cytisus battandieri
In a wall corner, such as it enjoys at Wallington, Northumberland.
× *praecox*
purgans
Daphne alpina
blagayana
cneorum
All like some shelter
mezereum
odora
pontica
retusa
Deutzia chunii
compacta
corymbosa
× *maliflora*
sieboldiana
Dianthus alpinus and progeny
barbatus
Dipelta floribunda
Should be all right
yunnanensis
Drimys winteri
Sheltered by wall
Eleagnus angustifolia
× *ebbengei*
glabra
macrophylla
Dislikes winter dampness, maintain a supply of cuttings
Elsholtzia stauntonii
Erica arborea
Succumbs to prolonged periods of low temperatures
australis
Can be damaged by snow, needs shelter
mediterranea
Reasonably hardy
Escallonia Donard Hybrids
rosea
virgata
Erysimum alpinum
linifolium
pumilum
Eucalyptus dalrympeana
Must be well sheltered among other trees, as at Howick, Northumberland
gunnii
Worth trying, quick to establish
pauciflora
Eucryphia glutinosa
The most reliable to try
lucida
Requires sheltered position
milliganii
Requires sheltered position
nymansensis 'Nymansay'
Requires sheltered position
Filipendula ulmaria
Foeniculum vulgare

Fothergilla gardenii
Require sheltered positions
major
Require sheltered positions
Fraxinus ornus
Galanthus spp
Galtonia candicans
Gaultheria forrestii
fragrantissima
procumbens
Genista aetnensis
hispanica
Gleditschia triacanthos
Not seen much in the north, but thrives in a pocket at Harlow Car
Halesia carolina
monticola
Hamamelis × *intermedia*
japonica
mollis
vernalis
virginiana
Heliotropium arborescens
As bedding, or as container decoration
Hemerocallis fulva
Hesperis matrionalis
Hosta plantaginea
Hyacinthus amethystinus
azureus
orientalis cvs
Hyssopus aristatus
officinalis
Iberis amara
Iris bakeriana
Short-lived
danfordiae
Short-lived
florentina
germanica
graminea
histrioides
pallida
reticulata
unguicularis
xiphium
Itea illicifolia
virginica
Probably prefers wall protection; grows among heavy shrub planting in Cheshire
Jasminum nudiflorum
officinale
Likes to scramble about a protective corner
Laburnum anagyroides
alpinum
× *watereri*
Laurus nobilis
Container grown out of doors in summer; known in sheltered walled garden
Lavandula angustifolia
Does not always overwinter
Ligustrum henryi
japonicum
lucidum
ovalifolium
quihoui
sinense
vulgare
Lilium auratum
candidum
cernum
chalcedonicum
duchartrei
hansonii
monadelphum
parryi
Fails in wet winters
regale
× *testaceum*
wardii
Liriodendron tulipifera
Lonicera × *americana*
augustifolia
caprifolium
fragrantissima
× *heckrottii*
Requires wall protection
periclymenum
× *purpusii*
Bad winter will affect flowering
setifera
syringantha
× *tellmanniana*
Lupinus arboreus
More popularly grown than in the south
Magnolia denudata
grandiflora
sinensis
× *soulangiana*
stellata

× *thomsoniana*
virginiana
× *watsonii*
Needs wall protection
wilsonii
Needs wall protection
Mahonia japonica
lomariifolia
In a sheltered pocket or suitable microclimate
Malus spp
Matthiola spp
Melissa officinalis
Monarda didyma
Muscari armeniacum
botryoides
comosum
moschatum
racemosum
Myrica californica
gale
pensilvanica
Myrtus communis
Requires wall protection, or put it in a container to grow outside in the summer
Myrrhis odorata
Narcissus calcicola
canaliculatus
jonquilla and forms
juncifolius
minor
poeticus
pseudonarcissus
rupicola
tazetta
triandrus concolor vars
Nepeta faassenii
nervosa
× Souvenir d'André Chaudron
Nicotiana alata and cvs
Cultivate as annuals
Nymphaea alba
odorata
tuberosa
Oenothera biennis
caespitosa
Olearia avicenniifolia
With shelter
× *haastii*
ilicifolia
Worth trying
nummulariifolia
solandri
With wall protection
Origanum majorana
onites
Survives only mild winters
vulgare
Osmanthus armartus
delavayi
Requires protection
× *fortunei*
heterophyllum
× *Osmarea* 'Burkwoodii'
Osmaronia cerasiformis
Successful in mild or very late springs
Pachysandra terminalis
Pelargonium spp
Container grown and taken indoors to overwinter
Perovskia atriplicifolia
Petasites fragrans
Petrocallis pyrenaica
Only in scree bed, or in troughs
Philadelphus coronarius
× *lemoinei* and forms
× *virginalis*
Phillyrea angustifolia
latifolia
Phlox maculata
paniculata vars
Pieris floribunda
Require sheltered positions with canopy of trees
formosa
japonica 'Christmas Cheer'
Pimpinella anisum
Very sheltered corners
Piptanthus laburnifolius
Likes protection
Populus balsamifera
× *candicans*
simonii
szechuanica
Requires shelter from early frost
trichocarpa
Primula florindae
helodoxa
nutans
prionites
× *pubescens*
sikkimensis

sinoplantaginea
viallii
veris
vulgaris
Rhododendron spp and hardy hybrids
Ribes alpinum
fasciculatum
gayanum
odoratum
sanguineum
viburnifolium
Robinia hispida
pseudoacacia
Romneya coulteria
Requires wall protection
Rosemarinus lavandulaceus
Often succumbs to winter wet and cold
officinalis
Roses, all
Usually better in the north
Salvia farinacea
glutinosa
haematodes
sclarea
Sambucus canadensis
nigra
racemosa
Saponaria officinalis
Santolina chamaecyparissus
Often fail in damp winters
virens
Sarcococca confusa
hookeriana
ruscifolia chinensis
Scilla spp
Skimmia japonica
'Fragrans'
'Rubella'
laureola
reevesiana
Smilacena racemosa
stellata
Spartium junceum
Stachyurus chinensis
praecox
Stewartia malacodendron
Worth a try
serrata
sinensis
Syringa × *chinensis*
microphylla
× *persica*
sweginzowii
tomentella
velutina
vulgaris
Tanacetum vulgaris
Teucrium chamaedrys
On warm walls
marum
Sheltered spot
polium
Sheltered spot
scordonia
Tilia × *euchlora*
oliveri
petiolaris
Thymus spp
Tropaeolum majus
Tulipa gesneriana
sylvestris
Base of wall, shelter
Ulex europaeus
gallii
minor
Viburnum × *bodnantense* 'Dawn'
× *burkwoodii*
× *carlcephalum*
carlesii
cinnamomifolium
Requires some shelter
farreri
grandiflorum
japonicum
× *juddii*
odoratissimum
Requires a warm wall
suspensum
Requires a warm wall
tinus
Vitis × *brandt*
riparia
Viola spp and cvs
Wisteria floribunda
macrobotrys
sinensis
Zenobia pulverulenta

A Catalogue of Fragrant Plants

Freesia. Many hybrids of Freesia refracts are intensely and sweetly scented, although it is a known fact that they are viodorous to some people

GREENHOUSE PLANTS

Only arbitrary decisions can be made, in a book of this kind, about which plants to suggest for greenhouse cultivation. Those requiring stove conditions have been omitted; many others will thrive with the protection of a domestic conservatory or house extension. Requirements vary from one area to another with altitude, prevailing winds, average rainfall and winter temperatures, so that a plant may thrive happily out of doors in one place and crave the umbrella of glass in another. Other sections of the book, notably those on Shrubs and Climbers and Bulbs, ought to be consulted for further ideas for fragrant plants to include in greenhouse cultivation.

Once the hardy fragrant plant has been grown with glass protection and in the environment provided there, two things will happen. Firstly, it will need to be hardened off again before being taken back to the garden, and secondly, and more relevant to the subject, fragrance of foliage will almost certainly be reduced. The resultant softer growth is less aromatic and this is especially true of those small-leaved, or twiggy, plants from the arid soils of the hills around the Mediterranean: such plants as rosemary, lavenders, hyssop and savory. Glass cultivation best enhances flower perfume; the higher temperature encourages it and confines it for enjoyment.

Orchids have been omitted here; they are a special consideration, but some fragrant ones are included on page 50.

BAROSMA *pulchella* (*Rutaceae*) (E) 3¼ft

Rare in cultivation, and grown as a cool greenhouse plant this South African heath plant was at one time widely cultivated for its leaves. They constituted *foliae buchu* when dried, an ingredient of some perfumes, and with a penetrating aromatic odour like rue. The leaves are thick, dense and heath-like, the flowers in terminal-rounded clusters a rather pretty mauve in summer. In really mild conditions, a sheltered corner out of doors with a neutral-to-acid soil may support this aromatic plant, so long associated with perfumery.

CEDRONELLA *triphylla* (*Labiatae*) 3–4ft

BALM OF GILEAD, MOLDAVIAN BALM

Often called, though incorrectly, Balm of Gilead (a name that really belongs to the Balsam Poplars) it is closely related to, and often confused with dracocephalum and nepeta. It is a tender shrubby herb, best grown in a conservatory for its aromatic leaves. Out of doors, cuttings need to be taken each year to maintain a stock, and it is, in fact, treated as a half-hardy perennial. The flowers are two-lipped, pale lilac-pink in August and September in terminal heads. The true delight is in three-lobed leaves, freshly aromatic and variously described as camphorous and lemon-scented.

GARDENIA *jasminoides* (*Rubiaceae*) (E) 3–6½ft

CAPE JASMINE GARDENIA

The one species generally available of this large evergreen species from the warmer parts of the world, *jasminoides* from Southern China, is the gardenia of the florists, used in bouquets and button-holes. The flowers are strongly and heavily fragrant, and dried the petals can be used to make a sweet-smelling tea or tisane. Grown as a greenhouse pot plant, the leaves are a deep lustrous green and the flowers large and pure white. The form *G. j. fortuniana* with large double flowers, and *G. j. f.* 'Veitchiana', a winter-flowering form, are wonderful fragrant plants where suitable temperatures can be maintained – usually up to 18°C (64°F) in winter, with good shade in summer and all-the-year-round humidity.

HEDYCHIUM *gardnerianum* (E) (*Zingiberaceae*) 4ft

GARLAND FLOWER, BUTTERFLY LILY, GINGER LILY

The most popularly cultivated perennial species of this genus of half-hardy rhizomatous plants, eminently suited to garden rooms and conservatories as evergreen pot plants. Very sweetly perfumed, intense like jasmine, especially towards the evening, the bold upstanding spikes of lemon-yellow flowers with protruding red filaments are held well above the broad leaves in late summer and autumn.

HELIOTROPIUM *arborescens* (Syn. *H. peruvianum*) (*Boraginaceae*) 6in–3ft

HELIOTROPE, CHERRY PIE

A Peruvian shrub, grown in a variety of ways, and most frequently as a half-hardy annual for effect in summer bedding schemes. It succeeds best in a light rich loam and is intolerant of shade, but is an interesting plant for the gardener to 'play' with. It can be cultivated in hanging baskets, or maintained from year to year and put out with the summer bedding, or used to decorate and perfume the conservatory and greenhouse during late summer and winter as it does in a pale flowered form at Wallington, Northumberland. Small tightly packed heads of purple, or sometimes white flower heads, richly and heavily scented, nestle among dark green leaves. The perfume often hangs on the air in the summer garden, and is thought by some people to resemble that of cherry pie, hence the vernacular name. However it is undoubtedly a heavy, fruity and distinctive perfume.

HOYA (*Asclepiadaceae*) (E)

WAX FLOWER

A large genus of oriental plants of which two or three

shrubs are commonly cultivated under glass in the temperate regions. Some are climbers, others epiphytes, all with richly perfumed flowers. Given a coarse loam the climbers will clothe a pillar or screen and clamber away along wires or rafters. Others make first-rate pot plants. All the flowers are borne on the end of spines which arise at the base of the leaf stalks.

bella 2ft

A somewhat procumbent species, best suited to cultivation in hanging baskets for conservatory and greenhouse decoration. As a pot plant it will demand support. The waxy flowers are carried in clusters or umbels and like most waxy-petalled flowers emit a heavy perfume, rich and sweet. The petals are glistening white and thick, and the centres are mauve. They have been likened to 'an amethyst set in frosted silver'.

carnosa 20ft

With thicker leaves than *H. bella* and a climbing habit the flowers are carried in pendant clusters with a fragrance reminiscent of incense. The form *H. c. exotica* displays leaves variegated from pale green to butter-yellow. The flowers of both forms are white and waxy with a pink centre, and age to pink. Usually spring-flowering, the plant will produce a succession of blooms when grown well.

MIRABILIS *jalapa* (*Nyctaginaceae*) 2–3ft

MARVEL OF PERU, FOUR O'CLOCK PLANT

The most commonly available tuberous-rooted species of this South American plant, cultivated often as a half-hardy annual, although a true perennial. Grown in pots, they make interesting flowering plants for the cold greenhouse, conservatory or living room, and where good tubers form they can be treated like dahlias and planted out in the summer months in the warmer districts. The flowers are gaily coloured, opening in the afternoon and evening and therefore only fragrant at that time – hence a colloquial name Four O'Clock Plant. The flowers are formed of a tubular coloured calyx opening into a flat starry face, varying from white to red, pink, and yellow in midsummer and remaining in flower over quite a long period, with a fruity scent.

NERIUM *odorum* (*Apocynaceae*) (E) 6½–13ft

SWEET SCENTED OLEANDER

Prized for its intense scent of almonds which surrounds the entire plant, it has the same colour ranges as the common oleander, but is not as frequently grown. A Persian plant, it can be pot-grown in conservatories which are frost-free in winter, and the pots may be stood out of doors in the summer during the flowering period. The foliage is long, narrow and shining and the flowers in white, pink and cream varieties come in high summer.

PELARGONIUM (*Geraniaceae*) (E)

Pelargoniums are perennials of various habits, but of special interest here are the scented-leaved sorts which make fine pot plants, for indoor or conservatory decoration. Some can be used in the warmer areas as garden plants, when foliage form is of value. As indoor plants they are sometimes lacking in vitality simply because they do not get nearly enough light, nor do they get potted on as frequently as they require. Natives of South Africa, where the light is far more intense than in the northern temperate regions, and where drought conditions are frequent, the variety of leaf form and scent is one of the plant's adaptations for survival. The strong scent discourages browsing animals.

A surprisingly wide range of volatile oils is given off by the leaves of various plants ranging through scents of eucalyptus, camphor, citrus, spice, pine, lemon, peppermint, nutmeg, ginger, rose, apricot and many pungent aromas not closely identified with other familiar plant material. Many of them are old in cultivation, having been introduced first in the 18th century, and subsequently caught the imagination of the florists. The named varieties, many of them first contributed to cultivation by the florists and the Victorian gardeners, are the collector's delight.

While the foliage comes in an assortment of shapes and sizes, the scents are of a yet wider range. Some examples are: 'Clorinda', (eucalyptus); 'Endsleigh' (pepper); 'Fair Ellen' (pungent); 'Fragrans' (pine); 'Lady Mary' (peppermint): 'Lady Plymouth' (rose); 'Lady Scarborough' (lemon); 'Pretty Polly' (almond); 'Prince of Orange' (orange); 'Queen of Lemons' (lemon).

Species with scented foliage:

abrotanifolium

Leaves deeply divided, scent: southernwood. Introduced from South Africa 1796.

graveolens

ROSE-SCENTED GERANIUM

Leaves roughly triangular, dark green and deeply divided. Shrubby growth. Scent: rose. The parent of many rose-scented varieties.

odoratissimum

APPLE-SCENTED PELARGONIUM

Leaves velvety, pale green. Scent: apple; the whole plant is miniature. Introduced from South Africa 1724.

quercifolium

OAK-LEAVED GERANIUM

Leaves roughly triangular, dark green, very deeply

indented. Commonly grown as a house plant. Growth shrubby, especially when put out of doors in the summer. Scent: pungent. Introduced from South Africa 1774.

tomentosum
PEPPERMINT PLANT
Rather a bushy spreading plant with soft felted leaves. Scent: strong peppermint.

triste
THE SAD GERANIUM
Little, but interesting because it is one of the oldest in cultivation, having been introduced by Tradescant in 1632. A tuberous plant with filmy fern-like leaves reminiscent of carrot foliage. The foliage is sweetly fragrant after dusk.

PETROCALLIS *pyrenaica* (*Cruciferae*) 2in

Few alpine plants are scented, so this tiny hummock-forming plant is invaluable for trough cultivation, or for growing in the alpine house where its fragrance may be enjoyed. Hailing from the Pyrenees, it has intensely green, wedge-shaped, notched leaves, over which clusters of sweetly scented lavender flowers are dotted in May and June. Like most minute plants it requires light, and sharp drainage.

PROSTANTHERA (*Labiatae*) (E) 3¼ft

Tender plants from Australia, and cultivated in Britain only in the most sheltered areas, or in a cool greenhouse or as a container shrub that can be stood out of doors in the summer months. Given a sheltered dry corner, they can be most floriferous and attractive shrubs, but are intolerant of chalk.

cuneata
ALPINE MINT BUSH
A species that has not yet stood the test of time in British gardens, but one that promises to be reasonably hardy. Pale mauve with purple marking at the throat in May and June, bell-shaped flowers with scalloped flaring mouth are pleasingly scented. The true mint aroma, with gives the plant its common name, is found in the ovate toothed leaves on bruising.

melissifolia
BALM MINT BUSH
True to its name, the aroma of the plant is locked in its foliage which is strongly scented of mint, the sharpness softened. The flowers are mauve, smothering the plumes of foliage in summer, bell-shaped with decorative scalloped mouths, and are pleasingly scented, but far less so than the foliage.

rotundifolia
ROUND-LEAVED MINT BUSH
The aromatic foliage is more rounded than in other species. The flowers in summer are deep lavender-blue in dense plumes, bell-shaped with scalloped flaring mouths and with a spicy aroma.

STEPHANOTIS *floribunda* (*Asclepiadaceae*) (E)

CREEPING TUBEROSE, MADAGASCAR JASMINE
A highly scented greenhouse twining climber with white waxy flowers from late spring until August. Requiring an average winter temperature of 13°C (55°F), where it flourishes it will furl along the rafters of the greenhouse, or may be trained on to wires or trellises. Cultivated in pots, its growth can be restricted and it is sometimes used as a room plant when in flower. The foliage is deep green and leathery, oval and highly polished, and matches perfectly the clusters of tubular flowers. Somewhat exotic and sturdy, they are impregnated with one of the most powerful sweet fragrances of the plant kingdom. They used to be cultivated in quantity for inclusion in bridal bouquets.

Some fragrant plants to grow under glass

Plants requiring stove conditions have been excluded, but many that are listed as requiring cool or cold protected conditions can be cultivated as conservatory or porch plants. Almost all, other than those needing a warm greenhouse and the attendant humidity, may be tried in a garden room, especially where domestic central heating is installed. Attention needs to be paid to watering and humidity.

S = shrub; P = perennial; B = bulb;
A = alpine; An = annual; Bi = biennial

PLANT	TYPE	HOUSE	SEASON
Acacia dealbata	S	cool	Dec-Feb
Achimenes longiflora	P	warm	June-Sept
Androsace pubescens	A	cold	May
A. villosa	A	cold	May
Bouvarida spp	S	warm	Oct-Jan
Buddleia alternifolia	S	cool or cold	summer
B. asciatica	S	cool or cold	
B. caryopteridifolia	S	cool or cold	May
Calycanthus floridus	S	cool or cold	May-June
Callistemon citrinus	S	cool	late summer
Cassia corymbosa	S	cool	all the year
Cedronella triphylla	S	cold	summer
Cheiranthus spp	P	cold	early spring-early summer
Choisya ternata	S	cool	all summer

PLANT	TYPE	HOUSE	SEASON
Citrus spp	S	cool	almost all the year
Convallaria majalis	P	cold	Dec-March
Coronilla valentina	S	cool	March-Oct
Crocus spp	B	cold	Dec-March
Daphne spp	S	cold	Dec-March
Datura suaveolens	S	cool	summer
Dianthus caryophyllus	P	warm	all the year
Erysimum spp	P	cold	spring and early summer
Eucalyptus citriodora / *E. ficifolia*	as S / as D	cool or cold	foliage all the year
Eucharis grandiflora	B	warm	winter
Freesia refracta hybrids	B	cool	Jan-April
Gardenia jasminoides	S	warm	autumn
Genista fragrantissima	S	cool	summer
Hedychium gardnerianum	P	cool	summer
Heliotropum arborescens	P (soft wood)	cold or cool	spring-summer
Hoya bella	S	cool	spring-summer
H. carnosa	S	cool	summer
Humea elegans	Bi	cool	foliage summer
Hyacinthus spp	B	cold	Dec-April
Jasminum grandiflorum	S	cool	summer
J. polyanthum	S	cool	summer
Lathyrus odoratus	A	cool or cold	spring-summer
Lavandula stoechas	S	cold	summer
Laurus nobilis	S con-fined	cold	all the year foliage
Lilium longiflorum	B	cold	summer late spring
L. speciosum	B	cold	summer
Lonicera fragrantissima	S	cool	summer
L. hider brandiana			

PLANT	TYPE	HOUSE	SEASON
Mandevilla suaveolens	S	warm	summer
Mattiola spp	A & Bi	cool	spring-summer
Muscari moschatum	B	cold	March-April
Myrtus communis	S	cool or cold	all the year foliage summer
Narcissus spp	B	cold	Dec-March
Nicotiana alata	P	cool	spring-summer
Osmanthus fragrans	S	cold	summer
Pelargonium spp	P	cool or cold	all the year foliage
Petrocallis pyrenaica	A	cold	May-June
Philadelphus coronarius	S	cold	summer
P. × lemonei & cvs	S	cold	summer
Polianthes tuberosa	S	warm	autumn
Primula malacoides	P	cool	Jan-March
P. polyantha	P	cold	Dec-May
Reseda odorata	P	cold	spring-summer
Rhododendron 'Countess of Haddington'		cold	March-April
R. fragrantissimum		cold	March-April
Rosa banksiae	S	cold	summer
Salvia rutilans	P	cool or cold	foliage all the year
Smilacina racemosa	P	cool or cold	March-May
Stephanotis floribunda	S	warm or cool	April-June
Syringa spp	S	cold	spring-summer
Teucrium fruticans	S	cool or cold	foliage all the year
Trachelospermum jasminoides	S	cool or cold	summer
Tulipa spp	B	cold	March-April

Scented plants to grow indoors

Achimenes tubiflora	April-May
Aloysia citriodora	summer
Citrus mitis	most of the year intermittently
Convallaria majalis	December-May
Datura suaveolens	July-August
Dendrobium nobile	February-May
Dryopteris oreopteris & forms	evergreen foliage
Hoya carnosa	summer
Hyacinthus orientalis (forced)	December-March
Jasminum polyanthum	February-May
Lilium Aurelian hybrids	June-July
'Brandywine'	July
'Royal Gold'	July
regale	July
tenuifolium 'Golden Gleam'	June
Muscari moschatum	March

Myrtus communis 'Microphylla'	July-August
Narcissus Tazetta vars	December-March
Nicotiana affinis	May-August
Oxalis enneaphylla	early summer
Pelargonium graveolens	all the year round
odoratissimum	foliage
quercifolium	
tomentosum	
Salvia rutilans	evergreen foliage flowers August-Sept
Stephanotis floribunda	spring-early summer
Trachelospermum jasminoides	summer

BULBS

Here, the term 'bulbous plant' is interpreted liberally to include corms and tubers, all of which are remarkably tolerant and rewarding plants. Labour-saving in the extreme, innumerable bulbs will simply fend for themselves year after year once established; a valuable attribute for natural gardening. Naturalized bulbs in drifts in the woodland garden or on grassy banks or lawn boundaries are a salient feature of the English 20th-century style of gardening. Many of the spring-flowering ones hover close to the ground and their scent is not immediately detectable, which has probably prompted the cultivation of bulbous plants in pots and other containers to bring them more easily to nose level.

When pot-grown many of them score enormously as indoor plants, especially appreciated when they can be forced, like hyacinths, crocus and narcissi, to flower in the shortest days of the year. Under glass, perfection of flower is assured, spared the blemishes of wind and sleet, and the perfume is trapped within the structure for enjoyment.

Dramatic emphasis can be given to the garden scene by the larger bulbous plants such as lilies. Naturalized in woodland where they associate happily with rhododendrons and camellias, they spill their fragrance on the air, or collected into bold clumps, or grown in tubs, they can punctuate a terrace or border.

Many are tender, needing conservatory or greenhouse cultivation in most areas of Britain: freesias, *Eucharis grandiflora*, *Polyanthes tuberosa*, and the white Easter Lily are obvious ones. In the alpine house, the tiny flowered bulbs come into their own; crocus, fritillaria, miniature narcissi, iris and species tulips are all successful.

The following catalogue includes a selection of those bulbous plants most popularly cultivated, but others to try might include *Alstromeria ligtu*, *Crinum asiaticum*, *C. bulbispermum*, *C.* × *powellii*, *Cyclamen* spp., *Lachenalia glaucinda*, *Notholirion thomsonianum*, and fragrant species of *Scilla*.

ACIDANTHA bicolor (*Iridaceae*) 2½–3½ft

The corms require treatment similar to that for gladiolus, but they are less hardy, lending themselves to greenhouse pot culture. The best form *murielae* had superseded the type and is the plant in general cultivation, flowering at the end of September. The flowers are quite large, drooping, and a white flared bell in shape, each petal blotched at the base with maroon. The perfume is sweetly penetrating. Out of doors, in mild localities, they can be grown in open well-drained borders, and lifted after flowering.

ALLIUM (*Liliaceae*)

Some graceful plants are included in this genus, though generally not considered fragrant because of the sulphurous content. In general, the onion odour is only released on bruising, but one or two generally cultivated species are pleasantly fragrant. They grow in well-drained soil in sunshine or broken shade. *Allium triquetrum* is generally listed as 'scented' but is a plant considered to be a menace!

moly 6-12in

A garden favourite and one to be included in the fragrant garden where the flowering coincides with many blue and purple flowered herbs and makes an attractive plant association. Numerous golden-yellow star-like flowers form a loose rounded head atop an upright stem in June. Leaves are deep green and glaucous, spearing the ground in spring as a single leaf. Rather gentle of scent, they are good plants for naturalizing.

neapolitanum 8–12in

An early-flowering species, March to May, and totally devoid of any onion smell, and for this reason sometimes grown in the greenhouse, especially in the form of *A. n. cowanii*. Under glass the warmth and sunshine persuades a delicately sweet perfume from the flowers in characteristic heads with mid-green strap-shaped leaves. Really only for the milder counties.

rosenbachianum 2–2½ft

Perhaps the most handsome Asiatic species and useful for the herbaceous border where the rounded flower heads stand out, unique in shape among other late-spring herbaceous plants. Flowers are purplish violet or rosy purple in late spring and fragrant. The leaves, unlike those of most alliums, are hairy.

BABIANA (*Iridaceae*)

BABOON ROOT

Low-growing cormous plants from the warmer regions of South Africa, cultivated in Britain in a cool greenhouse. The leaves are sword-like, and strongly ribbed or pleated, and the upturned flower faces are in small clusters.

disticha 1ft

HYACINTH-SCENTED BABIANA

Flowers are pale blue with a yellow throat, bloom in June and emit a pleasing perfume, richly reminiscent of that of the hyacinth.

plicata 6in

Flowers of pale lilac mauve, with darker basal markings, bloom in May and June with a scent like that of carnation.

stricta 1ft

Flower colour covers a wide range from pale blue, to brighter blues, lilacs, mauve and crimson in the late spring. *B. s. rubro-cyanea* is the more highly perfumed, blue with a rich plum-red centre, and aptly named Wine Cups.

CROCUS (*Iridaceae*)

Winter-flowering cormous plants that give a succession of displays from October to March when several species are grown. Crocuses are best suited to naturalizing beneath trees and shrubs or in the lawn, but thrive also grown in troughs and tubs which bring them nearer to the nose. They all close up at night, but a bowl brought indoors from the cold greenhouse will reward you with their startled open faces and delicate perfume, giving pleasure the whole evening.

chrysanthus 2–2¾in

A species from Greece and Asia Minor, usually flowering about mid-February, and the parent of a vast range of seedlings of tremendous variability, many of them named after birds by the late E. A. Bowles. The species itself and the progeny are particularly attractive when cultivated in pans under glass, or in troughs or window boxes. The one most noted for its fragrance is 'Snow Bunting' flowering in February very freely, white with purple feathering on the outer three petals.

longiflorus 3¼–4in

A primrose-scented species from Italy and Sicily, quite hardy and producing rather goblet-like flowers in November. They are lilac, deeper bluish mauve within and with prominent orange stigma and orange feathering deep in the throat.

sativus 3¼–4in

SAFFRON CROCUS

From the hills of Southern Europe and Turkey whence in the Middle Ages its stigmas were the source of saffron, this large rose-lilac flower has a very long stigma of deep orange yellow and flowers in September and October giving off a perfume described as mossy.

versicolor 4in

Farrer wrote of its 'hundred forms', and it is the 'Party-coloured Crocus' of Phillip Miller; the named varieties are so variable that they tend to merge. A large, pale lilac, grey-mauve flower, feathered with dark purple, flowering in March and scented of primrose.

GALANTHUS (*Amaryllidaceae*) 6–12in

SNOWDROP

In all snowdrops the flowers are pendulous and white with green markings on the under-segment of the perianth. They form good clumps, naturalize well and with the exception of *G. fosteri* are among the hardiest plants grown in Britain. Unselective of soil, tolerant of storm and snow, the only thing they dislike is animal manure in the soil, or compost. They can be grown in pots for cold greenhouse or indoor decoration. There are many variable forms, probably because of the widespread extent of their natural areas and some of the garden forms are so close in appearance that they are virtually indistinguishable even to the experts.

alenii

A little-grown species, with green, strap-shaped leaves and comparatively large flowers. It is late-flowering about March, and is almond-scented.

elwesii

A larger-flowered species than most with broad dark-green markings at the base of the inner segments, and it is normally scentless. But, a violet-scented form has been exhibited in recent years at the Royal Horticultural Society's shows, which is distinctly and strongly suggestive of violets. Given the right atmosphere its perfume is perceptible from the upright position – a true asset in the depth of the winter.

nivalis

A native British woodland plant which flowers very early in the year and is said to have a distinct mossy smell. Its subspecies *reginae-olgae*, which often starts to flower in October, is reminiscent of heather honey in aroma. Other garden variants of *nivalis* are G. 'Magnet' and 'Straffan', both honey-scented, the former imaginatively named for the flower literally dangles on the slender pedicle, seemingly held in position by some mutual attraction with the stem.

GALTONIA *candicans* (*Liliaceae*) 3ft

A summer-flowering bulb very slight of fragrance bearing glistening white dangling bells around a tall stem in July and August. The real attraction of the fragrance develops after the flowers have been cut and taken indoors. The leaves are strap-shaped and somewhat glaucous green. The flowers are exquisite upon examination, tipped green, and green within the throat, and provide the flower-arranger with marvellous material for 'church flowers'. The bulbs demand well-drained humus-rich soil and a sunny sheltered site. Although considered to be the only hardy species of a rarely cultivated genus, it certainly flourishes in Cumbria.

HYACINTHUS (*Liliaceae*)

HYACINTH

One of the few genera to include all the primary colours in its various flowers. Native of the Mediterranean regions it is seen at its best, perhaps, in the florists' forms derived from *H. orientalis*, used for spring bedding, pot culture in the conservatory, and indoors as winter flowering plants. As they open, their rich heavy scent pervades the air. Quite large robust and uniform flower spikes can be produced affording a dramatic effect indoors during the winter.

Some popularly grown cultivars include the following: White: 'L'Innocence', 'Mont Blanc', 'Queen of the Whites', 'White Pearl'. Yellow and orange: 'Carnegie', 'City of Haarlem', 'Gipsy Queen', 'Yellow Hammer'. Pale blue: 'Blue Haze', Delft Blue', 'Myosotis' (particularly richly scented), 'Queen of the Blues'. Deep Blue; 'Ostara'. Purple and mauve: 'Amythyst', 'Lord Balfour', 'Purple King'. Pink and red: 'Ann Mary'. Cherry Blossom', 'Cyclop', 'John Boss', 'Lady Derby', 'Pink Pearl', 'Princess Margaret'.

The double-flowered cultivars, reminiscent of the Dutch flower paintings of the 18th century, are not often seen, but 'Ben Nevis' (White) and 'Hollyhock' (red) are probably the most easily available.

Altogether daintier and more graceful, and especially useful for window boxes or ribbon borders, are the Cynthella hyacinths in such varieties as 'Gainsborough' (blue), 'Sunflower' (yellow) and 'Apple Blossom', (pink).

On the whole the quality of hyacinths as fragrant garden plants is not very rich, their flowering so often coinciding with March winds; but taken indoors they will mark their appreciation with perfume. Indoors, both when they can be used as cut flowers and pot-grown plants, the perfume changes perceptibly as the flowers mature and fade; the cloying sweetness disappears and a far more 'down to earth' fragrance is experienced.

amethystinus 8in

An early spring-flowering species for the rock garden, with drooping bells of pale Cambridge blue. Useful for the rock garden.

azureus 8in

A densely clustered head of brilliant azure blue bells from the mountains of Asia Minor, and particularly attractive in the rock garden in spring.

orientalis 1ft

The species from which all the popularly grown cultivars listed above have been derived, and from which they have inherited their fragrance. The species itself varies in flower colour from white, through pale blues to mauve, with somewhat sparse bells, but a delicious perfume. From the form *albulus* the Roman Hyacinth has been derived; this flowers earliest of all, well before Christmas with encouragement. The fragrance is not as pronouced as that of the later-flowering cultivars. It is an altogether more slender plant often producing several stems.

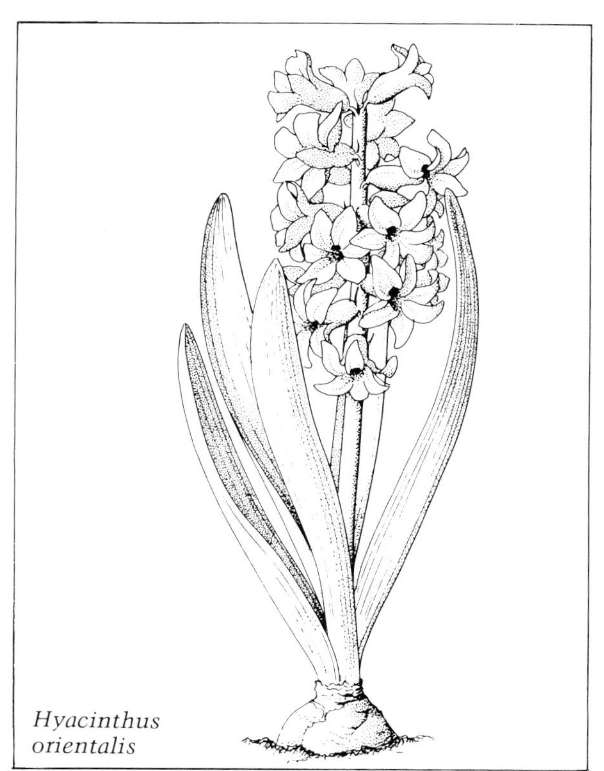

Hyacinthus orientalis

romanus 1ft

Included for its powerful scent, which is rich and heavy, but a plant dingy of flower. The flowers are greenish yellow carried in a globular head. A plant of the Mediterranean regions of southern Europe, sometimes described as *Bellevalia romana*.

HYMENOCALLIS (*Amaryllidaceae*)

SPIDER LILY

South African and South American bulbous plants, closely allied to Pancratium; the somewhat spidery flowers have long, narrow, recurved stamen filaments, strap-like, the bases of which are united by a wing to form a cup, the whole flower looking rather like a pleated funnel with shaggy ribbons. One or two scented species are nearly hardy and can be cultivated out of doors in very protected corners in the Channel Isles and south-western England.

narcissiflora (Syn. *calathina*, sometimes *Pancratium calathina*) 1½ft

PERUVIAN DAFFODIL

The flowers are white in March and April under glass, or in summer out of doors, funnel-shaped, the filaments long with fringed margins. A rich honey scent lingers about the flowers. The leaves are broad and shining green, strap-shaped, narrowing towards the base.

speciosa (Syn. *Pancratium speciosa*) 1½ft

From the West Indies, a winter-flowering species, grown under glass with large pure-white flowers which are very showy and spidery and exceedingly fragrant.

IRIS (*Iridaceae*)

Irises are plants of open sunny positions, usually liking some lime in the soil, and, although some are considered difficult of cultivation, they are most rewarding little plants. This is especially true where some baking out can be achieved after flowering, or at least dryness maintained at that time emulating the harsh dry soils of the hilly areas around the Eastern Mediterranean which is home to so many of them.

bakeriana 4–6in

Perhaps failing in cultivation because the bulbs do not survive for long, *Iris bakeriana* is well worth growing for its strong violet fragrance alone. The flowers in January and February consist of pale ultramarine standards and deep violet falls held horizontally, the white downward-hanging tip dotted with purple-black.

danfordiae 3in

A dainty, rather squat flower, canary-yellow lightly blotched with brown, blooming during January and February. A good plant for the alpine house or cold greenhouse where the soil-hugging flower may be better enjoyed and its faint perfume brought out.

histrioides 4–6in

A stout little plant braving the mid-January weather to produce a lovely deep royal-blue, rather spiky flower before the rush-like foliage develops. The form *major* is usually grown and they are at their best on good loam.

reticulata 6–8in

One of the loveliest of all spring bulbs, and totally reliable even in the worst winter. Hailing from the Caucasus and Russia the flowers are a deep blue-mauve, and the haft of the falls is upstanding to reveal a golden yellow-and-white marking. The violet perfume pervades the garden, and is markedly strong when the bulbs are cultivated in the cold greenhouse or as indoor plants. The leaves are ribbed and rush-like.

xiphium 2ft

SPANISH IRIS

Found extensively throughout the Iberian Peninsula, Southern France and maritime tracts of N. W. Africa, *I. xiphium* itself is seldom seen in gardens, unless it has been collected, say, from the alpine meadows of the Pyrenees. It is delicately scented, but a number of forms are strongly fragrant of violets, notably 'King of the Blues'. Most flower in May, The flower colour varies from deep to light purple with a pronounced central yellow band along the paler fall.

LILIUM (*Liliaceae*)

LILY

The lilies form a large genus, mostly grown from a scaly bulb and only a comparatively small section of them is sweetly scented, but these are probably among the best loved of all perfumed plants. Most scented lilies bear whitish, creamy yellow or purple flowers and are usually native of the higher altitudes – as indication of their cultural preferences. Generally they are most effective in the garden in groups together and fail in impact in association with other flowering plants. They therefore seem to give of their best away from the herbaceous border and planted in groups against some softer background. They are also successful employed for decoration when grown in pots, out of or in the conservatory, and make excellent patio plants when they can be transported to the proximity of the house as they come into flower.

The more difficult of cultivation have been omitted, but the specialist will probably wish to try the fragrant *L. bakerianum*, *iridollae*, *kelloggii* and *polyphyllum*.

auratum 6–8ft

GOLDBAND, GOLDEN-RAYED LILY OF JAPAN

The open funnel-shaped white flowers are thickly spotted, the colour varying in different varieties, but always with the central yellow band on each petal which gives the flower its common name. Stems bear lanceolate leaves and support about 10 blooms, occasionally more. Numerous hybrids are cultivated, difficult to distinguish from the various forms of *auratum* itself, but all bear the sweet scent which in a sheltered spot will pervade the air for some distance around for several weeks in August and September.

brownii 2–4ft

The large trumpet-shaped flowers with glistening white petals are pure white inside and a deep mahogany purple outside, with prominent brown anthers. Although the fragrance is faint, its sweetness excels, is stronger in the form *viridulum* (better recognized by some gardeners as *colchesteri*) and perhaps less easy to grow than *brownii* itself.

candidum 4–5ft

WHITE MADONNA LILY

The flowers are widely bell-shaped, the petals curving backwards, of the purest white, with golden anthers, in June and July. Tradition has it that this lily prefers the companionship of cottage garden plants, but this may be merely the supportive shelter afforded to the leaves and rising stem which appear in the autumn. For this reason, the bulbs are best transplanted in July or August immediately after flowering. The honey scent is perpetuated in the Cascade Hybrids.

cernuum 18in

A dainty low-growing Turk's-cap lily in form, which is often short-lived in our gardens. However, it provides an attractive splash of rosy-lilac in midsummer, and is a useful plant for dappled shade on the borders of the rock garden or in raised beds. The nodding flowers are spotted with damson and are sweetly fragrant.

chalcedonicum 4ft

More brilliant in colour than any other lily, this tangerine martagon-type flower is worth the patience needed to establish it. Give it good drainage in a really sunny spot on a calcareous soil. The waxy petals are strongly reflexed, scented, though with a perfume not universally acceptable as sweet. Up to 10 blooms can dangle from a stem where the plant is happily established.

ducharteri 4ft

MARBLED MARTAGON, FARRER'S LILY

This rather slender plant is one of the most graceful of all lilies, scented, and once established forming good clumps because of its stoloniferous stems. White nodding flowers spotted deep purple appear in June and July and love dappled shade, where some leaf mould is available at their feet. The plant is lime-tolerant and will need to be supported.

formosanum 3–4ft

A good plant for the cool greenhouse or conservatory, where it flowers quickly even from seed. Glistening white trumpets flared at the tips emit a deliciously spicy perfume in August and September. The outer edges of the petals are suffused with crimson purple. A somewhat capricious plant because of its susceptibility to virus disease.

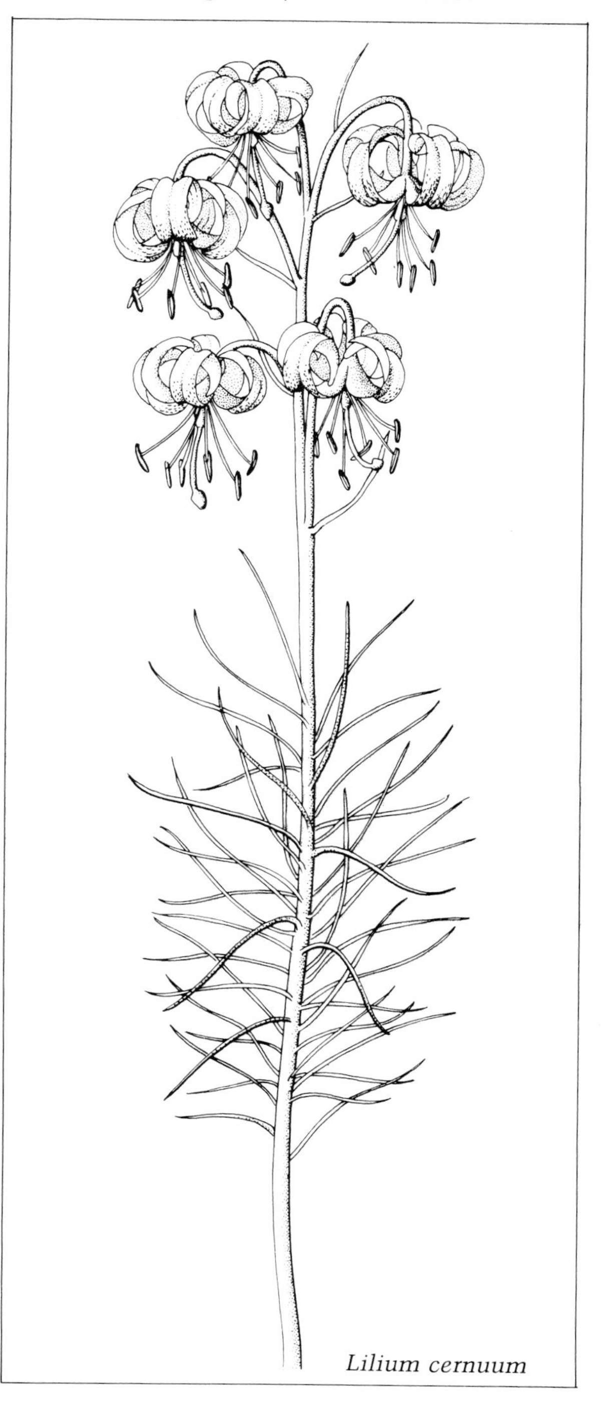

Lilium cernuum

hansonii 4ft

The thick reflexed golden-yellow petals of this martagon-type lily are slightly spotted with milk-chocolate brown, and are perhaps seen to best advantage where the sun catches the petals. Being thick, they really need light to enhance their colour. Fragrance is sweet, perhaps fleeting at times, but the summer garden is the better for it, especially perhaps on the border of shrubberies or open woodland where the roots can enjoy some shade.

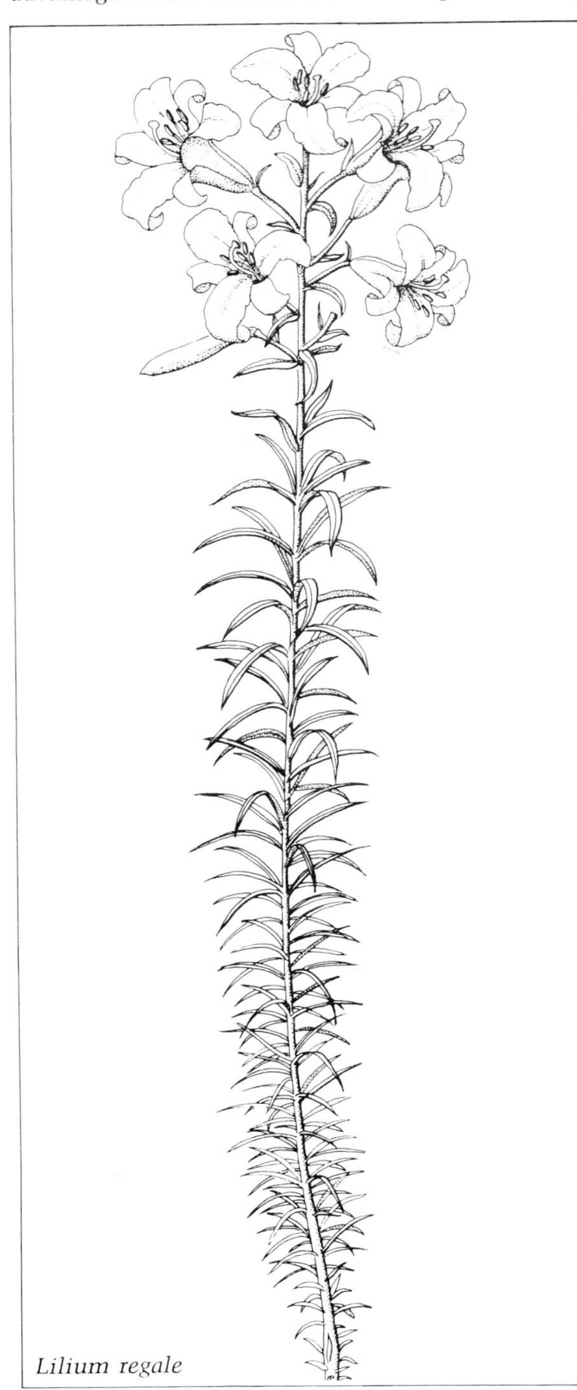

Lilium regale

henryi 8ft

ORANGE SPECIOSUM LILY

A splendid species for the uninitiated gardener to try! Tolerant of lime soils, *henryi* never fails to give a good display of deep yellow or apricot-orange flowers of the martagon type, with 20–60 or more nodding flowers to each stem in July. The flowers are spotted with a deeper golden brown and are sweetly fragrant in August. The outstanding Aurelian Hybrids (*L. sargentiae* × *L. henryi* × *L. leucanthum*) are among the most rewarding of fragrant garden plants, noteably the aptly named chartreuse 'Limelight'.

longiflorum 2ft

EASTER LILY, BERMUDA LILY

L. longflorum is the lily of the florist's shop, a good cool greenhouse plant never failing to flower in March and April. Its variety *giganteum* obviously produces more spectacular blooms. Remove the anthers before they shower their golden pollen, as the florists do, to retain the purity of the flower. Out of doors, especially in sheltered areas, because it is a doubtfully hardy plant even when the shoots are protected from late frosts, the glistening white trumpet flowers in July are fragrant of jasmine. Especially useful as conservatory plants are American raised plants such as 'Croft', 'Estate', and 'White Queen'.

parryi 5ft

A lily for open woodland planting where generous leaf mould or peat can be provided. Generally, it is not long-lived, but the beautiful clear-yellow funnel-shaped flowers, recurving at the tips of the petals, are gracefully displayed around the tall stem. It blooms in May and June and an exquisite perfume hangs about its domain when it can be persuaded to flourish.

regale 6ft

A beginner's lily, very easy of cultivation and tolerant of lime. It has erect stems each carrying numerous trumpet-shaped flowers. Streaked brown externally and of purest white flushed gold at the throat inside, the flowers are strongly fragrant, in July. The spring growth requires protection from late frosts and often it suffices to plant the bulbs among flowering shrubs.

sargentiae 4–5ft

Although *L. sargentiae* resembles *L. regale*, it comes into flower as the latter is finishing, and is less tolerant of lime and generally less easily managed.

The fragrance is perhaps enjoyed best in the conservatory. About 10 trumpet flowers are borne per stem. They are of glistening white, flushed pale green deep in the throat, and purple-brown on the outside. Its fragrance is delicious, fruity but fresh.

× *testaceum* 4–5ft
THE NANKEEN LILY

Fragrance has been inherited from both its parents (*L. candidum* × *L. chalcedonicum*) so the golden apricot-yellow flowers give off a strongly sweet perfume in June and July. Tolerant of chalk, it is a useful plant for a sunny position provided the cold spring winds can be kept at bay and some enrichment is supplied in the autumn in the form of a top dressing.

wardii 5ft
In broken shade where the flowers can be held in the open, as among low-growing shrubs, this martagon-type lily is happy, though seemingly rather short-lived. The purple stems, usually stoloniferous, carry racemes of up to 30 flowers at a time. Each is nodding and pinkish-purple, some deeper than others, and all are spotted with deep maroon-purple within the strongly recurved petals. They bloom in July and August.

MUSCARI (*Liliaceae*)
GRAPE HYACINTH

A genus of small bulbous plants that spread quickly and are very easy of cultivation in all temperate regions, with the possible exception of *M. moschatum* which needs a really sunny spot.

Somewhat grass-like leaves in tufts appear during the winter to herald the spring flowers. Most flowers are urn-shaped and globular in dense racemes and are most often blue. They are happy in any well-drained garden soil, but object to shade. Planted beneath a window or by a doorway, their perfume can be snatched on calm spring days.

Ruskin described grape hyacinths he saw growing in the South of France as 'a cluster of grapes and a hive of honey . . . pressed together in one small boss of celled and beaded blue.'

moschatum 8–10in
MUSK HYACINTH

The most sweetly scented member of the family, strongly perfumed of musk which atones for its dingy appearance. The leaves are wider than those of most species and the flowers purplish-green maturing to a yellowish-olive in the lower flowers of the head. It blooms in April, preferring a really sunny position. A slightly more vigorous form *M. m. major* is more powerfully scented. The name *moschatum* has been replaced by *muscarini*, and the plant is also seen as *Muscarinia moschata*, but there are few instances of this being accepted, and trade catalogues certainly cling to *Muscari moschatum*.

NARCISSUS (*Amaryllidaceae*)
DAFFODIL

Perhaps the best known of the bulbous plants, the genus *Narcissus* encompasses a range of very divergent plants, from the tiny to the grand, spring-flowering, autumn-flowering, scented and not so scented. Their native habitat is mainly the Iberian peninsular but they grow also in most countries bordering the Mediterranean, and farther north, even as far as Scandinavia and Scotland. *Narcissus pseudonarcissus* is a wild native plant, the plant that enchanted Wordsworth in the English Lake District.

The whole range provides plants for naturalizing in woodland and wild garden, and for underplanting, especially useful on banks and for cutting. At the other end of the scale, there are some treasures for the alpine house and trough cultivation. They almost resent forcing, and when grown in bowls and pots indoors they bloom but a week or two earlier than in the garden. The *Narcissus* 'Paper White' however is popularly grown for the Christmas market and is one of the few that can be brought into flower when cultivated in water and supported by pebbles.

This is not the setting in which to explore the merits of the various groups, but rather to select those that are particularly attractive and scented. Their name 'narcissus' is derives from *narce* ('dullness of sense') from which is derived the word narcotic. In some forms the perfume instigates headaches and light-headedness when deeply inhaled. Within a room, even the aroma of cut flowers changes perceptibly as the blooms fade. Among the most highly scented are:

jonquilla 1ft
JONQUIL

A plant perhaps for outdoor cultivation in more sheltered districts, the jonquil provides marvellous cut flowers in April, highly perfumed and really almost overpowering. The single-flowered ones are less intoxicating in scent than the double forms, and *N. j. florepleno* 'Queene Anne's Double' is the most highly perfumed of all.

When grown in bowls in a conservatory or greenhouse the flowers of the jonquils are perhaps the most perfect; they are flat-cupped and borne bunched. Their true home is the Iberian Peninsula and those regions of North Africa that border the Mediterranean.

Very close to the true jonquil is the so-called Campernelle Jonquil, *N.* × *odorus* and its form *N. o.* 'Rugulosus' (sometimes known as *N. campernelli*). It is in fact a hybrid between *N. jonquilla* and *N. pseudonarcissus* and has rush-like foliage and bright yellow flowers carried in clusters. *N.* × *o.*

'Rugulosus Florepleno', the double form of the sturdier 'Rugulosus', is even more powerfully perfumed than the type. A number of lovely varieties have the same heavy perfume of the jonquil itself: 'Bobbysoxer', butter-yellow with brighter golden-yellow corona; 'Cherie', cream-white with shell pink flushed corona; 'Orange Queen', a form of 'Rugulosus' with the deepest golden-yellow flowers, perhaps less fragrant; 'Suzy', primrose-yellow with tangerine corona; 'Sugar Bush' snow-white with amber corona edged silvery white and 'Trevithian', soft lemon-yellow with shallow yellow corona and very popularly forced in bowls for its long-lasting scented flowers.

juncifolius 4–6in

Grown in a pan in the alpine house where its delightful fragrance may be enjoyed, this lovely miniature has enormous charm. It may be grown also on the rock garden or in troughs and scree beds out of doors to flower in March or April. Native mainly of the Iberian Peninsular and southern France it bears 2–5 clear yellow little flowers on a stem. Its rush-like leaves wither quickly after flowering time, so the plant dies tidily. A lovely little *juncifolius* hybrid is 'Lintie', clear yellow, the cup edged with orange, and very fragrant.

minor 6in

The powerful scent given off by these small flowers is perhaps at its best in the variety *conspicuus*, slightly smaller in every way than the form. It is sometimes sold as *nanus* and has a pale yellow flower. *Narcissus minor* itself is a little taller and a little earlier in flower, usually coming about February, and has a slightly darker yellow corona giving it the bicolor appearance. *Narcissus minor* 'Pumilus' is all pure golden-yellow, not a bicolor, and is richly scented in flower in March. It is a strong-growing form.

poeticus 2ft

POET'S NARCISSUS

Narcissus poeticus recurvus, the old Pheasant's Eye Narcissus, has pretty flowers with reflexed snow-white perianth and yellow eye trimmed with tangerine, and is well known for its fragrance.

The latest-flowering of the spring narcissi often not appearing until early May, the named forms provide some of the best possible cut flowers with a strong perfume, possibly a little less cloying than that of the jonquils. Its native regions are the shores of the Mediterranean from Spain to Greece and its best recommended forms are: 'Actaea', white with orange-red 'eye'; and 'Queen of Narcissus', white with an astonishing yellow 'eye' trimmed with red.

tazetta 15–20in

THE POLYANTHUS NARCISSUS

Narcissus tazetta itself does not flourish very well in Britain but its varieties are the mainstay of the spring-flowering display, especially in the milder areas or where sunny corners can be found. In Cornwall and the Channel Isles they can be persuaded into bloom at New Year, and are all very reliable for indoor or cold greenhouse cultivation. The so-called Paper White Narcissus, *N. t. papyraceus*, responds to cool greenhouse forcing and can be had in flower before Christmas. This is one of the narcissi which can be relied upon to give first-class results when grown in water supported by clean pebbles. The flowers bloom during the shortest days of the year indoors or under glass. Other reliable varieties are: 'Cheerfulness', 3–4 sweetly scented creamy-white flowers with double 'centre', and good both for indoors or for naturalizing; 'Yellow Cheerfulness', a good sport which to naturally yellow in flower scented; 'Gernaium', unsurpassed for its perfume with 4–6 pure white flowers in a head with really bright orange-scarlet frilly cups; and 'Winston Churchill' with tight double flowers of pale yellow with bright orange tucked away at the heart of the flower and 4–5 flowers together atop a single stem

PANCRATIUM (*Amaryllidaceae*)

Only two European species are in general cultivation in England, and are worth seeking out for their intensely sweet strong scent. These are bulbous plants for the base of a sunny wall where the bulbs can ripen, in a warm area, excellent in maritime regions and sometimes needing covering in winter Useful also for pot cultivation under glass or in the cold frame.

illyricum 1½ft

The leaves are strap-shaped, glaucous green and blunt-ended. The white flowers are starry with tufted or fringed stamens giving a general narcissus like appearance, but ornamented with protruding thread-like stamens. Very fragrant in May and June

maritimum 2–2½ft

SEA DAFFODIL, SEA LILY

More commonly grown and somewhat hardier than the foregoing species, the leaves are slightl glaucous and persistent. Flowers, white, narcissus like with a green stripe along the back of each petal and again a fringed and toothed edge to the cup an rather more frivolous stamens. Very fragrant from July to September. Hailing from the Mediterranea shores, especially in Greece, it earns the name of Se Lily.

TULIPA (*Liliaceae*)

TULIP

Native of Asia Minor and the Caucasus region around the Black Sea, and Turkestan, the tulip bul is one of the most easily recognizable with it smooth brown skin and aquiline nose. Tulips ar tolerant of a wide range of soil including chalky ones, where good drainage is provided. After flowering in April and May it is best to lift them because they need to be well dried off during the summer, and this condition cannot often be met during the British summers.

Their stately carriage begs use of the cultivars for bedding schemes; a few of them are scented; but the species are best used in block planting where their beauty of flower and leaf can be better appreciated. Some, such as *T. humilis*, thrive best in pans in the alpine house, where their perfume can be enjoyed in late winter.

The garden cultivars available today are the result of extensive breeding and several hundred are always grown. Even more fall out of cultivation. A recent standard classification by the Royal Horticultural Society and the Royal General Dutch Bulb Growers' Society allocates each cultivar into one of 15 classes. A few of these named cultivars carry perfume, obviously inherited, but it is in the species that the sweetest scent is to be found.

aucheriana 3in

Now considered by many authorities to be a variety of *T. humilis*, the flowers open to a lovely shade of pink and are striped greenish-yellow on the outside, in April. The flowers open flat and are very sweetly scented, perhaps more so than any other tulip species.

gesneriana 9in

Generally considered to be the species from which most of the garden cultivars have arisen, the flower of *gesneriana* startles with its brilliant red flower with an olive black blotch at the centre. The flowers come in May and early June on stems arising from glaucous leaves, and are sweetly scented, with a fruity fragrance.

sylvestris 4–6in

Some forms of this species are quite strongly scented and because *T. sylvestris* itself is sometimes quite shy to flower they are more useful in the fragrant garden. It extends its range by stolons and may need to be contained, but the twin flowers of yellowish green are nearly always faintly scented. The form *celsiana* is the best choice for perfume, its flowers opening out like flat stars of yellow on branched stems usually in June, and is one of the latest of all tulip species to come into flower. The handsome green leaves are banded with crimson. It naturalizes well and is perfectly hardy.

SHRUBS

Today, shrubs are used as permanent features of the garden, giving a greater sense of scale and character than any other group of plants. Gone are the dull 'shrubberies' of laurel, *Rhododendron ponticum*, aucuba and privet, a legacy from the Victorians, and by considered selection a labour-reducing display of extreme interest can be achieved.

Plant-hunters have explored the five continents and the British climate enables gardeners to cultivate shrubs from almost every country of the world, providing an astonishing variety of form and colour. During the last 30 years, the popularity of shrub planting has increased in both private gardens and public areas. Wall-shrubs and climbers have become favourites and their value as fragrant plants in the proximity of the house and terrace are of special importance.

The suggestions for shrubs, wall-plants and climbers given below are not definitive by any means, and it is in this section that I have experienced the greatest difficulty in selecting what to include. The joy of garden-visiting, which so many gardeners indulge in these days, is frequently enhanced by the discovery of a rare or hitherto unfamiliar shrub. Thus, if the visit coincides with its brief flowering period, and moreover if the flowers are fragrant, then one has made an acquaintance that will remain for the rest of one's life!

Any gardener who persists in his hobby will surely become eventually a shrub addict!

Reference should be made to the section on planning (pages 60–68) because the selection of shrubs for any garden is important. It is so easy to choose indiscriminately, with the result that while the stronger shrubs will stand, the remainder abandon the fight, and the whole form, shape and purpose of the planting is disastrous. Shelter is the key to successful shrub gardening, and where even temporary protection is given to allow plants to establish themselves, the results will be satisfactory. Apart from the general rules of suitability to soil and area, some thought needs to be given to ensuring a continuity of interest; evergreen or deciduous, leaf and bark colour, period of flowering *and* overall effect and form. The ensuing lists give flower colour and season, but this may not sufficiently describe the overall effect. For example the outstanding attribute of *Actinidia kolomikta* is its jester-like leaves, and the total effect is not changed by its fragrant white flowers in early summer. Alternatively, the lilacs are planted mainly for their highly perfumed flowers when colour may be selected also, and not for their general visual effect for the remainder of the year, although they happen to become good shelter for smaller shrubs.

Other shrubs may be considered – space has not allowed us to include them in the detailed catalogue. They include the vigorously climbing, fragrant *Actinidia* species, *Callistemon citrinus*, good for conservatories and tubs; the Chilean *Cestrum parquii*, strongly fragrant at dusk; *Datura suaveolens*; *Edgworthia chrysantha*, offering February flowers for the conservatory; the fragrant species of *Erica*; the pretty *Freylina lanceolata*, an evergreen from South Africa for the mildest corner, or to grow under glass for late summer flowers; the curious *Hakea microcarpa*, whose fragrant white flowers nestle in early summer among the needle-like foliage; the handsome Chinese evergreen *Gordonia chrysandra*, with fragrant creamy white flowers, and strictly for a lime-free soil; the evergreen *Itea illicifolia* and *I. virginica*; × *Osmarea burkwoodii*, chalk-tolerant with ivory-white flowers in April and May; and the tender *Ozothamnus*, shrubs for the milder districts.

There is *Pachysandra terminalis*, useful for underplanting shrubs and really shaded corners; *Petteria ramentacea*, from the Albanian coast, closely resembling a laburnum, vanilla-scented in the early summer, and offering winter flower interest; *Phlomis fruticosa* with leaves fragrant of sage; *Plumeria rubra*, with highly perfumed showy leaves in summer and autumn; deliciously scented *Poncirus trifoliata*, a suckering shrub with large, deep-rose flowers; *Sarcococca* spp., happy on any fertile, humus-rich soil as borders and corner fillers; *Ulex* spp, whose mellow fragrance is often carried on the breeze for great distances; ornamental vines – some of which are fragrant of flower and most of which are fragrant of fruit; and, finally, *Zenobia pulverulenta*, whose pure white flowers in midsummer have a strong anise perfume.

ABELIA (*Caprifoliaceae*) (D)

A group of attractive shrubs that revel in full sunshine. Given a well-drained leafy soil in a protected position or sheltered garden they are eminently successful in most districts. Two species merit attention for fragrance.

chinensis 3ft

A much branched bush with light-green ovate leaves in pairs and bearing flowers in groups in July and August. The flowers are white suffused with rose, formed like little funnels with flaring or reflexed mouths, and are held in rose-pink calyces which add a decorative air to the plant. Their fragrance is sweet.

triflora 5ft

Elegantly upright in habit, this Himalayan species has light-green ovate leaves and flowers in dense groups, blooming in June. They are very richly scented and are like miniature white trumpets tinged with pink.

ABELIPHYLLUM *distichum* (*Oleaceae*) (D) 9–10ft

A winter-flowering shrub from Korea, useful as a wall plant, where it will get the support and protection it requires, as well as a well-drained soil. Flowers sweetly fragrant appear from January to early March and are white, open-bell-shaped, with brown-pink at the centre. Lovely on the house wall where its winter fragrance may be appreciated.

ACACIA (*Leguminosae*) (E)

The wattles of Australia, drought-tolerant plants of which one or two are fragrant and hardy in our temperate climate in sheltered gardens in the south and west. Good cool greenhouse or frost-free conservatory shrubs. Out of doors they need a warm sunny wall and neutral-to-acid, fertile, well-drained soil.

dealbata 33ft

SILVER WATTLE, MIMOSA

A half-hardy tree, but usually grown as a very decorative wall shrub in sheltered areas. Foliage blue-green-silver and fern-like. Flowers in January to April in globose heads, fluffy and lemon yellow. They are highly fragrant of almond, the scent fading or disappearing totally as the flower matures. This is the Mimosa of the florist's shop.

rhetinoides 33ft

Again a small tree, usually grown as a wall shrub and possibly the most lime-tolerant of the genus. Foliage is narrow grey-green, willow-like, and the lemon-yellow globose fluffy flowers are carried in loose panicles in late winter, spring and early summer, dependent upon season and locality. Fragrance of almond but less intense and lighter than that of *dealbata*.

ALOYSIA *citriodora* (Syn. *Lippia citriodora*) 4–6ft

LEMON VERBENA

A highly aromatic shrub, probably far less tender than it has always been considered to be; in many places it survived the winter of 1978–79. Often the growth dies back completely during the winter and flushes late in spring, often not until the middle of May. The leaves are shining green, long and narrow and strongly scented of lemonade crystals. Growth is lax, except when cut back to the wall each autumn in the wall-grown specimens. The not-very-attractive flowers are small and insignificant – it does not always flower. Ensure shelter from cold rough winds; give it a dry root run at the foot of a wall of cultivate it as a tub plant for porch or conservatory where the leaves will surrender their lemon scent to passers-by.

AZARA (*Flacourtiaceae*) (E)

Shrubs or small trees often grown against a wall for shelter, where some species will flourish through hard winters. Good drainage and friable neutral soil and sunshine for part of the day is all they ask. They may be grown as free-standing bushes in the really mild areas.

Acacia dealbata

lanceolata 10ft

The shining bright-green leaves are long, narrow and toothed, on arching branches, and the flowers are borne deep at the base of the leaf in the axils all along the branches. Bright mustard-yellow flowers with fluffy abundant anthers are very sweetly fragrant in April and May.

microphylla 16½ft

Sometimes attaining the proportions of a small tree, *A. microphylla* also grows happily as a wall shrub. The foliage is rounded and toothed and of varying sizes. The leaves are bright, shining green, rusting with age. The vanilla-scented flowers, bright yellow in spring, again are in bloom in spring and are fluffy in general appearance. Grown as a wall shrub, the branches fan out well and so the effect is best appreciated only at close quarters. Not a wall shrub for garden effect.

petiolaris 9½–13ft

Earlier to flower than the foregoing species, with oval sharply toothed leaves, bright shining green and leathery. It flowers from Christmas to March. Perfumed highly of orange, the flowers are yellow and clustered in the axils of the leaves. The wood is a burnished red and it is possibly the most garden-worthy form, away from the milder counties.

BUDDLEIA (*Loganiaceae*) (D and E)

This is a large genus of shrubs and small trees, thriving in full sun, tolerant of a wide range of soils, but happiest, perhaps, on sandy loams (the exceptions are noted below). Their tendency to grow rapidly has encouraged a reputation for coarseness, but when severely cut back in the spring, or after flowering in the milder areas, they can be kept within bounds. Buddleias are remarkable for their ability to attract butterflies to the garden, as well as for their powerful heavy fragrance. A selection of scented species is suggested, but others to try would include: *B. crispa*, felted growth, mauve sprays of flower in August, rather tender; *B. forrestii*, pale lilac flowers in late summer, very fragrant, rather tender; 'Lochinch' (*B. davidii* × *B. fallowiana*) violet flowers with a deep golden eye, in July; 'West Hill', pale lavender flowers with an orange eye in late summer, deliciously fragrant; *B. farreri*, with a reputation for tenderness and which has deliciously fragrant rosy lilac flowers in April – in spite of this it flourishes in many sheltered areas, such as Howick garden in Northumberland.

alternifolia (D) 8ft

A good plant to grow as a specimen where space permits it to attain a well-rounded shape. Rather weeping-willow-like in habit, but a little more tangled, the branches are strongly wreathed in tiny mauve flowers in June and July, richly perfumed of heliotrope. They attract many bees, butterflies and moths. A cultivar 'Argentea' is available with silver foliage, bestowing a filmy appearance to the whole plant when in flower. They make very attractive weeping shrubs or small trees.

asiatica (E) 9½ft

Rather lax of growth, this tender evergreen bears drooping slender spikes of sweetly scented white flowers in winter. It is an excellent greenhouse shrub, where a frost-free temperature is maintained.

auriculata (D) 3–5ft

Lax and open of habit, with silver-white felting beneath the leaves, *auriculata* demands the protection of a warm wall to produce its flowers in winter. It is a good porch, conservatory or cool greenhouse plant where sufficient light can be given, and the creamy white flowers, yellow at the throat, will provide a strong honey fragrance in mid-winter.

caryopteridifolia (D) 8ft

Again, the tomentose nature of the leaves presents a woolly appearance especially on the young growth. A plant for mild areas, where there is protection from prevailing wind and rain. When grown under porch, loggia or conservatory conditions its fragrant lavender-coloured flowers in April and May are delightful. If cut back in spring it will flower in the autumn, both under glass and out of doors.

davidii (D) 15ft

BUTTERFLY BUSH

Universally grown and often maltreated, *davidii* and its cultivars give the best results when hard-pruned in March. Rewarding, in that it fills its allotted space quickly with its cane-like growth, it is accommodating for both towns and seaside districts. From the wide range of cultivars a required colour can usually be selected, and for this alone the plant is useful in garden planning. They appreciate some lime or rubble in the soil. Long panicles of small flowers give off a musky, honey-like fragrance in July, August and September.

All of them attract butterflies in profusion. Some recommended cultivars are: 'Black Knight', deep violet; 'Empire Blue', violet-blue with orange eye; 'Fortune', soft lilac with orange eye; 'Harlequin', red-purple with variegated creamy leaves; 'Ile de France', rich violet; 'Peace', white, and 'White Bouquet', white with a yellow eye.

fallowiana (D) 6½–10ft

Given a sheltered position, the felted growth is enhanced by pale lavender-blue flowers in summer, which are highly fragrant. It is particularly adapted to maritime areas.

globosa (*Semi-E*) 9½–16½ft

ORANGE BALL TREE

An erect-growing shrub of unusual but distinctive appearance from South America, carrying bright

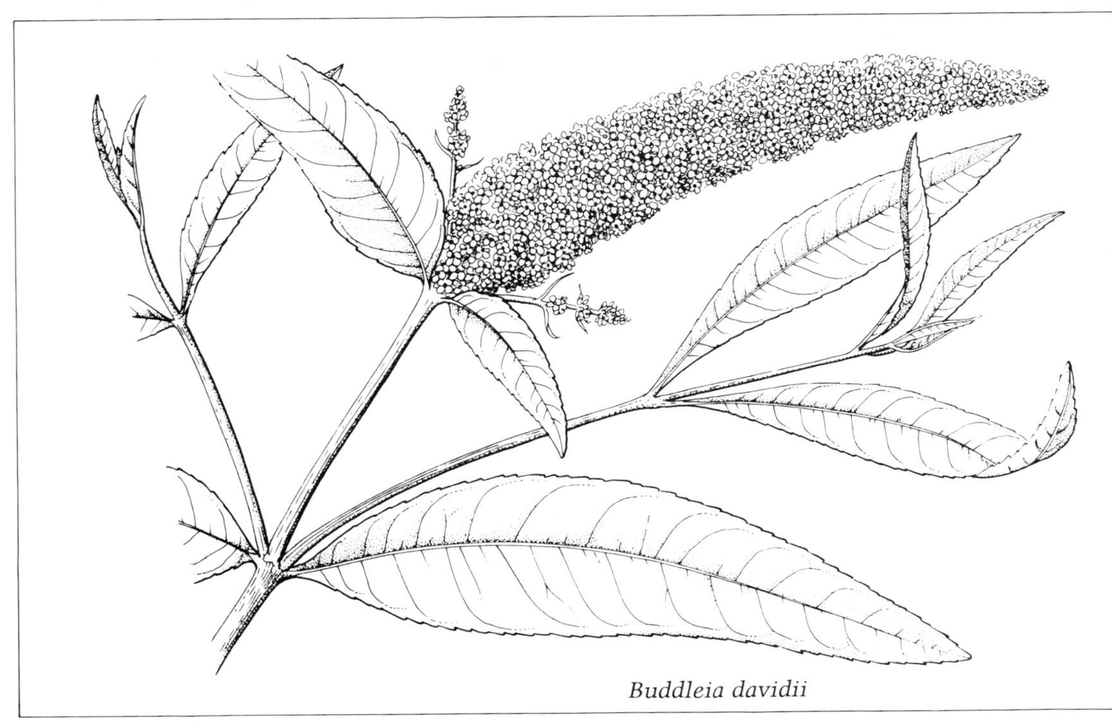

Buddleia davidii

1 *Catmint lining a path in the rose garden*

2 *A collection of thymes planted in chequerboard fashion, and forming a small patio*

orange balls of flowers resembling xylophone hammers in May and June. One of the buddleias that enjoys lime and is totally hardy in all districts of the British Isles. Even in the coldest of seasons it perfumes the air around it with a sweet honey-like fragrance.

officinalis (*Semi-E*) 8ft

Preferring cool greenhouse cultivation, this delicate plant provides delightfully fragrant mauve flowers in winter. The silver-green leaves, tomentose beneath, add an air of filmy silver to the whole plant.

CALYCANTHUS (*Calycanthaceae*) (D)

ALLSPICE

A group of American plants with scented wood, happiest on peaty or loam soil with added moisture-retentive material.

fertilis 6ft

Rather spreading in habit with oval leaves aromatic of camphor, dull green and downy beneath. Curious dull crimson-brown flowers resembling a small bunch of ribbons appear in June to August, and are scented. The scent is perhaps best described as 'rough' and slightly spicey. The wood, roots, bark and foliage carry the perfume, as well as the flowers. Plant it in a sheltered corner where the sun is not going to scorch the flowers.

floridus 8ft

CAROLINA ALLSPICE

Straggling in habit, it is often confused with or even grown as *fertilis*, although it is rarer in cultivation. Leaves downy and paler beneath and aromatic of camphor. The flowers like a bunch of ribbons – or described as having tongue-shaped petals of a dusky brown – are aromatic, scented of ripe melons, in June and July. All parts of the plant are hauntingly aromatic.

occidentalis 12ft

More robust but rather ungainly in growth with similar leaves, but paler larger flowers than the previous species. The scent of the flowers in June to August is stronger, quite pungent and sharp, but that of the leaves, wood and bark more pleasantly aromatic than in other species.

CARYOPTERIS (*Verbenaceae*) (D)

BLUE SPIRAEA

Reasonably spreading, low-growing shrubs tolerant of chalky soils, needing good drainage and protection from wind and frost.

× *clandonensis* (*C. incana* × *C. mongolica*) 3ft

Leaves narrowly ovate, sometimes coarsely toothed, and hairy beneath in pairs along the stem and harbouring decorative lavender-blue flowers with protruding anthers. On close inspection the petals can be seen to be fringed but it is for the value of its aromatic foliage that it is included here. The forms 'Ferndown', and 'Kew Blue', 'Heavenly Blue' with deeper blue flowers and a little more compact of habit, and 'Arthur Simmons' with bright blue flowers are superior. All flower in August and September and are useful late-flowering shrubs, and provide a remarkably attractive foil for silver-leaved plants.

incana

One of the parents of × *clandonensis*, it is altogether a greyer plant and not very hardy. The leaves are more felted and the flowers seem powdery-blue and pale. The reward comes in the stronger-scented foliage. *Caryopteris mastacanthus* and *tanguitica* are listed as the same plant, or forms of it, but in the herb garden at Cranborne Manor, Dorset, the two latter grow nearly side by side and are quite distinct plants, redolent of sweet turpentine when bruised.

CEANOTHUS (*Rhamnaceae*) (D and E)

Only one or two of this large tribe of decorative garden shrubs carry any fragrance. Usually given the protection of a wall or building as they are only marginally hardy, many did not survive the brutal winter of 1978–79. One of the floriferous plants that look as though they ought to be fragrant, and always disappoint except for the following cultivars.

arboreus 'Trewithen Blue' (E) 12ft

A spring-flowering tree-like shrub with lightly fragrant deep blue flowers in panicles in May. The leaves are oval, shining green, and fresh in appearance. Marginally hardier than other *arboreus* forms.

× *delinianus* 'Gloire de Versailles' (D) 12ft

One of the most widely cultivated of ceanothuses, it carries large panicles of deep powder-blue fragrant flowers in summer. The leaves are deep-green, paler beneath.

CHIMONANTHUS *praecox* (*Calycanthaceae*) (D) 8ft

WINTER SWEET

One species commonly cultivated, and sometimes catalogued as *C. fragrans*, is a winter-flowering shrub with strongly scented flowers carried on the bare branches. Later, the leaves carry the same fragrance, slighter and less elaborate than that of the flowers. Reluctant to flower when young, it forms a nicely open bush, or planted against a wall a taller plant with whippy branches. The flowers are yellow, bell-shaped, in stiff tufts held downwards along the branches and with brown centres. The perfume is

Ceanothus × delinianus
'Gloire de Versailles'
Choisya
ternata

very sweet and is carried on the winter air. The summer foliage is a lustrous green, rough to the touch and lanceolate. *Chimonanthus p.* 'Grandiflorus' has larger flowers of deeper yellow and more marked brown-red centres, and 'Luteus' is without the brown marking. They are happy in any friable garden soil, love being on chalk, and need good drainage and shelter from the cold winds. Best in a sunny corner where the wood ripens well for the provision of growth buds.

CHOISYA *ternata* (*Rutaceae*) (E) 8ft

MEXICAN ORANGE, MEXICAN ORANGE BLOSSOM

A bushy shrub with good, bright shining green leaves always giving a lustrous appearance of clean growth and often looking like so many small fans. Foliage strongly pungent when bruised, of a peppery orange, flowers in clusters as sweetly fragrant as orange blossom.

The flowers are white with a dark eye, appearing mainly in summer, but often flushing again in the late summer and often speckling the shrubs in the meantime. Given protection from wind, most drained garden soils suit it, and it tolerates chalk and shade, though when grown in full shade it fails to flower properly. It makes a fine evergreen hedge in southern gardens, and is useful as a weed suppressor in wild gardens when planted in groups.

Of the same strong prickly fragrance is *Choisya arizonica* growing under the wall of the laboratory at the Royal Horticultural Society's Garden, Wisley, Surrey. Obviously not commercially available, but its spiky leaves when rubbed claim its family relationship without doubt.

CLEMATIS (*Ranunculaceae*) (D and E)

Scrambling or lax-growing and climbing shrubs and herbaceous perennials. They are certainly not to the forefront for the scented garden, and those with dramatically large and brightly coloured flowers are scentless, though some people detect a 'woody' scent in them. A number of the species are reputed to have some perfume, a few certainly do. Cultivation demands a cool, moist but well-drained root run, and a spot where they can get their heads into the sunshine.

flammula (E) 13–16½ft

FRAGRANT VIRGIN'S BOWER

Invaluable for the autumn scented garden, when its tangled growth is enveloped in creamy white, sweetly scented flowers. The scent is so strong that it proves to be an anticlimax on close investigation, but at some distance from the source resembles that of meadow-sweet or hawthorn. A vigorous climber with three or five leaflets which it retains well into the winter, to accompany the silky seed heads that bedeck it in late autumn. A marvellous plant that drapes and transforms an otherwise unsightly host, be it rail, post or stump.

montana (D)

For clambering, the accolade always goes to *C. montana* which with age willingly produces a thickly gnarled trunk and tangled growth. Flowering in late April and May and into June in cooler gardens, there is always the vaguest hint of aroma in the open flower. But the form 'Alexander' with white sweetly fragrant flowers, in May and June, is good. *Clematis montana wilsonii*, late flowering in June with innumerable small white scented flowers, is a useful summer-impact plant for a north-facing wall. Used to full effect, the scented montanas are delightful when allowed to ramp over a fence or balustrade when their fragrant flowers are maintained at nose level.

recta 3–4ft

Rather floppy, nearer to a herbaceous perennial in habit, and tufted in growth requiring support so that it can form a loose mound of growth in the border. (Not a plant for the labour-saving garden.) Very sweetly scented small white flowers are borne in profusion in June and July. There is a double-flowered form *flore-pleno*, and also *purpurea*, very similar to the type, but one that dons purple foliage.

CLERODENDRUM (*Verbenaceae*) (D)

Attractive flowering shrubs, the hardy species thriving in sunny sheltered positions in a rich well-drained soil.

bungei (Syn. *foetidum*) 6–8ft

A suckering shrub which can be contained almost like a herbaceous perennial by cutting back, and looks attractive when used in block planting that can be looked down upon. Leaves are heart-shaped, with a most disagreeable smell if bruised, but the flowers are sweetly scented, rose red in tightly packed rounded heads, in August and September. At its best in hot summers and sheltered situations in the southern counties.

fragrans (D) 10ft

A little-grown tender scrambler, useful for trellis and pillars in conservatories and garden rooms, when it produces very sweetly scented double or semi-double white flowers from July to September. The fragrance is likened to that of dianthus with strong overtones of clove.

trichotomum (D) 10ft

Large three-lobed lower leaves, downy beneath and oval higher up the plant, and much veined. Grown mainly for its autumn effect, the flowers bloom late in the summer, with pink maroon calyces which persist to form claw-like decoration for the turquoise-blue fruits, which finally turn black. The flowers are white and highly scented. The form *C. t. fargesii*, formerly known as the Glory Flower, has smooth leaves, pinkish when young, and is preferable as it sets fruit with greater freedom. Some people find the fragrance of the white flowers in late summer unpleasing. It is heavily scented like the Pheasant's Eye Narcissus. The leaves when bruised have the roast beef smell of *Iris foetidissima*, mixed with that of elder bark.

CLETHRA (D and E)

Tender shrubs needing some protection, flourishing in light neutral-to-acid moist humus-rich soil. Although *C. alnifolia* manages in the wild garden at the Royal Horticultural Society's garden, Wisley, 'manages' is perhaps the best word, as the shrub probably lacks light there.

alnifolia (D) to 8ft

MIGNONETTE TREE, SWEET PEPPER BUSH

A handsome shrub of branching habit with oval tapering leaves and erect sprays of small sweetly scented white flowers in August. The form 'Paniculata' transcends the type, because the flowers are held in quite generous panicles, as they are in 'Rosea' where the buds are gently tinged pink, and there is a suspicion of pink in the flowers as though a paint brush had been passed over the protruding anthers. 'Rosea' has also beautifully glossy leaves and the shrub has sacrificed scent for its enchantment; for the fragrance is slight. Otherwise *alnifolia* is very sweetly scented, something between balsam and honey, in both flowers and foliage, perhaps with a suggestion of lilac.

arborea (E) 12–15ft

LILY-OF-THE-VALLEY TREE

Sometimes cultivated under glass in conservatory or cold house for the pervasive sweet scent of its flowers, and grown out-of-doors only in the very mild south-western regions of England. The leaves are shining green and tapering, and the chalk-white flowers resembling lily-of-the-valley in quite substantial terminal racemes in August and September.

delavayi (D) 8–10ft

A handsome shrub, not quite as tender as *arborea*, bearing striking dark-green deeply veined leaves with serrated margins. The flowers are in sprays held horizontally about the bush, in August. Again, the perfume is sweetly pervasive and the flowers resemble those of lily-of-the-valley.

COLLETIA (*Rhamnaceae*) (D)

These plants are peculiar in that they are composed of grey-green fleshy branches with rigid stems, rather thorn- or needle-like in shape, and form a tangled mound of growth. Leaves seem few and far between but the pitcher-shaped flowers are highly fragrant. Hardy in most places and requiring a light soil and a warm spot, they flourish best in warm summers that recall their South American home.

armata 6½–9½ft

Much-branched and tangled thorns, all of which are completely enveloped in creamy-apricot flowers in August, September and October. The blooms are small, waxy and richly fragrant of almonds. The form 'Rosea' provides a rose-pink mass when in bud, but only slightly deeper apricot-rose flowers, again transforming the evil-looking mass of growth into a flowering ornamental plant.

cruciata

The green branches bear strange wing-like thorns in opposite pairs, producing a shrub of formidable appearance. But again, the bell-shaped white flowers, carried in great profusion in September and October, transform the scene. They are highly scented, rather sweeter than those of *armata*. A particularly slow-growing shrub which will for several years remain small, and needing a succession of good seasons in full sunshine and well-drained fertile soil.

COMPTONIA *peregrina* (*Myricaceae*) (D) 3¼ft

SWEET FERN

Given a warm spot in full sunshine, a lime-free soil and sharp drainage, the Sweet Fern makes an unusual aromatic shrub. The foliage resembles that of the spleenwort, and is astonishingly resinous giving off a rich spicy scent on to the breeze. On touching, the fragrance is stronger and lingers on the skin and when the leaves are dried the scent increases. It is likened to that of cinnamon but with a fruity overtone. The rather downy foliage is a good foil for the shining brown catkin-like flowers in high summer.

Flowers are borne in broad panicles, in spring and summer and are very sweetly fragrant. The roots too, are aromatic, pungent and hot, earning the plant its common name of Ginger Plant.

CORONILLA *valentina* (Syn. *glauca*) *Leguminosae* (E) 3½ft

Delicate and decorative small Portuguese shrub with glaucous leaves, rather blue-grey, and bearing bright-yellow small flowers smelling of ripe peaches in late spring and early summer, and perhaps intermittently afterwards. Strictly only for well enfolded sites, but a winner in the conservatory.

CORYLOPSIS (*Hamamelidaceae*) (D)

A group of very dainty, hardy Asiatic shrubs with drooping inflorescence of scented flowers on bare wood in early spring. They welcome good rich soil, acid or neutral, but *C. pauciflora* will tolerate some chalk.

glabrescens 5ft

A spreading shrub, with somewhat horizontal branches, decorated with dangling primrose-yellow tassels of flower before the leaves in April. The scent is admittedly slight, but sweetly fragrant, and seems to get trapped beneath taller shrubs, as at Westonbirt Arboretum.

pauciflora 4ft

A small rounded dense shrub of twiggy habit with drooping catkin-like sprays of two or three sweetly fragrant, pale yellow flowers in March before the leaves break. The scent is likened to that of cowslips. The young foliage adopts pretty pink colours, turns green for the summer and then resumes the coloured outfit for the autumn.

spicata 4–6ft

A spreading shrub with rather large heart-shaped hazel-like leaves silky and glaucous beneath, which colour well in the autumn. Long drooping racemes of bright yellow flowers with purple anthers appear on bare wood in February and March and are faintly fragrant of cowslip.

willmottiae up to 8ft

A quick-growing species from Western China, whose foliage is often reddish purple when young, and again sometimes in the autumn. The soft primrose-yellow flowers are sweetly fragrant and held in long showy racemes which droop from the bare wood in April.

CYTISUS (*Leguminosae*) (E and D)

BROOM

The brooms are essentially sun-worshippers, rather selective of soil, preferring neutral fertile soils that are well drained. They have a reputation for being short-lived, but for them it really is a 'short life and a gay one' for they are superbly decorative and graceful plants. All come from southern Europe or the Mediterranean regions, the Canary Isles and Madeira.

battandieri (Semi-E or D) 15ft

Soft and silky trifoliate leaves add a sheen to the whole plant; white woolly stems, almost jade green

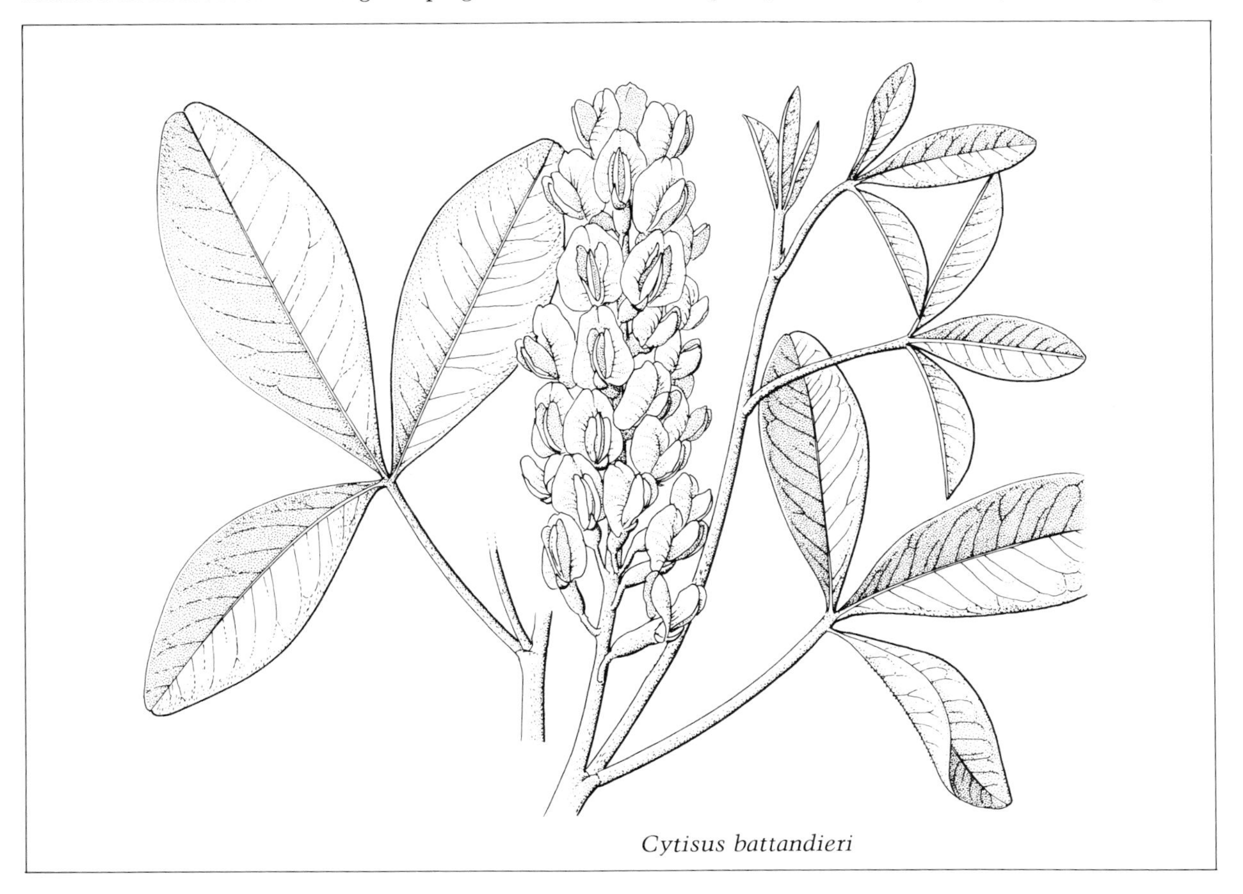

Cytisus battandieri

in effect, form a well-rounded shrub. Grown with the protection of a wall it towers with silvery outstretched growth. Yellow flowers are carried in cone-shaped dense erect heads in July and the fragrance is strongly of pineapple. The remarkable coincidence is that the shape, colour and perfume of the flower head is closely identified with the pineapple. Hardy in many areas, but really at its best against a wall where the reflected warmth will enhance the scent.

fragrans (of gardens) (E) 16½ft

C. racemosus, *C. canariensis*, more recently *C.* × *spachianus* – whatever one chooses to call this plant it will give a good performance when cultivated as a pot plant in the conservatory or greenhouse and restricted to size. The golden-yellow flowers in late winter to early spring, and again in the autumn, are deliciously scented and earn the plant the name of Fragrant Broom. The foliage is typical trifoliate, soft green and, if constantly cut back, always fresh. Sometimes cultivated as *Genista fragrans*.

'Porlock' (Semi-E) 4ft

A quick-growing conservatory shrub with ravishingly sweet-scented flowers in April and May, on slightly arching branches.

× *praecox* (D) 4ft

WARMINSTER BROOM

Of truly graceful habit with arching branches of sulphur-yellow flowers bursting forth in a fountain-like spray in May and June. Foliage bright green and small and stems whippy. A most useful plant for banks where its sprays may tumble to advantage. 'Albus' has white flowers and 'Allgold' is a slightly more solid yellow than the type, with rather longer-lasting flowers.

purgans (D) 3ft

A useful shrub for small gardens because it carries its branches upright and they are crowded with masses of deep golden-yellow along the branches in May and June, and sometimes again in the autumn. Occasionally virtually leafless, but the flowers appear in the 'leaf axils' and are sweetly scented with a truly flowery fragrance.

DAPHNE (*Thymelaeaceae*) (E and D)

The daphnes number among the hardiest and the most beautifully perfumed of all shrubs and the various species span a flowering period from November to August. Tolerant of most soils, provided that it does not dry out in summer, but best in a humus-enriched medium, daphne enjoys sun or shade, rock garden or tub cultivation, if the appropriate species is selected. Some are difficult to establish; one or two have only the slightest of scent, and scent is sometimes wanting, as in *D. acutiloba*. The native Spurge Laurel, *D. laureola*, is quite unpleasant in aroma. A selection of species is suggested here, but there are other fragrant examples that may comply with personal requirements.

alpina (D) 1ft

Dwarf-growing, useful in the rock garden, with grey-green leaves and clusters of sweetly scented white flowers in May and June, followed by orange berries.

blagayana (D) 9in

Not the easiest of plants to establish, but when the bare wood, which splays out to carry leaves and flowers, is pegged down and buried in leaf mould (as for propagating), a pool of flowering tips will be produced. The flowers are creamy white, delicately scented in March and April.

cneorum (E) 1ft

GARLAND FLOWER

Reluctant to stay in some gardens, and slow growing, this southern European native has prostrate growth well clothed with bright green leaves. In May and June the rose-pink flowers, typically tubular with starry mouths, are very sweetly scented. The form 'Exima' is more prostrate, with larger leaves and flowers of rose-pink, waxy and emitting a strong sweet scent.

Daphne cneorum

mezereum (D) 3ft

MEZEREUM, MEZEREON

One of the best known of the winter-flowering shrubs, variable in flower colour from pale lilac-pink to purplish red, which spatters the stems from January to March. Red shining berries follow later in the year, and are poisonous. The blossoms are highly fragrant, lasting well, and are tolerant of wind and rain. The form 'Grandiflora' is perhaps more robust and flowers so 'early' that it often comes late in the autumn when there is little else with such a delicious fragrance in the garden. (It is sometimes catalogued as 'Autumnalis'.) A white-flowered form, 'Alba' is sweetly scented but sometimes the effect is lost in the greyness of the shortest days of the year.

odora (E) 3ft

Even among this fragrant tribe, the accolade goes to *D. odora* for its outstanding sweet rich scent. Not reliably hardy everywhere perhaps, except in southern counties, it needs good protection from cold winds and from morning sunshine, or better still the pampering of a cool greenhouse so that its winter scent can spill into the air and be trapped. Deep rich pink buds open to a paler flower backed by a collar of leaves from February to April. A hardier and attractive form is 'Aureo Marginata' with cream leaf margins and similar rich pink flowers deliciously scented.

pontica (E) 3ft

For woodland planting, *D. pontica* is to be recommended because it tolerates the drip of trees and enjoys shade. Of rather open, spreading habit with exceptionally glossy bright lettuce-green leaves, it bears flowers which are slightly fragrant on inspection, but do not scent the air as do many other daphnes. Rather stringy greenish-yellow flowers in April, followed by black-purple round berries.

retusa (E) 6in

A lovely little plant for the rock garden or pan cultivation in the cold greenhouse. For so small a plant the leaves seem stout and the clusters of waxy rose-purple flowers resemble posies in a collar of the leaves. Exceptionally frangrant in May and June.

DEUTZIA (*Philadelphaceae*) (D)

A group of very floriferous shrubs with starry flowers produced in clusters, and opposite serrated leaves like those of the philadelphus, to which they are allied. When they were first introduced from the Far East they were considered to be only half-hardy.

chunii 4–6½ft

A truly delightful July flowering plant introduced during the last 50 years from China. An arching habit and peeling bark of grey-green willow-like leaves, glaucous beneath, lend a subtlety to the whole shrub when it flowers. The blooms are white and starry, flushed rose behind, when open, and eventually reflexing to reveal deep-yellow anthers. The scent has the same depth as that of hawthorn, and is very similar, but without the fishy overtones.

compacta 5ft

Slow growing and for a sheltered spot; the creamy white flowers in July are hawthorn-scented, remaining fresh without the mustiness of that plant. Rough leaves, pale brown beneath, and pale brown bark which peels away on the older stems, lend an air of great elegance. *Deutzia compacta* 'Lavender Time', now offered by Hilliers, bears pale creamy-lilac flowers, darker at first, and well accompanied by light green foliage.

corymbosa 4ft

Arching growth and slender pointed leaves, with white flowers rich with yellow anthers, give a creamy froth to the whole plant when in flower in June and July. It emits a hawthorn-like scent.

gracilis 3¾ft

Best perhaps when gently forced under glass to flower in spring. A Japanese species, tender in most areas, with white large flowers, frothy and milky in appearance in May and June, and strongly scented.

sieboldiana 4ft

Another Japanese species with heart-shaped-to-elliptical leaves which flower in June. The pure white flowers are small, carried in loose panicles, and are honey-scented.

× *maliflora* (*D. lemoinei* × *D. purpurascens*) 6ft

Flowering in June, the form grown for its fragrance is 'Avalanche', well named for the branches literally arch under the weight of snow-white blossom in June. The fragrance is strongest of all deutzias.

DIPELTA (*Caprifoliaceae*) (D)

Useful because they are shade-tolerant and floriferous, and of great interest to flower-arrangers for the clusters of elm-like winged bracts to the fruit. They require a good fertile soil, properly drained, and can be grown as a wall shrub where there is some shade. However, they are quite happy in the sunshine also.

floribunda 9¾ft

Stout upright-growing shrub, with attractive peeling bark which comes away in cigar-like rolls. The leaves are long and narrow and the sweetly scented flowers are borne in rich profusion clustered near the stem. They are pale pink with yellow throat and weigela-like in shape, in April.

yunnanensis 9½–13ft
Larger and more arching in growth than *floribunda* but every bit as floriferous, with deep-cream fragrant flowers in May, deeper at the throat and with orange markings on the lip of the flower. Again, followed by clusters to winged papery bracts about the fruits.

ELEAGNUS (*Eleagnaceae*) (D and E)
Useful hardy shrubs really cultivated for their good foliage. They are quick-growing and wind-tolerant so the evergreen species make first rate informal hedges or shelter plants, even in seaside gardens. Accommodating to all types of soil, with the exception of shallow chalk. The spring-borne fruits are said to be edible and sweet but do not always develop in the British climate.

Eleagnus pungens

angustifolia (D) up to 33ft
OLEASTER

Large shrub or small tree, spiny and heavily covered with silvery scales when young. Leaves silvery grey, narrow and lanceolate. Flowers bell-shaped in June, sweetly and deliciously fragrant, creamy yellow within and silvery-scaled on the outside.

× *ebbingei* (*E. macrophylla* × *E. pungens*) (E) 13ft
Reliable and vigorous as a shelter-providing shrub, especially attractive when planted in groups. The leaves elliptical, green-silver-bronze especially when young, and remaining a metallic gilt beneath. Flowers fragrant, cream and silver-scaled in September, followed by spiny fruits which are dull orange, speckled with silver.

glabra (E) up to 20ft
When established, adopts a semi-climbing habit of thornless growth with rather glossy leaves, bronzed beneath. October-November flowering with the creamy, scaled flowers of the genus, sweetly fragrant and tucked well down among the foliage. Fruits in spring, a dull orange, speckled silver.

macrophylla (E) 10ft
A pretty shrub with rounded habit and rather broad elliptical leaves, shining grey-green, and silver beneath when young. Of spreading habit, often producing a shrub wider than it is tall. Flowers fragrant, bell-shaped, creamy silver and scaled in October; red fruits come in early spring.

pungens (E) up to 15ft
Vigorous and quick-growing, and widely cultivated in its coloured-leaved forms, providing a splash of golden yellow in winter. Leaves somewhat leathery with undulating margins, silver beneath and speckled with bronze scales. Attractive forms include 'Maculata' ('Aureo-variegata') with a central splash of butter yellow; the leaves of 'Dicksonii' have a wide irregular margin of gold; they are variegated, with a paler cream margin. The small flowers are all creamy yellow late in the year, fragrant. Some forms of *pungens* have aromatic leaves, peppery when crushed.

ELSHOLTZIA *stauntonii* (*Labiatae*) (D) 3–5ft
This sub-shrub is unusual in appearance, but when bruised the foliage is reminiscent of calamentha and aromatically sweet. The leaves are oval and narrow, dark green, paler beneath. The plant carries spikes of violet-pink flowers in September and early October. It needs a sheltered site where it will prove to be perfectly hardy in a sunny position and well drained soil. It may die back in winter but will break again.

It thrives happily at the base of a wall in the fragrant garden at Elvaston Castle, Derbyshire.

ESCALLONIA (*Saxifragaceae*) (E)

The thick, small-toothed leaves, although glossy, are surprisingly sticky to touch, leaving a resin on the skin reminiscent of Balsam Poplar or walnut leaf.

Some species have fragrant flowers. This is a shrub for maritime areas, excellent as a decorative informal hedge and a good garden shrub for the milder regions. In less clement parts of the country it is a good wall shrub, soon blocking out fences and screens. Tolerant of dry conditions and accommodating to most soil types. One or two species have a positively evil smell, such as *E. illinita* and *viscosa*.

macrantha 13ft

Strong-growing, and a really good hedging plant for coastal areas, with large shining leaves, pungently aromatic. The flowers bloom from July to October and are bright red, lending an air of general carnival brightness to the whole plant. It forms a really rewarding wall shrub when grown inland. 'C. F. Ball' with crimson flowers and aromatic leaves is a seedling of *macrantha*.

× *rigida*

A group name for cultivars derived from *E. rubra* × *E. virgata*, and including most of the popular escallonias raised at the Donard Nurseries in Northern Ireland. They all bloom profusely, and are of arching habit, and several bear scented flowers. 'Donard Beauty' slender habit and bright rose red flowers, and aromatic leaves; 'Donard Gem' of neat compact growth with sweetly scented pale pink flowers rather large than most escallonias, and slightly aromatic leaves; 'Slieve Donard', of rather open habit with pendulous branches, and sweetly scented pink flowers in June and July and sometimes again in September and October, and quite hardy.

rosea (Syn. *pterocladon*) 5–10ft

Winged or angled branches and small leaves, set off the sweetly scented white flowers which are held in loose racemes. This is an ideal shrub to grow against a wall where the pure white flowers can be shown off to advantage from June to August.

rubra (Syn. *punctata*) 5–10ft

A dense shrub with small leaves, which bears clusters of flowers over a long period from June to September. The red flowers are scented and the glossy leaves aromatic when bruised. A low-growing form 'Woodside' (sometimes catalogued as 'Pygmaea') is a dwarf compact growing mutant up to 2ft high, a neat plant suited to the rock garden. Again the flowers are crimson, smaller than the type and sweetly fragrant. It has a strong tendency to revert to the type, so the more vigorous branches need to be constantly pruned.

virgata (Syn. *philippiana*) (Semi-E) 4ft

A treasure where it can be accommodated on totally lime-free soil, for its graceful arching habit. The white flowers are sweetly scented, in bloom from July to September, and seem a little more startling than those of other species.

FOTHERGILLA (*Hamamelidaceae*) (D)

Given a lime-free soil enriched with humus-producing material, these North American plants have bottle-brush-like, fragrant flowers just before the leaves are in evidence in spring. They show a predilection for a sandy peat in a semi-shaded spot

Escallonia × rigida
'Donard Gem'

where they associate well with other spring-flowering shrubs and bulbs.

gardenii (Syn. *alnifolia*) 5ft

A slow-growing plant from the eastern United States with spreading habit and slender branches, bearing creamy white erect bottle-brush-like flowers in March and April decorated with bright yellow anthers, and enveloped in a heavy sweet scent. The leaves resemble those of the witch hazels and assume brilliant colours in the autumn.

major (Syn. *monticola*) 6ft

Slow growing, but rather taller when fully established and bearing rounded spikes of sweetly scented white flowers in March and April. It provides an exciting range of autumn leaf colour. Some authorities list *monticola* as a separate species suggesting that it is lower-growing with slightly less conspicuous flowers and less perfume.

GAULTHERIA (*Ericaceae*) (E)

Sub-shrubs useful for associating with ericas on peaty soil, or for using in a woodland situation on acid soils where summer sunshine is excluded. The habit is tufted and spreading, thus affording splendid ground-cover. One of two are fragrant, the scent enhanced when sprays are cut and taken indoors.

forrestii 1½ft

A spreading plant, best cultivated in groups or as a border to woodland paths. The stems are white and carry delightful drooping lily-of-the-valley-like flowers which are waxy and richly perfumed, in May and early June. They are followed by blue berries in the autumn.

fragrantissima 5ft

A spreading species with markedly red stems and dark green leaves turned back at the edges. White bell-shaped flowers in small sprays appear over quite a long period from June to September and are refreshingly fragrant. The foliage when rubbed is aromatic of camphor. *G. fragrantissima* is a good greenhouse plant, or may be grown to advantage in a pot for balcony or loggia embellishment.

procumbens

WINTERGREEN, CHECKERBERRY

A North American species, creeping in habit with polished rather rough foliage, some of it rusting to a bronze red in the autumn, when it makes a good accompaniment to the red berries. The flowers are lily-of-the-valley-like, waxy, white and borne on red stems in summer.

All parts of the plant are aromatic, rather than fragrant, and the essential oil of the leaves is that used in the manufacture of wintergreen. A truly ground-smothering plant.

GENISTA (*Leguminosae*) (D)

With its spined growth obscured by the bright yellow flowers, the genus is one of those ubiquitous ones that gardeners quickly recognize but never 'quite know which it is'. Remarkably useful on banks, associated with other sub-shrubs and at best in full sunshine, they are tolerant of most soils and one or two species are fragrant.

aetnensis 10ft

MOUNT ETNA BROOM

Native of Sicily and Sardinia, the golden-yellow flowers smother the bush in July and August emitting a strong vanilla fragrance. It is a fast-growing, quite rewarding and elegant plant, good for a newly planted garden, rabbit-proof and soon attaining its full height.

hispanica 1½–2ft

SPANISH GORSE

From the Iberian Peninsular, a dwarf rounded spiny sub-shrub, seldom more than a cushion of growth, but very useful for the rock garden and in raised beds. Bright golden-yellow flowers envelop the entire plant in May and June obscuring the tiny leaves completely and giving off a fruity scent. To some it is reminiscent of pineapple, but to others of apples being cooked.

HAMAMELIS (*Hamamelidaceae*) (D)

WITCH HAZEL

The spider-like yellow and reddish flowers appear in winter, usually on bare branches, and seem to withstand the severest weather; for additional interest the foliage gives rich autumn colour.

× *intermedia* (*H. japonica* × *H. mollis*) 9–15ft

A large shrub, or when established, a small tree, usually quite open in shape and useful when planted in groups to give a yellow or bronze haze to the winter garden. A number of reliable cultivars are available, all with the characteristic crumpled, strap-shaped petals balanced in clusters along the bare branches. Fragrant, or quite strongly scented, sometimes recalling incense. Free flowering cultivars include *H* × *i.* 'Jelena' with rusty red and brown-yellow petals; 'Moonlght', sulphur yellow, very sweetly scented; 'Ruby Glow' coppery red; and 'Winter Beauty' golden-yellow.

japonica up to 7–9ft

Variable in habit and flowering early in some areas, starting for Christmas and going on until March with pale yellow flowers of undulating strap-like petals. They emit an unusual perfume, honey-like and pungent at the same time. The form 'Sulphurea' with very pale lemon crumpled flowers has but a faint perfume, while 'Zuccariniana' though less robust of form and flowering late in February and March has the same haunting fragrance as the type.

mollis 9ft
CHINESE WITCH HAZEL

The most commonly cultivated of the witch hazels, a large shrub carrying flowers of broad strap-shaped petals from December to March. These flower clusters are golden yellow with a scarlet calyx and are strongly scented. The good autumn colour is especially rewarding in the form 'Brevipetala' (Syn. 'Aurantiaca') whose perfume is sweeter and heavier than that of the type. 'Pallida' produces pale lemon, clustered flowers in profusion and a much lighter fragrance, still very sweet but rather more elusive.

vernalis 6ft
THE OZARK WITCH HAZEL

Upright in habit, this medium-sized shrub can truly be said to flower once the bright yellow autumn foliage has been shed, so it is welcome in the very shortest dismal days of the year. The flowers are bronze-red and emit a pungent heavy scent.

virginiana 8–16ft
SPOTTED ALDER, WINTER BLOOM, VIRGINIAN WITCH HAZEL

Less worthy of a place in the scented garden because it flowers in autumn before the leaves fall, and the impact is subdued. Providing but a faint perfume in the garden, it is the commercial source of witch hazel, and that of the Pond's Extract of witch hazel, so favoured by our grandmothers, and still useful to soothe bruises.

JASMINUM (*Oleaceae*) (E and D)
JASMINE

An extensive genus of scandent shrubs and twiners for which support has to be provided to the feeble stems, so the jasmines are popularly grown on posts and pergolas, and used to obscure gate posts or to blur the outline of such objects as oil storage tanks, or to camouflage an awkward contour.

The leaves are dark green, the stems often glossy and green, and the flowers usually white or yellow. Many species are native of the warmer regions of the Old World, and so require some protection, which always enhances the enjoyment of their perfume. Tender species thrive in the sheltered areas of Britain and several provide rewarding decoration for conservatories, or rooms, where their captive perfume is strongest. Hardier species withstand town conditions and establish themselves happily even on industrial sites, provided some sunshine finds them. Tolerant of most soils, except waterlogged places, they all need some tying in and respond to light pruning after flowering because the blossoms are carried on young shoots.

anguiare (E) 10ft

Although rarely seen in cultivation this South African species bears large sweetly scented flowers during the late summer and is best treated as a conservatory plant. It may be grown in troughs or borders, or large pots in a compost of two-thirds loam, one-third leaf mould with a little old manure and some sand.

azoricum (E) 13ft

In the mildest localities, this evergreen species will bloom summer and winter, or intermittently. It is seen at its best as a conservatory plant when the purple-flushed buds open to white fragrant flowers. Out of doors it requires good protection from cold winds and early morning winter sunshine, is tolerant of most good garden soils, and does not need any great depth of soil. It was introduced into cultivation in the late 17th century from Madeira.

beesianum (D) 10ft

Something of an individual in the jasmine tribe, *J. beesianum* flourishes with dark velvety-red flowers in summer, whose scent is spicy rather than sweetly fragrant like the rest of its relatives. Black polished berries follow, often persisting well into the winter in considerable abundance to spangle the scandent tangled growth. It has been cultivated in Britain since the first decade of the present century when it was introduced from Western China.

grandiflorum (Semi-E) 30ft
SPANISH JASMINE, CATALONIAN JASMINE.

Originally from India, this is the Jasmine of the perfumery trade, the fragrance thought to be the most distinct of natural odours, and not accurately reproduceable. The intensely fragrant white blooms, tinged pink outside especially in bud, open early in the morning and are collected then when their fragrance is at a peak.

In temperate climates *J. grandiflorum* is a plant for the warm house where it will flower from June to early September pouring out its fragrance onto the whole atmosphere.

officinale (D) 10–13ft
COMMON JASMINE, JESSAMINE

The common White Jasmine, thought of as a cottage garden plant because it has been popularly grown in Britain since Tudor times, is a scrambling twining vigorous climber on house walls. It is deciduous and flowers continuously from summer until autumn with terminal clusters of sweetly fragrant chalk-white flowers, produced on young shoots. Two commonly grown forms are 'Affine', a superior plant with white flowers flushed rose-pink on the outside and particularly over the tube of the corolla, and the variegated or mottled leaf form 'Aureum', whose flowers often appear to be ivory-white.

Jasminum officinale

polyanthum (E) 19½ft

PINK JASMINE

Closely allied to *J. officinale*, but tender, *J. polyanthum* requires a really warm wall to encourage it to flower. It makes a good porch or loggia plant where a trellis or frame can be provided to support its pliant twining growth, and where it is kept within bounds by vigorous pruning in the early autumn. As a conservatory plant it can be allowed to trail (or travel!) according to the space available, and will be highly decorative. On the other hand, pruning to restrict its range will be rewarded by an even greater abundance of flowers. These bloom slightly earlier than *Jasminum officinale* and are suffused with deep rose pink on the outside as a flush of youth. This is the jasmine offered by florists as pot plants – the growth is usually trained over an arched cane.

× *stephenense (J. beesianum* × *J. officinale)* 23–26ft

The only known hybrid jasmine has inherited the pink flowers of its parent *beesianum*, and carries them in terminal clusters. It has almost the angular growth of *nudiflorum*, but is a vigorous supple climber, and looks really splendid when encouraged to form a canopy over a garden shed or summer house. In the latter situation the fragrance could be enjoyed in June and July when the pale pink flowers are in bloom.

LAVANDULA (*Labiatae*) (E)

LAVENDER

Cultivated from ancient times for its refreshingly agreeable perfume, lavender has been long used commercially for the value of its extracted essences! The good grey-foliaged sub-shrubs are of immense garden value for emphasis at the corner of a bed, at the side of steps or to form a low hedge. Given tip top drainage, and full sunshine away from frost pockets, the lavender will flourish for some years. They usually live up to their reputation for being short-lived and become leggy after four or five years but judicious cutting back helps to prolong their effect. An excellent seaside plant.

angustifolia (*L. spica, L. officinalis*) 2–4ft

Dusty grey green leaves, which can look singularly lifeless in winter, form a rounded sub-shrub which in high summer is pricked all over with pale mauve flower-heads, so that the whole effect is one of a huge pin-cushion pierced with flower-headed hat-pins! It surely requires no detailed description. The leaves and flower bracts are fragrant, and the older the plant grows the richer its perfume. Various cultivars are available, all fragrant, the pink-and white-flowered forms less so. 'Hidcote' has narrow grey-green leaves, violet flowers with a silken sheen in long flowerheads, and is sweetly scented; 'Folgate' has grey-green leaves arranged rather in a shuttle-cock fashion around the stems, flowers blue-mauve, fragrant and rather later to flower; 'Munstead' is a compact form with narrow green leaves and bright lavender-blue flowers; 'Twickel Purple' has grey-green leaves comparatively wide and almost at right-angles to the main stem, flowers deep mauve and the best fragrance of all lavenders; 'Nana Alba' has compact grey-green leaves, white flowers; 'Rosea' has narrow green leaves, lavender-pink flowers a rather washed out colour but a good foil for the purple forms. *L. a.* 'Vera' the Dutch lavender, the source of much lavender oil, has broader, silvery grey foliage and sparse flowers of lavender-blue. We will group them into dwarf- and tall-growing forms – for this is the way in which they are selected at most garden centres: 'Munstead', 'Folgate' 'Nana Alba' and 'Rosea' are dwarf-growing, not more than 2ft, 'Hidcote' and

'Twickel Purple' are slightly taller, perhaps reaching 3ft where really happily established.

dentata 1–3ft

As the name implies, the green leaves are notched into narrow symmetrical lobes, resembling a miniature dandelion leaf in shape. The flowers are pale mauve in July, and these and the foliage are meagrely endowed with fragrance, more reminiscent of rosemary than lavender. An unreliable plant in damp cold winters but forming a stout shrub where it is happy. There always seems to be a small one somewhere at Kew, which reminds us that a constant supply of cuttings ought to be maintained of all lavenders.

stoechas 1–2ft

FRENCH LAVENDER

A wholly different plant, and one that varies quite considerably from garden to garden. Its grey-green, narrow leaves with tiny rolled-back edges form the body of the plant, from which flower stems burst upwards terminated by a blob of symmetrically arranged flowers with a frilly top knot of purple bracts, quite unlike any other lavender flower. The colour is generally described as indigo-purple, but it can vary to a madder pink-purple. They spike the plant from July to September, and do not dry as do other lavender flowers. *Lavandula stoechas* often raises comment!

The foliage when bruised gives a sharply refreshing fragrance, like lavender with overtones of mint. A good plant for container cultivations and quite rewarding when grown in a conservatory.

LIGUSTRUM (*Oleaceae*)

PRIVET

Quick-growing trees and shrubs accommodating themselves to town conditions, shade or semi-shade and tolerant of all but really soggy soils. Happy on chalk. Hardy in the north and well above sea level, but in such conditions more often assuming a semi-evergreen habit. The berries are oily, sometimes with a smell of olives. The Asiatic species provide some good garden plants, and their evergreen or semi-evergreen habit can really be said to reflect the location in which they are grown.

henryi (E) 6ft

One of the Asiatic species useful for its compact form, pyramidal shape and lustrous dark green foliage, paler beneath. Long panicles of honey-scented flowers bloom in July and August.

ovalifolium (Semi-E) 4–9ft

COMMON PRIVET, OVAL LEAVED PRIVET

Ubiquitous, mainly as a hedging plant in suburban gardens and very popular in its gold leaved form, *L. o.* 'Aureum', of which the oval leaves are tough, and richly yellow usually with a pale green central zone, but often this is lacking. The type bears tough bright green leaves which persist in most areas, but in the north the shrub, or hedge, is often totally deciduous. Cultivated as a shrub, the golden form is especially useful in dark gardens; semi-shade can be enhanced by its presence, either in towns or in dark woodland gardens. The flowers are carried in small dense upstanding panicles in August, heavily scented and richly sweet, the fragrance easily carried on the breeze.

quihoui (D) 8ft

Tiny white flowers carried in large outstanding plumes in August and September are the chief merit of this Chinese shrub. Heavily fragrant, and a gem of a late-flowering shrub.

sinense (Semi-E) 6ft

Most freely flowering of privets, and starting to do so in July, earlier than most, *L. sinense* can be grown into a graceful symmetrical bush. The flowers are creamy white and sweetly scented and are followed by autumn berries, shining black. Tips of the branches somethimes flop downwards, a quality more pronounced in the form 'Pendulum' with truly pendulous branches.

vulgare (Semi-E or D) to 9¾ft

Widely distributed native and naturalized plant of Central and Southern Europe including Britain, where it seems to select rather stoney calcareous soils in sunny spots. Not as frequently cultivated as it was formerly, supplanted by *L. ovalifolium*, except in areas of heavy air pollution where its leaves persist longer, sometimes loaded with grime. It is also highly tolerant of dripping trees. The forms 'Glaucum' with blue-green leaves and 'Chlorocarpum', remarkable for its yellowish berries, are both grown by flower-arrangers. Both have the heavily scented flowers of the type, but perhaps less pleasant than some other species; the fragrance can really only be said to be sweet when borne on the breeze and thus diluted. The flowers are all upstanding little panicles in July and August.

LONICERA (*Caprifoliaceae*)

HONEYSUCKLE

The name honeysuckle immediately brings to mind the ornamental twiner of the hedgerows and marginal woodland of Britain. There are several good cultivated twiners, none quite as wonderfully perfumed as the Common Honeysuckle *Lonicera periclymenum*, which can be enlisted for garden decoration. Always twining from east to west – or clockwise – their special gift is to cover tree stumps, or to unfurl over other bushes as they do in the wild. The shrubby species make small or medium-sized bushes totally different in habit. The whole genus offers both evergreen and deciduous plants; leaf sizes vary considerably.

Both those of climbing habit and those of shrubby form thrive best in dappled shade or where they have shade for part of the day. Well-drained, moisture-retentive soil is best, although they are tolerant of limy conditions, particularly *L. caprifolium*, which chooses chalky soils for itself in the wild. Support needs to be provided for the climbers, and the shrubby forms respond to thinning-out of the old wood in the autumn.

The honeysuckles do not berry well on the whole except in really good summers.

× *americana* (Semi-E or D) 30ft

One of the finest vigorous climbing honeysuckles when well grown. The flowers borne in whorled spikes are intensely honey-scented, in July and August, first appearing white or cream and deepening to yellow tinged with purple. Although it is deciduous, or at best semi-evergreen, its spectacular summer display and rich perfume excuse its winter drabness.

angustifolia (D) 5–6ft

A graceful shrubby plant of somewhat arching habit, and bearing perfumed pale-pink flowers, flushed pink in April. Scarlet berries mature later in the year and are edible. The whole plant assumes a gentle nature, and its perfume is delicate.

caprifolium (D) 30ft

GOAT-LEAVED HONEYSUCKLE, PERFOLIATE HONEYSUCKLE

Occasionally, this splendid climber is found growing in the wild in chalky districts of southern England, and has long been known as a cottage-garden plant –goats are reputed to have feasted on its leaves. Hence its vernacular name.

Distinguish it from the popularly known *L. periclymenum* by its perfoliate upper leaves. A native of the Middle East and Southern and Central Europe, it is seen at its best when festooning arches, porches or trellis. It is the most accommodating of its tribe for growing near the sea. The leaves are mid-green and glaucous; the flowers, carried in terminal whorls, appear in June and July and are highly seented, and creamy white. They are followed by sealing-wax-red berries. Fragrance is at its strongest in the evening when the long-tongued moths are flying.

etrusca (D or Semi-E) 33ft

A native of the Mediterranean regions, *L. etrusca* revels in sunny positions and appreciates the drier soils and localities. Seemingly, it takes time to settle down and does not flower when young. It has been grown in English gardens for more than 200 years.

The fragrant cream flowers deepen to yellow on maturity and are carried on the ends of the shoots in May and June. The soft downy foliage is tinged purplish, especially when young, and on the flowering shoots becomes perfoliate. Once established, the plant climbs vigorously, looking especially attractive on pergolas.

fragrantissima (Semi-E) 10ft

One of Robert Fortune's introductions from his first expedition to China, arriving in England in 1845, *L. fragrantissima* now graces our winter gardens with its sweet scent. Flowers appear in the winter and early spring discouraged only by prolonged periods of low temperatures and, as with most winter blossoms, by exposure to cold winds. They are cream, carried in pairs back-to-back, and are followed by red berries in early summer. A rambling grower with smooth leathery leaves, for the greater part retained through the winter, with a somewhat dense appearance. A good shrub for a border near the house.

× *heckrottii* (D) 8–12ft

Hybridization sometimes affects perfume, but × *heckrottii* has the hybrid × *americana* as one of its parents (the other is probably *sempervirens*), and seems to have inherited the same honey-like scent. A shrubby, rather lax climber, it bears its yellow flowers in whorls strongly flushed purple from June to September. A form 'Goldflame' sometimes produces flowers of a richer yellow, but is generally considered to be a variant of *L.* × *heckrottii* itself.

hildebrandiana (E) 20ft

GIANT HONEYSUCKLE

For mild localities, and even there for really protected corners, the Honeysuckle is a splendid evergreen species. But, to be seen at its vigorous best it needs to be grown as a conservatory plant. With such preferential treatment it will soon festoon the rafters and sometimes needs to be checked. In its native Burmese and Chinese locations it is a rampant climber and in cultivation lives up to its English name in all respects. The flowers in high summer are creamy white, ageing to deep amber yellow; they are as long as 6in and lusciously fragrant, scenting the entire conservatory.

periclymenum (D) 12–20ft

WOODBINE

The common honeysuckle of our hedgerows, a native of Europe and Western Asia with a trailing, wandering habit, has perhaps the best recognized perfume of any wild scented plant. The creamy white flowers, often purplish on the outside of the tube, appear in terminal clusters from June to September or October. They are followed by red berries. *L. p.* 'Belgica', early Dutch Honeysuckle with reddish purple flowers, 'Serotina', late Dutch

Lonicera periclymenum

Honeysuckle or 'Late Red', with even deeper-coloured flowers, are old established forms – or maybe only one form according to some growers. 'Belgica' however does give the added bonus of two flowering periods, May-June and August.

× *purpusii* (*L. fragrantissima* × *L. standishii*) (D) 4ft

Another valuable winter-flowering shrub from China, with stiff twiggy growth. The creamy yellow flowers are borne in pairs on bare brown wood, from the New Year onward. It may be distinguished from *L. fragrantissima* by the bristle-like hairs edging the leaves. The flowers are richly perfumed.

syringantha (D) 4ft

Sweetly fragrant lilac-pink flowers, as might be supposed from the name, appear in May, set in the axils of small sea-green leaves, to make this a most attractive shrub. It is of medium height with a graceful, somewhat arching habit, forming a rounded clump of growth.

thibetica (D) 6½ft

Like *L. syringantha*, which it strongly resembles, the mauve flowers of this shrubby lonicera are sweetly perfumed similar to lilac when in bloom in May. The foliage distinguishes itself by being tomentose beneath and slightly more glossy above. It forms a good vigorous shrub.

LUPINUS *arboreus* (*Leguminosae*) (E) up to 6½ft

TREE LUPIN

For quick results few plants surpass the Tree Lupin, so easily raised from seed. In fact it seeds itself and once introduced will stay in the garden – a useful attribute for a short-lived plant. Put in a well-drained sandy or chalky soil in full sun it forms a rounded soft bush with dark matt-green leaves, often as many as 10 leaflets arranged like the spokes of a wheel, and spangled with long panicles of lemon-yellow flowers in mid-summer. They last quite well and are vanilla-scented; some people find them clover-scented. A mauve-flowered form is less scented, and one or two cultivars are offered; the yellow flowers of the type are richly fragrant.

MAHONIA (*Berberidaceae*) (E)

Ubiquitous hardy shrubs, mahonias grow well on all soils and in full sun or dappled shade, and are remarkably attractive as under-planting on the borders of woodland areas. Interest is maintained throughout the year, from the winter and very early spring flowers to the polished beauty of the bronzed and red autumn foliage.

japonica 6ft

(This is often confused with *M. bealei*, which is much less cultivated, but both are outstanding winter-flowering shrubs.)

Tolerant of town conditions, excellent for forming dense cover to a slope, frequently used as an informal hedging plant, and yet at its best as under-planting in the wild garden. Although invaluable in this role, it justly deserves a place near the house where its winter beauty can be fully enjoyed. Long deep-green shining pinnate leaves, with delicately sharpened points, arch to frame racemes of pale yellow flowers in winter, from January to March or April. The fragrance is that of lily-of-the-valley and in both crisp or mild weather they scent the surrounding atmosphere. Blue-black berries embellished by a bloom follow and the foliage adopts a burnished glow of reds and brown in late summer and autumn.

lomariifolia 6ft

A refined plant with elegant slender pinnate leaves tending to explode from a central stem rather like a palm. Less hardy than other mahonias, but a gem for the milder counties. The lily-of-the-valley fragrance is carried by the rather dense, bright yellow flowers; again the black-blue berries and good colour-burst follow in late summer and autumn. Where it suffers from winter damage, the regeneration seems good.

× *media* (*M. japonica* × *M. lomariifolia*) 5–7ft

A group of hybrids, hardier than *lomariifolia* with characteristics strongly orientated to one parent or the other, and some second generation crosses also, provide shrubs which perpetuate the fragrance of the winter flowers. Long erect racemes seem to spout from the terminal collar of pinnate leaves as in *lomariifolia*. *Mahonia* 'Charity' especially has slightly reflexed leaves, and 'Buckland' lax racemes.

MYRICA (*Myricaceae*) (E and D)

Resinous and aromatic diocious plants growing in moist soil and sun and most ideal for the bog garden.

californica (E) up to 26ft

A vigorous glossy-leaved plant sometimes attaining the proportions of a small tree. A balsamic odour pervades the entire plant; the leaves are less aromatic because of their waxen sheen. Greenish flowers in early summer are followed by clusters of dark purple berries which persist well into the winter.

gale (D) 3–6ft

SWEET GALE, CANDLE BERRY, BOG MYRTLE

A plant native to both Britain and the North American continent. Given a really boggy acid home, Sweet Gale will sucker well and soon fringe the margins of a pool. It forms a close-growing bush with small grey-green leaves toothed at the tip, which are strongly aromatic when bruised. The glistening catkins of warm horse-chestnut brown flower on separate plants in April and May.

pensylvanica (Syn. *M. caroliniensis*) (D) 6–8ft

BAYBERRY

Unlike most bog myrtles, *M. pensylvanica* revels in arid conditions, loves the sunshine and will happily sunbathe by the sea. It is sometimes semi-evergreen, but usually the lemon-scented leaves fall in winter to reveal the frosted attraction of the small grey-white waxy fruits, which persist.

MYRTUS (*Myrtaceae*) (E)

MYRTLE

There is always the risk that the leaves of myrtle will suffer damage from cold winds in most districts, and they are really plants for sheltered areas. Good for planting near the sea and tolerant of most soils including chalk, they need good drainage. Grown as greenhouse evergreens they make attractive shrubs and can be planted directly into the borders or in containers, when they may be stood out of doors in summer at flowering time to scent a sheltered patio where the perfume can be enjoyed.

apiculata (Syn. *M. luma*) 23ft

In mild localities and when tucked into a sheltered corner this Chilean shrub luxuriates, spangled with white flowers in the late summer or early autumn. In the walled garden at Elvaston Castle, Nottinghamshire, its fragrant flowers and cinnamon-brown branches against the dull green leaves make a memorable corner. The bark is of special attraction, peeling to reveal creamy patches.

communis 5–10ft

COMMON MYRTLE

Of ancient cultivation in England, small dense aromatic leaves are speckled with many-stamened, almost fluffy, white flowers in June. Both leaves and flowers are used in making *pot pourri* and retain their aroma on drying. In very favourable conditions near the sea in south-west England it is known to climb the walls of houses surmounting the first floor windows.

The form *tarentina* has fragrant wood like the type, but is more compact with tiny leaves and masses of white fluffy stamened flowers in June.

nummularia 1ft

A small prostrate shrub considered hardy in all but the coldest counties of Britain, with a twiggy trailing growth of reddish stems and small shining aromatic leaves. The fragrant flowers are white in May and June, usually followed by pink berries. A good plant for the rock garden, spreading about and rooting as it goes where it can be provided with a moist pocket of acid soil.

ugni (Syn. *Eugenia ugni*) 3¼–6½ft

CHILEAN MYRTLE

A stiff, erect-growing shrub with thick leathery leaves and dangling cup-shaped pink flowers with tiny turned back petal tips. These rather waxy fragrant flowers are followed by sweet dark-red edible berries, which are aromatic.

OLEARIA (*Compositae*) (E)

DAISY BUSH

The genus has a reputation for tenderness which perhaps it does not altogether deserve. Even as a challenge some olearias are worth planting for their rewarding clean daisy-like flowers which rest like snow over the bushes. Aromatic foliage and fragrant flowers beg a place in the fragrant garden on most soils, provided that there is some sunshine. The olearias are of special value in maritime regions.

albida 6–13ft

Some vague confusion appears to surround the true

albida, possibly encouraged by other 'garden' names, but the true one would appear to be rather tender and in need of wall shelter in most southern localities. The pale green undulating leaves are felted beneath, and panicles of white flowers appear in July and August.

arborescens up to 13ft

Vigorous of growth, *arborescens* is again rather tender, but with pale green leaves rather glossy, and felted beneath and the margins toothed. In May and June daisy flowers with prominent yellow centres appear sweetly fragrant.

avicenniifolia 13ft

Hardy in all but harsher districts, attaining the habit of a small tree where it is happy. The large leaves are dark green, buff below, and the scented white flowers are held rather upright in August and September and have a habit of drying and persisting wall into the winter. A good plant for both seaside and town conditions. More pronounced in every feature is the cultivar 'White Confusion'.

× *haastii* (*O. avicenniifolia* × *O. moschata*) 3–8ft

Ubiquitous, hardy and commonly grown, × *haastii* makes a good decorative hedging plant with its dark green foliage and tough habit. The daisy-like flowers are vaguely hawthorn-scented in July and August. Suitable for industrial areas.

ilicifolia 6–10ft

The tough leathery leaves are coarsely toothed rather like those of the holly, beige-felted beneath, and when crushed strongly musk-scented. The cream flowers emit the same perfume in June. It is rather slow-growing and forms a spreading bush.

macrodonta 8ft

NEW ZEALAND HOLLY

The foliage again is holly-like, but the toothed leaves are without spines and silvery-white beneath. Fragrant flowers heads of daisies appear in June. A plant widely cultivated and advantageously employed as a hedge, screening or shelter plant as it appears to be wind-tolerant.

nummulariifolia 8ft

One of the hardiest species, stiff of habit and tolerant of, if not revelling in, dry conditions. The yellowish-green leaves are crowded along the stems and hide rather small daisy flowers in the axils, richly fragrant, in July and August.

phlogopappa 5ft

TASMANIAN DAISY BUSH

Where this species can be made to feel at home, it is well worth cultivating, but it has a reputation for being unreliable. The narrow leaves are aromatic and the large trusses of flowers appear in May long before those of most olearias. Compact in growth.

solandri 3–8ft

Given some protection from wind, and planted ideally in sunshine where the prevailing wind is sifted by larger evergreens, *solandri* ought to be included in fragrant collections for its vanilla scent. Growth is upright, the leaves pale green and golden buff beneath. The daisy flowers are yellow so the whole shrub offers a golden-yellow effect and is attractive in flower in August and September.

ORIXA *japonica* (*Rutaceae*) (D) 8ft

A small spreading shrub, little grown, but of interest for its leaves, highly aromatic of spicy orange. Its value for garden decoration lies in the lime green foliage which turns cream in the autumn – a useful contrast to other autumn colours. There is an interesting form 'Variegata' which bears the same aromatic foliage.

When Siebold found this plant the Japanese were using it as a hedging plant, and it gave off puffs of aromatic fragrance when brushed by their loose clothing.

OSMANTHUS (*Oleaceae*) (E)

The winter-flowering species of osmanthus are some of the most powerfully scented of all plants, and the foliage affords a splendid foil for the early spring-flowering plant in general in the decorative garden. Tolerant of most soils, one or two tender species are best grown as conservatory plants, especially in the colder regions.

armatus 10ft

Of rather dense and prickly growth, shade-tolerant but enjoying the sun, this species flowers in the autumn with sweetly scented creamy flowers. Probably hardier than is generally considered.

delavayi 8–15ft

A spring-flowering species with creamy-white flowers strongly and sweetly fragrant. It is quite commonly cultivated, especially in the southern areas of England. The arching habit of growth renders it as wide as it is tall. The flowers of purest white are tubular in shape and are very heavily scented. The cultivar 'Latifolius' is taller growing but retains the fragrant perfume of the flowers.

× *fortunei*

Flowering in the autumn, when there is a dearth of scented blooms, this holly-like shrub is really valuable in the garden. Again, the flowers are pure white and go on until the end of the year.

fragrans 8ft
FRAGRANT OLIVE
As the name implies, the perfume from the white flowers is delicious and powerful in early summer. Unfortunately it is a shrub for the mildest of localities, and worthy of a place under glass where space permits, so that it will survive all winters.

heterophyllus (Syn. *aquifolium*) 16ft
A Japanese species somewhat rounded in growth with holly-like leaves tending to become free of teeth at the extremity of mature branches. The flowers are white, highly fragrant and in little clusters in autumn. A good hedging plant when it can be lightly clipped. There are several forms mainly with leaf colour variation: 'Aureovariegatus' with yellow margins; 'Purpureus' where the young foliage is plum purple, maturing to purplish green (a specially hardy form); 'Variegatus' with creamy white borders; 'Myrtifolius' compact of growth with spineless glossy green leaves.

suavis (Syn. *Siphonosmanthus suavis*) 8ft
As the specific name suggests, very sweetly scented, some of the perfume coming from the glands on the stems, as well as from the white flowers. Rather erect in habit, and not altogether hardy, so advantage ought to be taken of this habit by planting it near the house wall where the perfume can be enjoyed from January to March.

OSMARONIA *cerasiformis (Rosaceae)* (D) 6 ft
INDIAN PLUM, OSO BERRY
A little seen shrub, but one easily grown on most fertile soils and valuable for its almond-scented dangling sprays of greenish-white flowers from January to March. Sometimes still listed as *Nuttallia cerasiformis*, the flowers on the female plants are followed by little plum-like fruits. Its tendency to sucker provides stock material and as the growth is upright and thicket-like, this is a most useful shrub for 'filling gaps' or corners. It has the added advantage that a bright green flush of fresh green leaves appears very early in the spring.

PHILADELPHUS (*Philadelphaceae*) (D)
MOCK ORANGE
A floriferous genus, at flowering time almost dominating the garden. They enjoy any fertile soil with good drainage and full sun, but will tolerate some shade and are hardy in all areas. Their densely branched and suckering habit makes philadelphus a good space-filling plant. The most fragrant species is *P. coronarius* introduced in 1562 from Turkey at the same time as the lilac by whose generic name it is still called. All the species are powerfully scented, sufficiently so to be repulsive to many people. The odour is generally reduced in the cultivars and hybrids, so these are mainly grown for preference. Many resemble orange blossom in perfume; hence its vernacular name.

coronarius 10ft
MOCK ORANGE
The most popularly grown species, it is a strong-growing medium-sized shrub. The flowers are borne in profusion along the whole branch and are very sweetly fragrant, the perfume, said to resemble that of the orange blossom, being carried on the breeze. The leaves smell and taste like cucumber. It is specially useful on dry soils, and also as a specimen shrub on lawns; it enjoys full exposure. The golden-leaved form, quite remarkable in the spring when the fresh growth is bright yellow, is *P. c.* 'Aureus'. The leaves fade somewhat to a bright lime-green later in the summer but the interest is repaid by the creamy flowers in June which retain the strong fragrance of the form. This is perhaps one of the best golden-leaved shrubs, especially for the fragrant garden. Its leaves will light up a shady corner, and it will enjoy being there too.

× *cymosus* 10ft
A group of hybrids carrying their flowers in loose clusters, highly scented in June. Perhaps the most fragrant of these is 'Bouquet Blanc' with double orange-blossom-scented flowers, held in fairly tight clusters. 'Amalthée' has flowers tinged with rose-pink and is sweetly fragrant, but less powerful. 'Voie Lactée' has large flattened flowers, glistening white and is outstanding among the single-flowered mock oranges.

delavayi 10ft
One of the prettiest mock oranges with pale green rounded leaves, paler and felted beneath and with lush sprays of small white flowers in May and June. One of the earliest to flower, the blossoms give off a strong sweet orange-blossom fragrance.

× *lemoinei* (*P. coronarius* × *P. microphyllus*) 3–6ft
This is a gracefully arching or erect-growing group of hybrids, the stems ornamented with flowers on numerous side shoots. All are highly decorative, providing some of the loveliest of white orange-blossom-scented shrubs. *P.* × *l.* 'Avalanche' has widely arching branches weighed down with dense sprays of single fragrant flowers. *P.* × *l* 'Erectus' has a more upright habit, especially when young, and is equally floriferous. *P.* × *l.* 'Manteau' d'Hermine' is a neat plant with double creamy-white flowers and the suggestion of pineapple scent. Fragrance is inherited from both parents, for that of *P. microphyllus* is described as between quince and melon.

× purpureo-maculatus (*P. × lemoinei × P. maculatus*) 10ft

Compact of habit, this group of hybrids is characterized by a purple flush on the flowers. *P. × p.* 'Belle Etoile' is particularly sweetly scented, and *P. × p.* 'Sybille' has a small flower, which in addition to the suffusion of plum-purple has fringed petals.

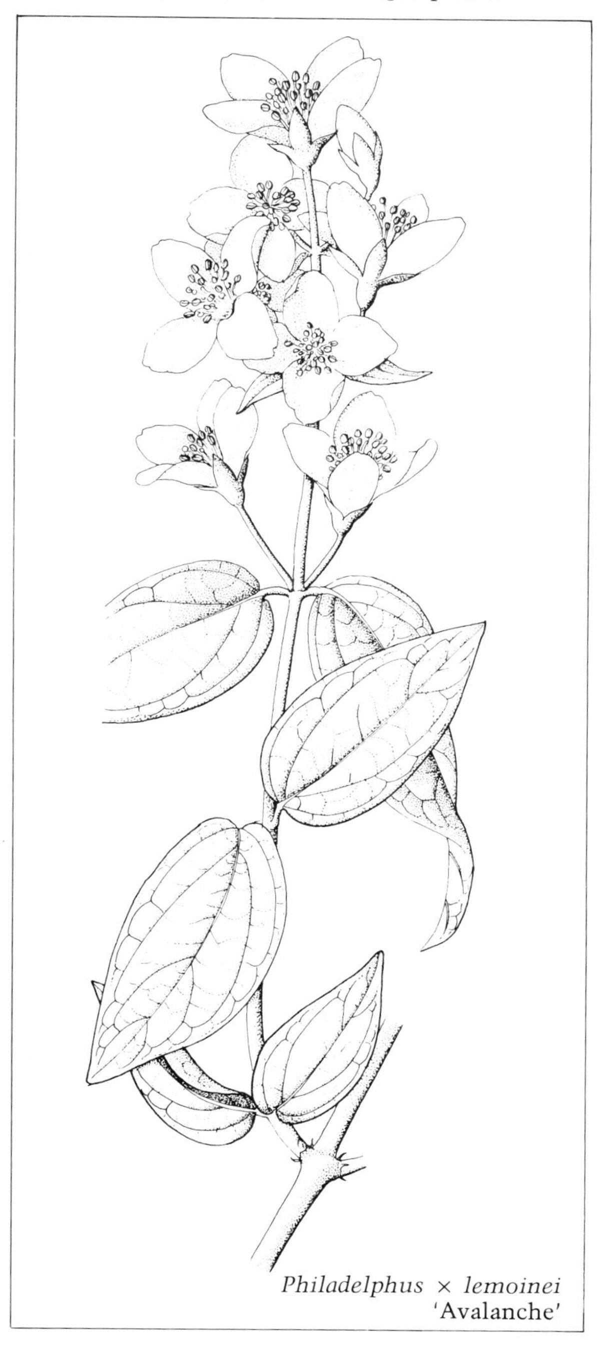

Philadelphus × lemoinei 'Avalanche'

× virginalis 8–10ft

A group of hybrids with semi-double flowers, of which 'Virginal' is the most widely grown and most readily recognized. This is a shrub with rather deeply toothed leaves on the non-flowering stems. The flowers are snow-white and powerfully scented.

PIERIS (*Ericaceae*) (E)

Woodland plants for the shaded site with humus-rich peaty soil. An intriguing attraction is the way the plants are covered with rose-pink buds for a considerable period in early spring, almost as if they were reluctant to open. Relatively hardy, but needing some protection from spring frosts, and morning sunshine, when the young growth is specially vulnerable. Not usually cultivated in cold elevated areas.

floribunda (Syn. *Andromeda floribunda*) 3–6ft

A North American species with dark green oval pointed leaves and sprays of white flowers which recall lilies-of-the-valley in shape, except that they appear to have a draw-string to pucker the mouth. Sweetly and intensely fragrant in March, April and early May.

'Forest Flame' 9ft

Elegant of habit and a plant in which the young foliage is least affected by frost. New leaves are pink-red and creamy white, decorating the branch tips in loose tufts. Flowers in April and May, richly scented.

formosa (Syn. *Andromeda formosa*) 6–13ft

Rather later to flower than other oriental species, with leathery glossy leaves and brilliant crimson young growth. The flowers bloom in late April and May in long rounded panicles, and are sweetly fragrant. It branches well close to the ground. In the forms 'Jermyns' and 'Wakehurst' the flower stalks, buds and youthful foliage are all blood-red, decking the plant with a glowing quality in the spring.

japonica 5ft

The brilliant coppery tints of the foliage of this oriental species followed by fan-like sprays of dropping pure white flowers in March and April make it a highly desirable garden plant. Each flower is perfectly pitcher-shaped, delicately fragrant. *Pieris j.* 'Christmas Cheer', with deep-pink-flushed flowers which bloom during the shortest days in all but cruel winters, displays its total hardiness. The recently introduced 'Flamingo' has coppery foliage and flower buds of deep carmine red, opening into rose and white flowers.

PIPTANTHUS laburnifolius (Syn. *nepalensis*) (*Leguminosae*) (E) 6½–12ft

EVERGREEN LABURNUM

Completely hardy in the south-western counties, this Himalayan 'evergreen' does reflect its inclement surroundings elsewhere by behaving as a semi-evergreen. Wall shelter is needed in all but the warmest situations. Vigorous and robust in appearance, the leaves are trifoliate, the flowers bright yellow in May and June carried in pendulous bunches like the laburnum. They are strongly scented of vanilla.

PONCIRUS *trifoliata* (Syn. *Aegle sepiaria*) (*Rutaceae*) (D) 3¼–6½ft

JAPANESE BITTER ORANGE

A tangled mass of bright green thick-armed stems, and one of those plants which once seen is never forgotten. A plant used to flourish by the old range of glasshouses at the Royal Horticultural Society's Garden at Wisely, Surrey, in a baked corner. Good in maritime areas and warm gardens, on well-drained soil, it is intolerant of lime. It produces white orange-blossom-like flowers at the axils of the spines before the leaves appear in early spring. They are deliciously scented and in very favourable areas and good seasons are followed by bitter small 'oranges'.

RHODODENDRON (*Ericaceae*) (E & D)

An enormous group of shrubs, ranging in height from tree-like proportions to pygmy bushes that embellish the rock garden. The majority come from the Hilmalayas, south-east Asia, and the mountainous regions of Malaysia.

Sheltered woodland conditions, where there is some canopy of trees, suit them ideally, where there is good peaty, humus-rich soil. The western regions of the British Isles, especially the western seaboard, provides the moisture-laden air they love so much. Devon and Cornwall and the west of Scotland abound in richly handsome specimens. To see rhododendrons in flower in some of the south-west Cornish gardens in April and early May is an exciting experience for a plantsman. Other collections of note are at Exbury near Southampton Water, in Hampshire (home of the famous Exbury Hybrids), Leanardslee, Sussex and the Royal Horticultural Society's Garden at Wisley where the wooded regions and dell garden of Battlestone Hill harbour the famous collection. There is also a remarkable collection in the Valley Garden in Windsor Great Park. Azaleas, as such, form a group or series of rhododendrons, and are included in the catalogue below.

arborescens (*Azalea arborescens*) 20ft

Carrying the quality of rich autumn colour of foliage, common to many azaleas, *arborescens* has oval glossy green leaves, pale beneath and assuming a good ornage before falling. Funnel-shaped white flowers flushed pink in June and July have a protruding long scarlet style, and are very sweetly scented.

Poncirus trifoliata

atlanticum (*Azalea atlanticum*) (D) 2–3ft

A rathr lax, mat-forming plant, with oblong bright green leaves. The flowers appear in May, white suffused pale pink and are particularly long-tubed. The scent is richly sweet.

auriculatum (E) 10ft

A Chinese species, particularly useful for its late flowering in July and August, but not coming into flower until it is well established, it is one of E. H. Wilson's introductions of about 1900, with huge trusses of funnel-shaped flowers, white and exquisitely scented. The heads of bloom are admirably set off by the deep-green oval leaves, rusty beneath. 'Polar Bear' is one of the best hybrids and also flowers in summer with long white flowers, green at the throat, and carrying the same richness of perfume. This also does not flower when young.

campylocarpum (E) 6ft

One of Hooker's introductions from the Sikkim in the mid-19th century and remarkable for its clear yellow bell-shaped flowers in April and May, which appear only on mature plants. Foliage is oval, glossy and very pale green beneath. The perfume is more delicate than that of most rhododendrons, but is clear and sweet.

canescens (*Azalea canescens*) (D) 10ft

One of the older species of rhododendron, with long narrow leaves of a fresh green, thickly tomentose beneath. Decorative funnel-shaped white flowers are suffused with pink and a far deeper pink in the throat. In April and May they are sweetly honey-scented.

cephalanthum (*Azalea cephalanthum*) (D) 2ft

One of the smaller-growing compact species with rather bay-like aromatic foliage. The glossy green leaves are tomentose beneath and set off the daphne-like white or pink flowers, which bear the same spicy perfume in April and May.

ciliatum (E) 5ft

Characteristically dome-shaped, with long narrow leaves edged with hairs, and an attractive golden-red peeling bark. The fragrant bell-shaped flowers in March and April are in nodding groups.

crassum (E) 6½ft

One of George Forrest's introductions with particularly tough, stiff leathery leaves, thickly rusty beneath. Very sweetly fragrant. The funnel-shaped flowers in June and July vary from white through shades of soft pink, sometimes with blotched petals. Only for the milder regions.

decorum (E) 10ft

A glabrous-leaved Chinese species with broad long leaves, pale on the lower surface. The funnel-shaped flowers are carried in rather floppy heads, white or pale pink, in May and June, and are deliciously scented with rather a light fragrance.

discolor (E) 12ft

Another of Wilson's introductions, useful for its mid-summer flowering. *R. discolor* has very large elliptical dark leaves, and enormous trusses of pink flowers in June and July. The individual flowers are bell-shaped with a wide flared mouth, and emit a sweet fragrance. One of the hardiest rhododendron species.

fortunei (E) 10ft

A mid-19th-century introduction of Robert Fortune's from the woodlands of central China, with pale green, long elliptical leaves and bell-shaped flowers. The rather rich fruitly scent in May comes from the mauve-pink flowers held in somewhat loose clusters. Its fragrance has been inherited by the Loder hybrids (*R. fortunei* × *R. griffithianum*), a group remarkable for the beauty of its scented flowers.

griffithianum (E) 15ft

An enormous plant when conditions suit it, and one of Hooker's early introductions from the forests of the Sikkim. It likes the south-western regions of England best and is really only hardy there and in similarly favoured spots. The bark peels and is of a reddish brown that lights up in the sunshine making a pleasing foil for the large dangling clusters of white flowers – among the largest of the genus. The fragrance is very sweet, in May. The foliage is suitably proportioned, sometimes reaching 1½ft, and dark glossy green.

myrtidiifolium (E) 2ft

MYRTLE-LEAVED RHODODENDRON

Its small aromatic leaves, with the same refreshing fragrance when crushed as those of the myrtle, are rather bronzed in appearance and small like those of its namesake. The flowers in May and June are in small clusters, and are a deep rose pink. A native of the mountains of central Europe and grown in English gardens for over 130 years.

occidentale (*Azalea occidentalis*) (D)

Richly coloured in autumn, the foliage is a bright glossy green, and opens simultaneously with the flowers in early May. The whole plant is very decorative and it is one of the American rhododendron species introduced by William Lobb in the mid-19th century. The flowers are creamy white and funnel-shaped, deepening to a peach-pink or yellow at the throat, and are richly honey-scented.

roseum (*Azalea rosea*) (D) 2ft

A small shrub with oval mid-green leaves, and rich spicy fragrance of flower in May. The flowers are a deep pink in colour, and the perfume has a distinctly clove-like overtone.

Rhododendron Hybrids

Some of the rhododendron hybrids bear scented flowers: 'Albatross', white, in May; 'Angelo', white; 'Argosy', white and cromson and very sweetly scented; 'King George', pink in bud, to white with green at the throat; 'Midsummer Snow', white and particularly sweetly scented; 'Polar Bear', white; 'Solent Swan', white.

Azaleas

Among the deciduous hybrid azaleas of immense garden worth for their rich autumn colour are the scented Ghent and Occidental hybrids. The former especially have long tubular flowers resembling those of the honeysuckle, with a fragrance every bit as intense and similarly carried on the breeze.

RIBES (*Grossulariaceae*) (D and E)

FLOWERING CURRANT

Easy of cultivation, tolerant of town conditions and enjoying chalk, but not unhappy without it, the genus is from the mountainous regions of the world, including Europe and Britain. The flowers are ornamental and in some forms the foliage is attractive also. They are tolerant of shaded positions, flourish without them and are generally useful shrubs.

alpinum (D) 4ft

MOUNTAIN CURRANT, ALPINE CURRANT

Native of mountain regions of Europe, and sometimes on rocky outcrops in Britain, of twiggy habit with coarsely toothed leaves and tiny greenish flowers, which are borne in erect racemes in April or early May and are sweetly fragrant. In cultivations the over-riding value is that it is very shade-tolerant. The attractive forms 'Aureum' with golden-yellow leaves when young and 'Pumilum', compact and dense with smaller leaves, retain the scented flowers and tolerance to shade.

fasciculatum (D) 3–6ft

A Japanese species bearing particularly fragrant flowers in drooping sprays in April. They are yellow and emit a fruity scent. The autumn fruits resemble red currants.

gayanum (E) 6ft

Hardy in southern countries or very sheltered gardens, not often encountered, this small suckering shrub forms a handsome plant with soft green velvety foliage. It has dense erect racemes of primrose-yellow flowers, later than most other species, in June. They are strongly honey-scented.

odoratum (D) 4–5ft

BUFFALO CURRANT, GOLDEN CURRANT

Frequently confused with *R. aureum* which is almost devoid of scent, this is a North American plant producing arching branches hung with long drooping sprays of yellow flowers in April. They are strongly fragrant and honey-scented with overtones of turpentine. Autumn foliage assumes the most beautiful colours and luscious looking black fruits accompany it.

sanguineum (D) 8ft

FLOWERING CURRANT

So commonly cultivated as to be overlooked or disdained, but well-known for its drooping sprays of rose-pink flowers blooming above many patches of spring-flowering bulbs in March and April, there are several forms; all have the pink flowers and soft foliage, downy beneath and curiously aromatic, literally sweet and dry. *Ribes s.* 'Brocklebankii', seen at its best in one or two dark corners at the Royal Horticultural Gardens, Wisley, Surrey, has golden-yellow armatic foliage, and pink flowers, and 'King Edward VII' bears deeper pink flowers than the type and retains aromatic foliage. 'Splendens' carries long sprays of pink flowers and retains the same foliage as the type, aromatic when bruised.

Ribes sanguineum

ROSA (*Rosaceae*)

ROSE

It matters not how the rose is used in garden decoration – there will be some sort available to meet the requirement. Roses look marvellous in natural groups of great flowering masses or festooned into old trees, clothing walls or fences, dangling across pergolas in the full blown, informal profusion of the old cottage-garden style. Alternately, they are admirable in the ordered formality of beds and borders, befitting palatial terraces and public parks, or in the trim plot of a semi-detached house on a housing development.

Native to the northern temperate-region zones and the mountainous regions skirting the Mediterranean, they can be grown in most soils and all districts, with more or less success, for there are certainly 'good rose areas'. The climbers show a shade tolerance not as happily displayed by the shrubs.

Fragrance has been a driving force in the cultivation of the rose over the centuries, not only commercially, but as a delight and stimulation to the senses. Contrasting nuances in aroma have been detected, and in spite of the highly personalized response to scent, varieties and species are recorded as claimants to the scent of apple, tarry tea, violet, lemon, or simple rose. A note from *Gardening World* (1885) claims 17 different sorts of scent in rose blooms. Present day conjecture may not attest to so many but the variations are sufficient to record scent reminiscent of several other plants. The lemon scent of 'Lafter' and 'Blue Moon' and 'Leverkusen'; raspberry of 'Adam Messerich' and 'Mme Isaac Pereire' and 'Golden Fleece'; the apple of 'Albéric Barbier' and 'New Dawn'; the sweet-pea scent of 'Bonn' and 'Vanity'; the musk of many, perhaps strongest in 'Penelope' and 'Moonlight'; violet scent in *R. banksiae-plena* and the clove of *R. paulii* and 'Fritz Nobilis'. The so-called tea scent, really a dry tarry tea, is detectable in numberless 'tea roses' in an almost chromatic scale of sensations, but particularly recognizable in 'Felicia'. Myrrh comes in 'Constance Spry', primrose in the climbers 'Adel d' Orléans' and 'Félicité et Perpétué', and mignonette in the wild *R. canina*.

Foliage also contributes to some extent to enjoyment of fragrance for the rosarian; the leaves, on bruising, can reveal aromatic and refreshing scent. That of the sweet brier, *R. rubiginosa*, is well known and the young growth also is scented almost like apples, rich and fruity. The scent glands are superficial so that a gentle brush is sufficient to release the perfume and during warm moist weather the aroma is carried on the air. *Rosa primula* is called the Incense Rose because of the rich aroma of the leaves, whose scent is again borne on the air. Some roses in the general cinnamon rose group stake claim to aromatic foliage, but it is not always readily detectable, except perhaps in *R. setipoda* where it is rather fruity; but as the whole plant is fragrant it is difficult to be precise. The Cinnamon Rose itself, *R. cinnamomea*, is perhaps spicy rather than fruity and in the same group is the Threepenny-bit Rose, *R. farreri*, which I first encountered as *R. f. persetosa* in the Ventnor Botanic Garden; I persuaded myself that the flimsy foliage was spicy. The rough, unusual odour of *R. foetida* is inherited with some variations in the Penzance briers, in particular the small-leaved 'Lord Penzance' and the foliage of 'Minna' and 'Meg Merrilies'. Perhaps the most remarkable of aromatic rose foliage is that of *Rosa glutinosa*, redolent of the pine forests of the Lower Alps. Superficial rather hairy glands can be seen on both sides of the leaf, and it is these that carry the astringent perfume. The plant is rarely cultivated, but ought to find a place in the true fragrant garden.

There is an interesting contribution to the study of rose fragrance in *The Rose Annual* (1980) where a system of points has been allocated over a period of time relating to the intensity of rose perfume, ranging from 'scent just detectable' to 'supreme scent'. Some of the roses listed have been cultivated for well over half a century, 'George Dickson' for example, suggesting that in spite of modern introductions a well-scented rose can remain a firm favourite.

centifolia 5ft

CABBAGE ROSE, PROVENCE ROSE

The species *centifolia* itself forms an open thorny shrub, very lax in habit and with rather coarse, rounded, floppy foliage. Cabbage Rose seems an inappropriate name – the reason, maybe, why some of them bow their heads! The flowers are very rounded, clear pink, fully double and deeply fragrant. Perhaps more than any other roses, in dull weather it keeps its fruity rose scent locked away, and only upon close inspection can the scent be detected. Of special interest of the fragrant garden are some of its forms: 'Fantin-Latour', pale rose pink deepening on maturity; 'La Noblesse', small rose pink, deliciously fragrant; 'Petite de Hollande' – perhaps the flowers ought to be described as 'miniature centifolia' – pale pink and very fragrant. 'Tour de Malakoff', magenta rose to deep parma violet, may seem a bizarre description for a rose, but the total effect is fascinating as the mature petals reflex, assuming a parma violet, and intermediate shades are suffused over the entire flower. 'Paul Ricault', has tight globular flowers clearly quartered in deep rose pink and with a good rich fragrance.

centifolia muscosa 6ft

MOSS ROSE

In these forms of the Provence Rose, scent glands on the flower stem and the calyx have become enlarged to form the moss-like growth, which seems to have endeared this type of rose to the Victorians. The growth is sticky, the oil retained on the skin after handling. White-flowered forms are less mossed as a general rule, but in all of them the fragrance is in both flower and these oil glands. 'Général Kléber' is one of the loveliest, with a deep rich scent, which is evident from the mossy glands, even when the flower is in bud. The flowers are neatly quartered, clear soft pink and with remarkably fresh green mossy trimming. Maréchal Davoust has deep carmine-magenta flowers fading to purple and set off by a dark moss trimming, the growth delightfully fragrant. 'Mousseline', which flowers intermittently over quite a long period, is not heavily mossed, but the flowers are of the very palest blush pink and the moss trimming is brown. 'William Lobb' heavily mossed buds are carried in great clusters, and split to reveal rich dark-crimson flowers tinted grey-pink on maturity and sometimes called Old Velvet Moss, and as richly fragrant as a blousy matron.

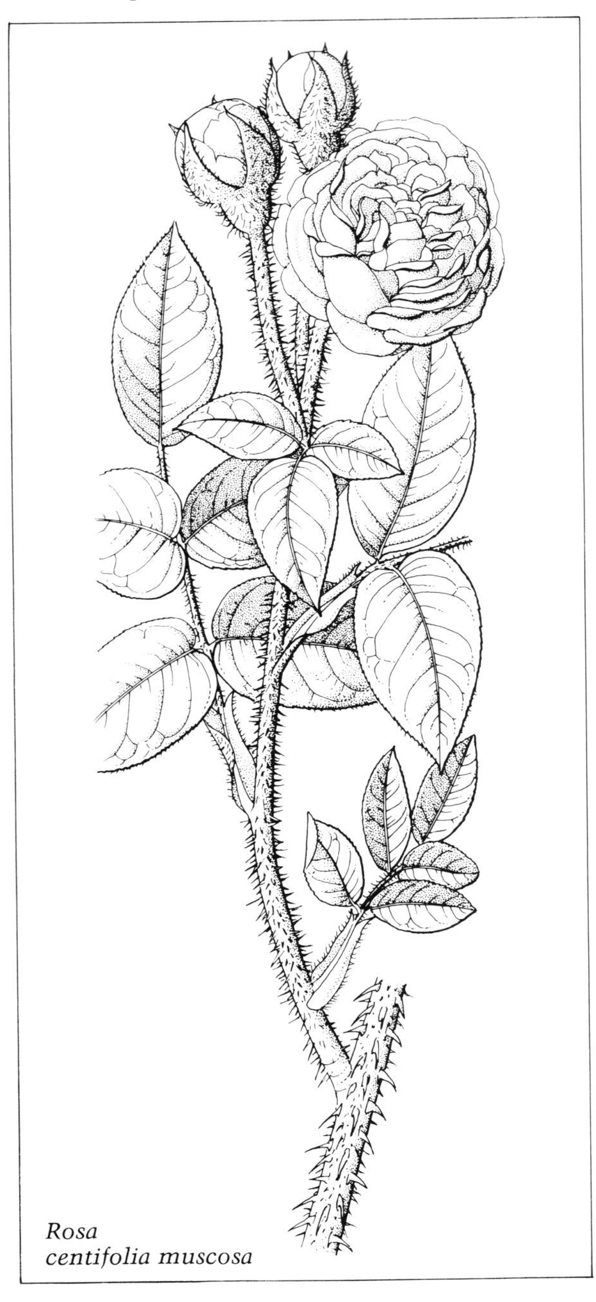
Rosa centifolia muscosa

damascena 4–5ft

DAMASK ROSE

For the fragrant garden, the damask roses have a role to play, not only by virtue of their true old rose perfume, but for their soft rather elegant growth. Some to plant are: 'Comte de Chambord', with full-blooded rose pink flowers which appear recurrently throughout the season; 'Jacques Cartier', very similar to the previous variety, but less floriferous with good big rich pink blooms and paler green foliage and a really intense rose perfume; 'La Ville de Bruxelles', a most luxuriant shrub, with very fragrant rich pink flowers – perhaps its only 'fault' can be said to be that its flowers are too grand, wrestling among the the leaves restrained by their own weight; 'Petite Lisette', a low-growing bush with perfect soft pink flowers, rather flattish and fragrant and enhanced by soft almost silken foliage, a plant that is truly described by the word 'damask', reminiscent of the richest patterned silks.

gallica 4ft

FRENCH ROSE, ROSE OF PROVINS

The true *R. gallica* is in fact a European weed, suckering badly and difficult to exterminate. It bears the largest pink flowers of any species rose, and for these reasons is superb as an informal hedging plant, or for covering informal areas. It always regenerates happily after cutting back. The flowers emit a true old rose perfume, clear and sweet, and when cut this will not fade, provided the flowers are not full blown and past their best. During the 18th century the French developed this rose with the result that some of the gallicas still cultivated today are richly scented, and these are the roses to grow for dried rose petals to incorporate into the most satisfying *pot pourri*.

Some forms to grow include 'Belle de Crécy', possibly the universally acclaimed 'best' rose scent of all the old roses. At first the flowers are a harsh cerise pink, but soon assume a softer parma violet shading flushed and powdered with lavender greys, and they cover the arching growth. The fragrance is rich, sweet and intensely satisfying. If one could grow only a single scented plant, this rose ought to be a contender for the role. 'Cardinal de Richelieu' is attractive for the dark dusky appearance of the whole

3 *Seat overlooking a small herb garden; scented-leafed plants are grown in containers and so may be enjoyed seasonally by being moved around*

4 *Sweet peas at the edge of a kitchen garden are grown to provide cut flowers for the house*

plant. At first the flowers are rich burnished lilac, but the strongly reflexed petals soon form a round mop head of velvety dark purple.

'Charles de Mills', is a good plant all round, but of interest for the flattened flowers that always look as though some whimsical force had sliced them through, removed the tops and scooped away the centre. The tightly packed petals are rich plum-crimson, lilac-bloomed like a plum on maturity. The fragrance is sumptuous and as rich and fruity as the plum itself. 'Duchess de Montebello' has rather light green foliage, providing the right note for the pale, fully double, blush-pink flowers, which are strongly fragrant. 'Président de Sèze' has striking flower colour and, again, good rose fragrance; the fully double blooms are a mixture of deep magenta red towards the centre and lilac pink at the circumference.

gallica officinalis 4ft

APOTHECARY'S ROSE, PROVINS ROSE

Probably the oldest cultivated form of *R. gallica*, because its petal perfume persists on drying, remaining perfectly fresh devoid of mustiness, it has a long history of utilization by man. This was the rose grown mainly around the town of Provins, south-east of Paris, for the production of conserves, confections and powders. (Unfortunately, it is often referred to as the 'damask' rose, adding some confusion, and a name that really bears no affinity to *R. damascena*. Rather, it is an old vernacular misconception, as it is thought to have arrived in England from Damascus at the time of the Crusades.)

gallica variegata (*versicolor*) 4ft

ROSA MUNDI

A sport of *R. gallica officinalis*, with light crimson petals splashed and striped with very pale pink, it gives a good display of flowers, rather showy and always reminiscent of peppermint rock! The perfume, however, is of the same true rose fragrance as the *officinalis* type. A sturdy and useful hedging plant.

primula 6ft

THE INCENSE ROSE

Twiggy dense growth is spangled with small single yellow flowers in May and June which are highly redolent of incense, hence its common name. On damp warm days the perfume hangs about the garden.

rubiginosa 8ft

SWEETBRIER, EGLANTINE

A wild English rose, a plant of the hedgerows, but cultivated for its fleeting, sweetly fragrant flowers, rose pink or pale blush, and for its strongly aromatic foliage. Heavily armed with prickles, the growth is arching and is useful for informal planting, or for use as an impenetrable boundary. The foliage fragrance is released to be carried on the wind, especially after rain or during moist warm periods. The so-called Penzance briars carry this rich fragrance of foliage. 'Amy Robsart', rich pink, 'Lady Penzance', golden copper; 'Lord Penzance', chamois yellow; 'Meg Merrilies', crimson; and 'Green Mantle', rose-red and white.

Modern Shrub Roses 5–7ft

Many 20th-century roses do not bear a direct relationship to the old shrub roses; so many have been derived from deliberate crosses in the ever widening search for something new. We cannot concern ourselves with a precise classification – they are included here simply as suggestions to introduce into the fragrant garden:

'Adam Messerich', deep pink and fragrant of luscious raspberry; 'Agnes', rich yellow-chamois with a unique and delicious fragrance; 'Black Boy', deep plum-crimson, scented of old rose; 'Bonn', salmon-magenta, the harsh colour once more accompanied by a crisp cheap sweet-pea scent; 'Cerise Bouquet', cerise-crimson, and scented richly of fruit, probably raspberry; 'Constance Spry', bright rose-pink redolent of myrrh; 'Fritz Nobis', rose-pink, crisp with the scent of cloves; 'Frühlingsduft', chamois to silver, almost ethereal, but its perfume leaving nothing to the imagination, a full rich-rose fragrance; 'Frühlingsgold', butter-yellow, with a rich rose scent that carries well on the air; 'Golden Wings', lemon-yellow and richly scented; 'Lafter', salmon orange-rose, unexpectedly lemon-scented; 'Macrantha', blush pink with a slight but very sumptuous fragrance; *paulii*, with white, spidery clematis-like flowers that are vaguely clove-scented on inspection; *paulii rosea*, a clear pink version with the same aromatic clove aroma; 'Scintillation', blush pink and highly and richly fragrant.

Hybrid Musk Roses 5–7ft

These are vigorous shrubs forming dense masses of stems carrying flowers in bold clusters from July onwards. They are invaluable for late autumn effect, because heps are borne profusely and retained, adding a glow to the entire bush. Many of them have superbly attractive foliage, and coloured stems, contributing enormously to decorative effect. Some of the scent is said to be carried in the stamens. Some to grow are: 'Buff Beauty', apricot yellow and with the true tea rose scent; 'Cornelia', copper pink and a strong fragrance; 'Felicia', silver pink, aromatic rather than fragrant of the true tea-rose scent, but with a dryness that is most attractive; 'Moonlight', creamy white and carrying the true musk rose scent; 'Penelope' creamy pink and again carrying the true musk rose perfume; 'Vanity', a deep hard pink with a scent as brittle and as cheap as its colour suggests.

Bourbon Roses 4–6ft

This group of old shrub roses displays the perpetual blooming characters of the modern Hybrid Tea rose, with rather opulent flowers. Some are fragrant, and bloom over a long period from June to October.

Some suggestions for the fragrant garden: 'Boule de Neige', creamy white and rather formal, richly scented of old roses; 'Bourbon Queen', giving a crêpe paper effect of pale and dark pink, and rose-scented; 'Honorine de Brabant', pale pink splashed with lilac and raspberry-scented; 'La Reine Victoria', a warm rose pink with a fragrance just as rose-like as the appearance suggests; 'Louise Odier', warm pink with lilac shading and formally arranged petals, giving a really strong rose fragrance; 'Mme Isaac Pereire', with large, formal flowers of deep rose red and a strong fruity fragrance suggesting raspberries; 'Lauriol de Barny', light silver rose and a strong fruity fragrance; 'Piere Oger', globular, formal pale pink deepening in warmer weather and giving a really rich and satisfying rose perfume.

Hybrid Perpetual Roses 4–5ft

In the complex history of the development of the rose, the hybrid perpetuals could be described as modern Bourbon-type roses. They have the same floriferousness, with a 'repeat performance' quality. One or two could be planted in the fragrant garden: 'Baron Girod de l'Ain', a dark crimson with a quaint white lace edging to each petal and highly fragrant; 'Ferdinand Pichard', a striped rose, not to everyone's taste in appearance, pink with plum-purple stripes and giving a rich perfume; 'Glorie de Ducher', a velvety dark plum crimson, very richly fragrant, and 'Souvenir de Docteur Jamain', also dark, rich, velvety maroon-crimson, and very fragrant.

Climbing Roses 8–30ft

There are many climbing hybrids and cultivars, as well as species roses of climbing habit, and climbing sports of Hybrid Teas and Floribundas. So for convenience, and because we are concerned here with fragrance rather than classification, here are some suggestions for climbing roses to use on posts, fences, walls or to festoon into trees or over summerhouses and pergolas. There is a wide range of flower form:

'Aimée Vibert', white opening to yellow, rich rose scent; 'Aloha', clear pink with a rich rose scent; *banksiae albaplena*, with white button-shaped flowers scented of violets; 'Celine Forestier', full-petalled pink and yellow with a sheen and powerfully scented of tea; 'Château de Glos Vougeot', climbing, dark velvety crimson and with a strong rose scent; 'Compassion', salmon bronze and deeply fragrant; 'Dreamgirl', coral pink and beautifully spicy; 'Étoile de Hollande', climbing, deep red and with strong rose scent; *filipes* 'Kitfsgate', creamy white, frothy and redolent of incense; *gentiliana*, creamy white and strongly rose-scented; 'Gloire de Dijon', large, buff pink with rich rose scent; 'Lady Hillingdon', apricot strongly scented of tea; *laevigata* (the Cherokee Rose), cream with a yellow centre, deliciously spicy; 'Lawrence Johnston', golden yellow and powerfully rose-scented; *longicuspis*, with single white flowers emitting a strong banana fragrance; 'Leverkusen', mauve and lemon-scented; 'Mme Alfred Carrière, white touched with flesh pink and wonderfully fruity of fragrance; 'Mme Grégoire Staechelin', large, deep pink and sweet-pea-like in scent; 'Maigold', semi-double tangerine yellow with a powerful rose scent; *moschata* (the Musk Rose), cream white with a rather delicate musk scent, especially noticeable in the autumn (somehow the fragrance for which this rose has always been famous is curiously elusive and really never very apparent); 'New Dawn', pale shell-pink with a fresh but fruity perfume; 'Parade', magenta, rich and quite powerfully scented; 'Paul's Lemon Pillar', pale yellow tea roses, with a full rose perfume; 'Paul Lede', climbing, yellow buff with apricot and a rich tea scent; *rubus*, pale yellow opening to white and a marvellously rich perfume; 'Souvenir de Claudius Denoyel', bright crimson and richly fragrant; 'Zepherine Drouhin', deep rose pink and richly rose-scented.

Floribunda Roses 2½–6ft

Rather showy cultivars resulting from crosses between Hybrid Teas and the Polyanthas, the Floribundas are vigorous, unusually clean growing but quite often scentless. However, some varieties to grow for perfume are: 'Circus', golden yellow, flushed cherry, scented of clove; 'Dearest', double, salmon pink, quite fragrant; 'Escapade', single rose violet and of musk fragrance; 'Golden Fleece', coral rose-apricot and smelling of raspberries; 'Iceberg', white and sweetly fragrant; 'Ma Perkins', double, silver-shrimp-pink, with the true rose perfume; 'Orange Sensation', traffic-stopper-vermillion with a good perfume; 'Pink Parfait', pink-apricot with a sweet but slight scent; 'Sweet Repose', rose to amber and gently fragrant; and 'Victoriana', tangerine-silver-grey and sweetly scented.

Hybrid Tea Roses 2½–3ft

One of the most popularly grown of all flowering shrubs, noted for the perfection of their high-pointed flowers, and the remarkably subtle colour combinations and perfection of flower form, there are literally hundreds from which to make a selection. Some of the most fragrant are: 'Amazing Grace', peach pink, sweet; 'Apricot Silk', apricot, sweetly scented; 'Blessings', salmon rose and sweetly scented; 'Blue Moon', silver-grey-lilac and lemon-scented; 'Bonsoir', cream-crimson and very sweetly fragrant; 'Buccaneer', cream yellow and richly perfumed; 'Chrysler Imperial', crimson and richly scented;

'Doris Tysterman', tangerine and very fragrant; 'Drambuie', a lovely tangerine-gold, beautifully scented; 'Elsa Arnot', cream to pink-amber, very strongly perfumed; 'Ernest H. Morse', bright crimson and very fragrant; 'Grace de Monaco', rose-pink and highly perfumed; 'Fragrant Cloud', coral scarlet with a scent that has been described as coarse; 'Just Joey', copper orange, richly scented; 'Lady Belper', bronze orange and fragrant; 'Lady Hillingdon', apricot and strongly tea-scented; 'Miss Harrop', light yellow and beautifully fragrant; 'Mme Abel Chatenay', rose-pale pink and sweetly perfumed; 'Papa Meilland', crimson and very fragrant; 'Prima Ballerina', bright rose-pink, richly scented; 'Sunblest', clear yellow and very fragrant; 'Super Star', a blazing vermilion and very fragrant; 'Sutter's Gold', golden yellow flushed pink with a sweet rose perfume that carries on the air; 'Tenerife', deep peach pink and very sweet; 'Troica', orange-amber and richly scented; 'Wendy Cussons', rose-red with a rich damask fragrance; 'White Wings', pure white and fragrant; and 'Whisky Mac', orange-gold and highly fragrant.

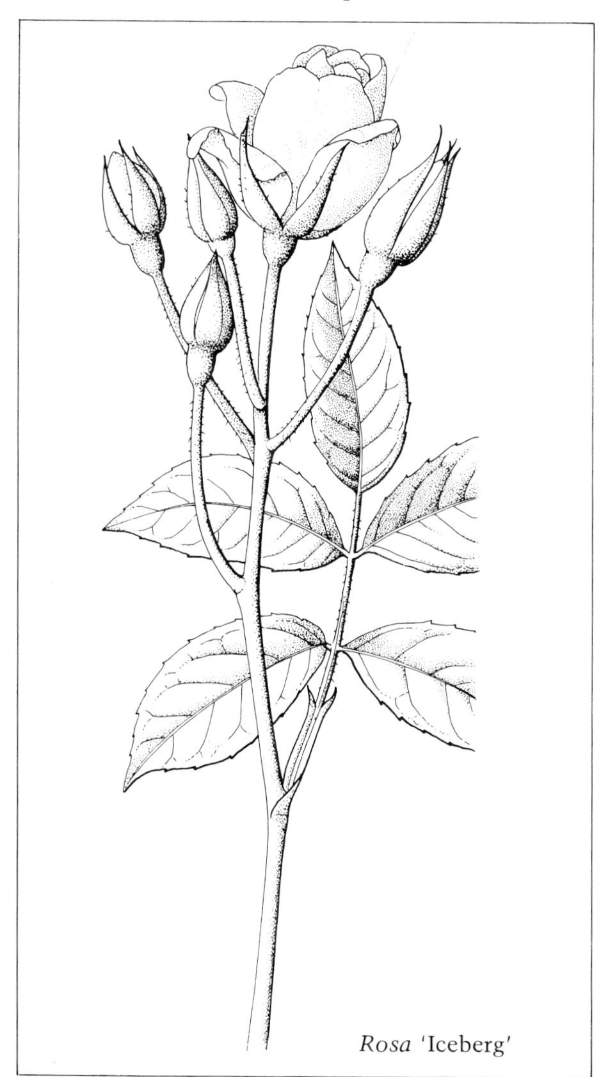

Rosa 'Iceberg'

Rambler Roses 20–30ft

These are climbing roses whose habit of growth forms a tangle unless well maintained. New growing stems are continually produced from the base. Many attain great height and provide huge blobs of colour as a backdrop to the garden scene. For the fragrant garden, some possibilities are: 'Adelaide d' Orléans', cream pink, fragrant of primrose; 'Albéric Barbier', cream, scented of apples; 'Albertine', salmon-copper with a strong rose scent; 'Auguste Gervais', copper-salmon heavily scented; 'Bobbie James', cream white, fragrant; 'Félicité et Perpétué', cream with a pink blush, fragrant of primrose; 'Frances E. Lester', single, white with a strong perfume that carries on the wind; 'La Perle', deep cream, strong fresh scent; 'Sander's White', semi-double and pure white, with a rich good fragrance; 'Seagull', single, white, most gloriously scented; *spectabilis*, shell pink to lavender, primrose-scented; 'Veilchenblau', garnet-mauve, smelling strongly of orange and 'Wedding Day', apricot-cream, with a sweet perfume.

Miniature Roses 6–18in

Literally miniature bushes, especially useful for window boxes, pot cultivation and border edges, these are not generally recommended for troughs, because they require a greater depth of soil to prevent the roots from drying out or baking. A few have fragrant flowers: 'Colibri', apricot and vaguely fragrant; 'Josephine Wheatcroft' (also listed as 'Rosina'), butter-yellow, slightly fragrant; 'Sweet Fairy', lilac-pink, fragrant; 'Yellow Doll', primrose-yellow and fragrant; 'Twinkles', white and sweet.

China Roses 2½ft

China roses are low-growing twiggy shrubs, with pretty flowers, the whole plant of a restrained appearance, sparse in foliage, which is often suffused pink. The species *R. chinensis* has played a vital role in the evolution of modern roses, especially for their long flowering period. Perhaps two to try for fragrance are: 'Hermosa', lilac pink, with rose-scented flowers and 'Le Vésuve', cream-coppery pink with tea-scented flowers.

ROSMARINUS (*Labiatae*) (E)

ROSEMARY

Clean-growing evergreens, these are aromatic in all their parts, revelling in sunshine and well-drained soils, at the same time appreciative of good humus-forming material at the roots. Hardy in most regions, wind-tolerant and rabbit-proof.

Rosemarinus officinalis

lavandulaceus (Syn. *R. officinalis prostratus*) 1½ft

A low-growing dense plant forming a mat of foliage speckled with pale blue flowers in April and May. It is perhaps susceptible to frost when not given good sharp drainage, and therefore at its best when grown along the top of a low wall or rocky bank where it can sprawl about and drape itself downwards, curtain-like. Sweetly and strongly aromatic when rubbed, with a sharp, satisfying scent that lingers on the skin.

officinalis 6½ft

COMMON ROSEMARY

A thickly growing semi-erect bush with small narrow dark green leaves, whitish beneath and highly aromatic when brushed with the hand, Common Rosemary bears dusty pale blue flowers in May. A good hedge plant where informality is required, although it can be formally clipped, but what a pity to sacrifice the flowers! The scent can only be described as 'rosemary', and it is an ingredient of eau de Cologne; although English oil of rosemary is considered superior to others, because of the English climate, it is now not produced commercially in England.

Various forms of the shrub are available: *R. o.* 'Benenden Blue', smaller growing than the type, with darker narrower leaves and bright blue flowers, less hardy; *R. o.* 'Fastigiatus' (also catalogued as Miss Jessop's Upright) of stiff erect habit with the pale flowers of the type; *R. o.* 'Roseus', lilac pink flowers and *R. o.* 'Severn Sea', small of habit but with attractively arching stems, useful for the borders of the rock garden, and bright blue flowers.

SAMBUCUS (*Caprifoliaceae*) (D)

ELDER

Thoroughly hardy in the greater part of the British Isles, the elder has, in the wild, become a characteristic roadside bush or small tree. In northern regions of Scotland, some forms are planted as game cover, and everywhere it is an excellent plant for semi-shade and the wild garden. Because it is quick to grow and regenerates equally quickly after cutting back, it is often used as a space-filler. Elder is happy on almost any soil, even on freshly turned building sites and extremely alkaline soils.

canadensis 8ft

AMERICAN ELDER, SWEET ELDER

An upright-growing shrub with large blue-green leaves and flowers in slightly flat domed heads up to 8in across in July and August. Deep cream in colour, they give off a strong muscatel scent, sweet and heavy, and are followed by purplish black edible berries in the autumn. An arresting form is *S. c.* 'Maxima', more robust in every way, the flower heads as much as 14in across. A good plant for the wild garden, along with the golden-leaved form *S. c.* 'Aurea'.

nigra up to 30ft
COMMON ELDER
A large shrub or small tree when allowed to grow naturally, with bright green leaves divided into four pairs, and creamy white flowers carried in flattened heads. Both the flowers and the shining black berries that follow are edible, commonly used in home wine-making. In June the bushes are laden with flowers, very strongly fragrant of musk, and when the air is warm and calm, the scent can be detected a considerable distance away from the plant. For garden decoration, there are several forms more decorative than the type; noteable perhaps is *S. n.* 'Lacinata', the Fern-Leaved Elder, with finely divided feathery foliage and the same sweet-smelling flowers and black fruits. *S. n.* 'Aurea' is the Golden Elder with golden yellow leaves, deepening in colour as the summer passes and retaining its attraction into the autumn when the shining black fruits contrast well – one of the loveliest of golden-leaved shrubs of easy cultivation. Mottled or variegated foliage, especially strong in the early summer, is a feature of *S. n.* 'Pulverulenta' and *S. n.* 'Aureomarginata', and there are one or two forms becoming available for the excellence of their edible fruits. All bear the typically sweetly musk-scented flowers, which drench the air with their perfume.

racemosa up to 4ft
HART'S ELDER, RED BERRIED ELDER
Rather earlier-flowering than most elders, the sweet smelling blossoms are carried in a more floppy way in pointed or panicle-like heads. This is a good shrub for open wild gardens and really at its best in the highly decorative form *S. r.* 'Plumosa Aurea' in which the deeply slashed leaves are golden-green. The berries, as in the type, are red-currant red, large and shining. A most attractive shrub.

SANTOLINA (*Compositae*) (E)
Given full sun in a well-drained spot, the santolinas are among the best sub-shrubs with aromatic foliage, variously green, grey or silver. Few forms are commonly grown; others can be seen in botanic gardens and special collections. All have bobble or button-like yellow flowers in late summer. All are hardy and are effectively used as drive-way edging plants, stop retaining walls and on the outskirts of the rock gardens and perennial borders. Santolina lends itself to clipping, but does tend to die out in patches.

chamaecyparissus (Syn. *incana*) 16–24in
LAVENDER COTTON, COTTON LAVENDER, GROUND CYPERUS
A plant, now old in cultivation, forming a compact low shrub with silver threadlike foliage and yellow bobble flowers on leafless stalks, all over the cushion of growth, in July and August. The foliage is pungent, and especially aromatic in the smaller form 'Nana'. The form *S. c. insularis* (Syn. *S. neopolitana*) is slightly taller, softer and looser of habit with feathered pungent foliage. *S. c. i.* 'Sulphurea' has primrose-yellow flowers set off by grey-green leaves.

rosmarinifolia 1½ft
A native of southern France and Portugal, this species is sometimes available and has bright green foliage and bright yellow flowers. The form 'Primrose Gem' is encountered more often, with pale yellow flowers, and both are more sharply aromatic than *S. chamaecyparissus*.

virens 1–1½ft
Another compact low shrublet, bushy of habit and a good edge-of-the-border or container plant, remaining a fairly good green throughout the winter, certainly in the south. The foliage is a bright emerald green, heath-like, and markedly oily to touch and very strongly aromatic, the scent adhering to the skin and clothes for a long time after brushing by. It is strongly camphorous, sweet and sharp at the same time. Small bobble yellow flowers appear in July, of little significance, rayless and not long lasting.

SKIMMIA (*Rutaceae*) (E)
Immensely useful slow-growing Asiatic plants, some with aromatic foliage, they are tolerant of shade and, where humus-rich soil is provided, thrive well in both town and maritime conditions. They have a reputation for disliking lime, but thrive in some Chiltern gardens without chlorosis problems. Some are less hardy than others, and some, noteably *S. japonica* and *S. laureola*, bear male and female flowers on separate plants. But these are good plants to grow in tubs, where acid, humus-rich soil can be provided and where two or more plants can be grown. The poisonous berries assume an importance possessed by few other shrubs, and persist as they appear to be distasteful to birds.

japonica 4ft
The rather leathery, large oval leaves give the shrub a dense dome-shaped habit. Slightly fragrant flowers, usually white, are carried in terminal stumpy panicles in April and May and on the female form are followed by the lovely coral-red shining berries. The cultivar 'Fragrans' is claimed to have lily-of-the-valley-scented flowers. The same perfume comes in 'Rubella' but the chief glory here is the pretty rose-pink flower buds which wait through the winter to open in early spring.

laureola 3¼ft

Dense of habit with bright green leaves, ovate and pointed, remarkably pungent when bruised, and dioecious pale yellow flowers in rather crushed panicles, in May. They are scented heavily and sweetly but are somewhat spicy and of the same pungent smell as the foliage. The fruits are shining bright red. A reasonably hardy plant, but not for winter in inclement areas.

reevesiana (*fortunei*) 2–3ft

Tender and small of stature, this Chinese species carries hermaphrodite flowers and so freely produces its deep crimson berries, which often persist into the following spring. There is the added joy of fruit and flower at the same time. The flowers are white, in small stumpy panicles, and fragrant. The foliage is mildly aromatic also.

SPARTIUM *junceum* (*Leguminosae*) (D) 5–10ft

SPANISH BROOM

A Spanish plant, and therefore revelling in sunshine in a light well-drained position, although it tolerates a wide range of soils. A superb plant for seaside gardens or windy banks and full exposure to light. The growth is whippy, the leaves almost inconspicuous but long sprays of deep yellow pea-like flowers are borne in high summer and through to September. The fragrance is sweet and orange-like, and lingering. Little black seed pods follow.

STACHYURUS (*Stachyuraceae*) (D)

Two species of stachyurus are hardy throughout the British Isles, tolerant of all types of fertile soil and really not very particular about sunlight or semi-shade. Immensely useful shrubs for town gardens or borders near the house where their very fragrant scent and early spring beauty can be appreciated. They ask only to be protected from very cold winds.

chinensis 6–8ft

A shrub of rather spreading and stretching habit flowering on the deep purplish-brown bare wood in February and March. With a jasmine-like fragrance the flowers are on stiff, downward-pointing stems, as many as 20 or 30 on each stem, and each flower beaker-shaped. They are primrose-yellow and the stems hang along the branches like icicles. The species is not seen as much as it used to be a generation ago, and is apparently difficult to obtain, but well worth tracking down.

Stachyurus praecox

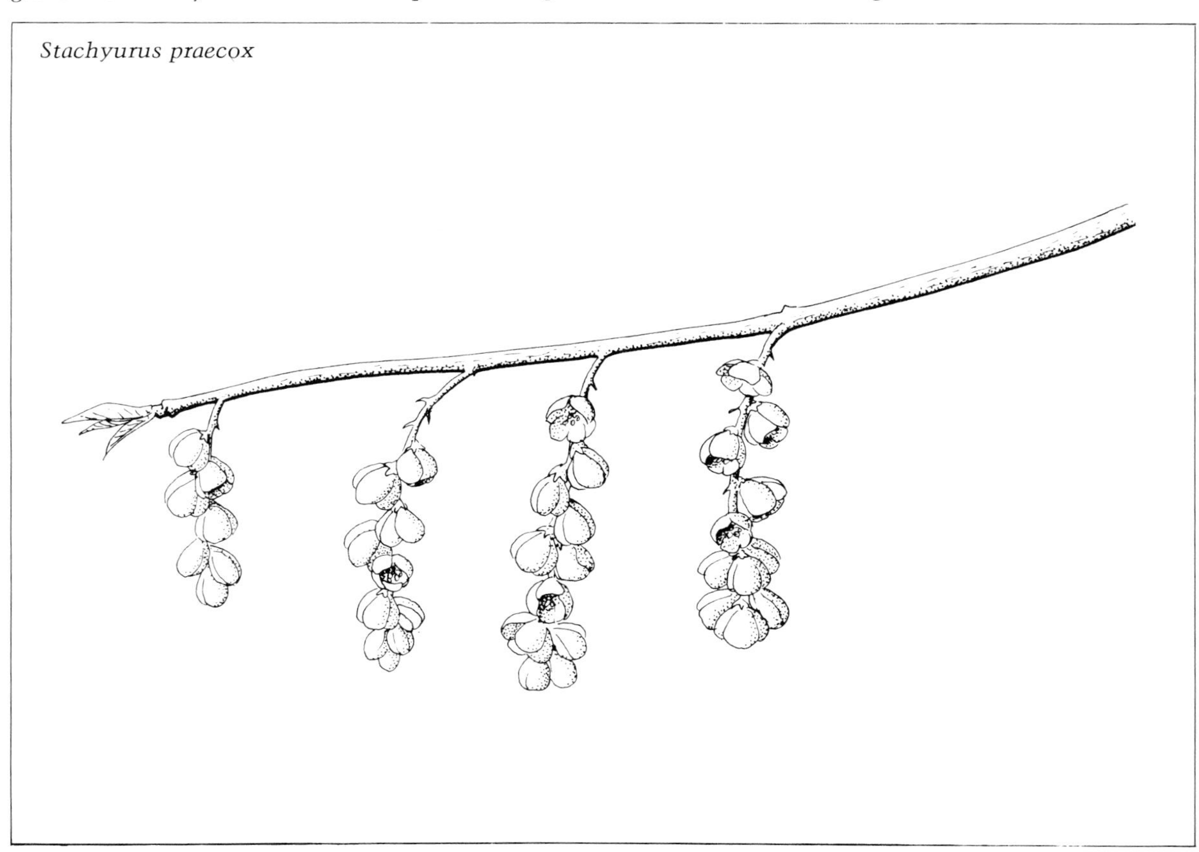

praecox 6–8ft

The flowers brave the coldest weather in January and February and are rather susceptible to frost damage. Again, the downward-pointing flower stems are strung along the bare branches and rich with pale lemon-yellow flowers, sweetly fragrant. The racemes of flowers themselves are rather shorter than in *chinensis*, and the ensuing leaves are narrower.

SYRINGA (*Oleaceae*) (D)

LILAC

Although the lilac is an old inhabitant of our gardens, it was only in the mid-19th century that French and German hybridists turned serious attention to it. One of the first hybrids was *S.* × *hyacinthifolia*, produced by Victor Lemoine at Nancy, France, crossing a Belgian-raised double-flowered form of *S. vulgaris* with *S. oblata* which Robert Fortune had found in a Shanghai garden. Today the temperate world seems to be filled with modern hybrids and cultivars, with lush and bulky flower heads in early summer. So numerous are they that they distract attention from the species, which not only prolong the flowering season considerably, but maintain the best perfume. Most species are scented, some extremely so, and offensive to some people, *reticulata*, *villosa*, *emodii* and *wolfii* in particular. Hillier's catalogue allows itself a sustained pause in its listing to describe the lilacs as 'accompanied by a delicious fragrance which has become an inseparable part of their magic'. Most soils in good heart suit them, chalky more so, and they appreciate the sunlight, growing twiggy where they are deprived of it. Some species to try are:

× *chinensis (S.* × *persica* × *S. vulgaris)* 6–8ft

ROUEN LILAC

The common name records its (chance, it seems) appearance in the Rouen Botanic Garden in 1777. A shrub of dense but graceful habit, with ovate leaves and drooping panicles of rich soft lavender-coloured flowers which can bear down the branches. A faint spiciness adds freshness to the perfume in May and June.

× *hyacinthifolia* (*S. oblata* × *S. vulgaris*) 6ft

A group of hybrid cultivars which combine parental characteristics, but appear nearer to *C. vulgaris*, characterized by early fragrant flowers. 'Lamartine' is an old favourite, grown by three or four generations of gardeners at least, with deep-lilac single flowers in enormous rather loose panicles, the early foliage suffused with bronze. 'Clarke's Giant', a progeny of work in California, begins to flower in April and early May with tight rosy-mauve buds, breaking into sweet-smelling blue-lilac single flowers. 'Plena' is one of the original crosses made back in the 1840s producing double violet flowers, of the shade our grandparents referred to as 'helio', which are royal purple in bud and deeply scented.

× *josiflexa* (*S. josikaea* × *S. reflexa*) 6–8ft

A group of Canadian hybrids, of which the best is 'Bellicent' with sumptuously fragrant rose-pink flowers in important-looking panicles and rather good deep-green foliage.

microphylla 5ft

A Chinese species with rather broad and pointed leaves and small heads of flowers that bring cross stitch to mind. They are a deep madder pink, darker on the outside – more rose-mauve and richly fragrant in June. Frequently a second crop of flowers blooms in September. The floriferous form 'Superba' bears larger heads of flowers in May and sporadically until the chilly days of October.

× *persica* 6–8ft

Cultivated in our gardens since the late 17th century, this lilac has a fragrance distinctly spicy and less intense than most lilacs, but even so it is sometimes called the Blue Persian Jasmine. It is a much-branched shrub with slender leaves and bauble-like heads of lilac-coloured flowers in May (here comes the difficulty of describing the flowers of the lilac, which though so varied in colour have lent their name to a soft old-fashioned mauve!). There is a white-flowered form 'Alba', though the whole shrub is less effective, and a curious slashed-leaved form with similar lilac flowers and the same clear fragrance.

vulgaris 3–6ft 9¾–19ft

COMMON LILAC

From the mountains of eastern Europe and grown in England since the 16th century, this is the Queen of plants for its progeny is the very essence of the poet's 'Lilac Time'. The species itself has rather rounded pointed leaves and lilac-mauve fragrant flowers in twin panicles in May. Cultivars are legion; it is almost presumptuous to recommend any in preference to others, and to quote Hillier's catalogue again, 'It requires a highly cultivated imagination to detect the differences in shade and colour, they vary from hour to hour.' It is perhaps permitted to observe that many cultivars, as with other genera, are less scented, and that they appear to be less 'talked about' or referred to than they were just after World War II. The choice is a personal one; all are scented to a greater or lesser degree. Some of the recommendations are: 'Congo', a wonderful velvety deep purple flower on rather dumpy panicles: 'Firmament', early-flowering in a clear mauve-blue more assocated with the stock (matthiola) than lilac;

'Hugo Koster', plum-purple; 'Maréchal Foch', creamy buds open to milky white, rather stumpy heads, and the plant grown by florists for forcing; 'Primrose', small rounded heads of pale yellow flowers and pale leaves, generally considered not to attain the peak of attraction that other cultivars may, but still flourishing well in a garden I made 25 years ago on Chiltern chalk; 'Charles Joly', deep-purple double flowers fading markedly to pinkish lilac, good dense panicles; and 'Mme Lemoine', an old form, clotted cream in bud and sugar-icing-white in flower, with numerous panicles and a scent rich and strong.

Syringa vulgaris cv

TRACHELOSPERMUM *jasminoides (Syn. Rhynchospermum jasminoides)* (E) 19½ft

STAR JASMINE

A tender evergreen with lustrous bright green foliage ovate and folded along the midrib, and climbing with aerial roots on the stems. Rather slow-growing, but a deliciously fragrant plant for the greenhouse or conservatory, or to grow in a pot for loggia decoration in mild areas. The ivory-white flowers spangle the growth in midsummer with some profusion and are very like the jasmine flower with reflexed petals. A sheltered wall which it hugs closely provides sufficient shelter on the terraces at Powis Castle, North Wales.

VIBURNUM (*Caprifoliaceae*) (E and D)

Not all the extensive tribe of viburnums bear fragrant flowers, but those that do are among the most attractively and strongly scented of shrubs. In addition they are highly ornamental excellent shrubs, many of them colouring in the loveliest fashion in the autumn when they are bespangled with shining fruits. The Asiatic species, particularly, bear scented flowers and are winter flowering on the bare wood, or evergreen and summer flowering. The notable exceptions are *V. tinus* which is evergreen and winter-flowering, and *V.* × *burkwoodii* which is of garden origin, although its parents were Asiatic, also evergreen and winter-flowering.

× *bodnantense* (*V. farrerii* × *V. grandiflorum*) (D) 4ft

A winter-flowering low-growing shrub with dense clusters of sweetly scented pink-flushed white flowers from October to March, in spite of frosty periods. Good in the form 'Dawn' with very sweetly scented blooms freely borne from autumn to spring.

× *burkwoodii* (*V. carlesii* × *V. utile*) (E) 4–6ft

Shining ovate leaves conspicuously felted beneath set off flattish clusters of white flowers of encrusted appearance, pink in the bud from New Year to May, emitting a very sweet fragrance, even on the coldest of days. A good wall shrub. Similar clones are available; the most notable for its perfume is 'Park Farm Hybrid' with large scented white flowers in April and May.

× *carlcephalum* (*V. carlesii* × *V. macrocephalum*) (D) 5–8ft

Compact of habit and presenting a rich colour spectacle in the autumn, the flowers are pink-tinted in May and are quite large in rounded clusters. They are said to be clove-scented.

carlesii 3–4ft

Oval leaves, downy, matt greyish-green beneath, and

Viburnum carlesii

changing to crimson in the autumn, from a bush of compact growth with rounded habit. The flowers are borne in rounded clusters, pink in bud expanding to pure white, and are scented of carnation. Happiest on lime-free soils, unfortunately it always seems to attract aphids. Pink-flowered, highly scented cultivars are 'Aurora', especially free-flowering, and 'Charis', whose flowers are eventually white but whose overall appearance is pink.

cinnamomifolium (E) 6–16ft

The elliptical dark glossy thick leaves are aromatic of cinnamon when bruised. Tolerant of semi-shade, it is not remarkable in flower because the blooms are rather small and dingy white, but compensation is made when the glossy black fruits arrive. It often makes a small tree. Flowers in June.

erubescens (D) 6–10ft

Rather tender, and best in sheltered sites, and favoured localities. Unlike most viburnums the white pink-flushed flowers are carried in pendulous clusters in July. They are very sweetly fragrant and are followed by drooping fruits which are first red, turning to black.

farreri (Syn. *fragrans*) (D) 5–7ft

Oval leaves conspicuously veined and flushed bronze when young give good colour to be followed immediately by the winter flowers. The blooms are pink, flushed in bud in January, and flowering through to March. They are strongly scented with an intensely sweet perfume Unfortunately, they deteriorate during cold wet periods. Fruit is rarely formed. Given the protection of a cold house it can be in bloom for Christmas.

grandiflorum (D) 6ft

Upright in habit and again with pronounced veins on the elliptical downy leaves. The flowers appear in February and March and are comparatively large, as the name suggests. Sweetly fragrant through the coldest days, coral-pink in bud, opening to a deep luscious shell-pink.

japonicum (Syn. *macrophyllum*) (E) 4–6ft

Rather large puckered leathery green leaves, paler beneath, really constitute the most arresting feature of the shrub. Once the plants are fully established, fragrant flowers are carried in rounded clusters in midsummer, and are deliciously scented and white. The ensuing fruits are red.

× *juddii* (*V. bitchiuense* × *V. carlesii*) (D) 4ft

Bushy of habit, and inheriting fragrance from both its parents, the shrub is free-flowering and bears white flowers, typically flushed pink, in April and May coming at the same time as the foliage. They are strongly fragrant.

odoratissimum (E) 8ft

A handsome Burmese shrub with striking obovate glossy foliage with conspicuous russeted leaf stalks. Sometimes, the mature foliage turns a bright carmine in spring, before falling, especially in mild areas and not too inclement winters, or where good shelter exists. The white flowers are carried in good panicles strongly fragrant in August, which is an unusual time for viburnums to be in flower. A shrub that really appreciates the midler areas and protected corners, and in these spots gives of its best.

tinus (E) 5–10ft

LAURUSTINUS

A very popularly grown evergreen, tolerant of town conditions and shade and never failing to produce clustered pink buds as early as October, and flowering spasmodically until April. The blooms are very fragrant, and last well when cut and taken indoors. Bushy of habit with oval glossy dark-green leaves, it offers late summer interest in the never-failing blue-black fruits.

WISTERIA *(Leguminosae)* (D)

GRAPE FLOWER VINE

Provided the soil is deeply worked and well prepared with some enriching and moisture-retentive material, the wisterias can be cultivated anywhere in the British Isles. They often attain a great age and often produce a gnarled and rigid but snaking woody stem which in summer is obliterated by the most filmy and decorative pinnate leaves; one needs never to be told that they hail from China and Japan, they display such an air of ancient elegance. So rigid is the stem that they may be trained as self-supporting standards, as at Knightshayes Court, Devon, when they assume the appearance of an oriental painting on silk.

floribunda 13ft

JAPANESE WISTERIA

One of Siebold's loveliest introductions, bearing long slender dangling racemes of flowers, mauve or violet blue in late May and June. Their fragrance is of sweet vanilla. The foliage is delicate, if covered when young, as are the inflorescences and pinnate leaves with numerous dark green leaflets. There is a white-flowered form, 'Alba', also fragrant, and 'Macrobotrys' with exceptionally long slender racemes of lilac-purple fragrant flowers, almost shaking their scent on to the breeze. Seen at its best when grown where the pendulous flowers can be seen to full advantage, as on a pergola or over an archway. I have seen this plant grown over a sloping frame to shade a patio, so that the flowers hung below the frame. Unfortunately, the stringy green flower stems remain looking like bell ropes for many weeks.

sinensis 100ft

CHINESE WISTERIA

Very popularly cultivated, similar in many respects to *W. floribunda*, but with rather more densely arranged panicles. The flowers are fragrant of sweet vanilla and are deep lilac-blue, and open as the foliage does, the whole plant silken in May. Foliage is pale green, prettily decorative again, with numerous pairs of leaflets.

GREEN AROMATICS

In general aromatic qualities are more subtle than those of fragrance, and plants with aromatic leaves often keep their secret locked away, until the leaf fabric is crushed. Plants that have come to be called herbs fall into this category. While their decorative qualitites may be somewhat lacking, they are of immense interest historically, and for the wide diversity of their individual aromas. With the exception of the evergreens, like sage and rosemary, their seasons are short, most herbs only providing really aromatic leaves during the three or four summer months of the year.

ANGELICA *archangelica* *(Umbelliferae)* 3–8ft

ANGELICA

Grown mainly for its tender leaf stalks which are candied for use in confectionery, this statuesque plant can be used to good decorative effect, and not be merely confined to the herb and kitchen garden. Given a reasonably rich and moisture retentive soil, to encourage steady growth, it flourishes best in light shade. Accommodating itself to tub culture, but not in full sunshine, it really makes an excellent impact on garden artistry. Bright-green deeply lobed leaves and bamboo-like stems display great round mop heads of green-white flowers in late May and June. All parts of the plant are aromatic and pleasant. But the true aroma is in the seeds and roots, alluding to musk, and is there stronger than in the bruised leaves or flowers.

ANTHRISCUS *cerefolium* *(Umbelliferae)* 1½ft

CHERVIL

An annual plant grown in the herb garden, in any good garden soil except a heavy clay, and given a sunny spot. The flowers are white in loose umbels, blooming from May to June, and the leaves very deeply divided and fernlike. The seed ripens in August or a little later depending on the season, and is highly aromatic, more so once completely dry.

ANTHEMIS *nobilis* *(Compositae)* 6–9in

CHAMOMILE

The English name chamomile is the general name for several perennial plants; most important here are Roman Chamomile (*A. nobilis*), German Chamomile (*Matricaria chamomilla*), and Scotch Chamomile (single-flowered form of *A. nobilis*). *Matricaria chamomilla* grows some 2–3ft; the flowers have a good apple-like fragrance and can be dried and put to the same uses as those of *A. nobilis*.

The main chamomile for the scented garden is *Anthemis nobilis*, fragrant of fruit, in foliage and flower with creeping rootstocks. It flourishes best on level ground, sandy or loamy and loves the sunshine. The flowers are white and daisy-like in July, those of the double-flowered form superior in fragrance and substance. This is the kind used for making chamomile paths or lawns or for planting between paving stones to enjoy the fragrance when walking on the plants. A non-flowering form 'Treneague' is available for lawns and retains the apple-banana scent.

ARTEMISIA (*Compositae*)

Artemisias are grown for their foliage and the insignificant flowers can for the most part be disregarded. There are many for the scented garden, some of them quite humble plants, all of them strongly aromatic; all are perennial. All grow best in well-drained fertile soil, but some are tolerant of neglect and poor soil, and, as if in an effort to make themselves noticeable, the aroma is more pronounced on such occasions. Most are plume-like or feathery and silvery and are first class ground-cover plants, *A. pontica* becoming invasive. They are lovely plants with which to cool down the flower border and most are marvellous plants for the outlying parts of shrub borders.

abrotanum up to 3ft

OLD MAN, LAD'S LOVE, SOUTHERNWOOD

A shrubby plant dying back in winter to a 'gnarled old man' and a denizen of old cottage gardens, preserved over the year only for its outstanding soft silky silver grey green thread-like foliage. Sweetly aromatic with a crisp refreshing fragrance, it, more than all the artemisias, appreciates a friable soil with some moisture-retentive material.

arborescens up to 3¼ft

A shrubby plant of rounded habit, tender, except in milder localities, with fern-like leaves forming a billowy mass of silver-grey sweetly aromatic foliage, when bruised.

chamaemelifolia 1½ft

LADY'S MAID

A species devoid of the greyness of foliage, but retaining the sharp sweet camphor-like aroma on bruising. The leaves are very finely cut and green, the growth soft and upright, and it tolerates some clipping when used as an edging plant. Good for block planting.

dracunculoides 3–5ft

RUSSIAN TARRAGON

Less aromatic, more pungent and harsher than most of the artemisias in scent, and often cultivated in the herb garden as 'tarragon' - from which it is hard to distinguish it, except that it seems less glabrous, and generally taller.

dracunculus 2–3ft

FRENCH TARRAGON

Grown in the kitchen garden and herb border for its culinary use. The leaves have a biting flavour and are warmly aromatic, lacking the welcome sweetness of others of its tribe. A somewhat stockier plant than *A. dracunculoides*, leaves glossier, glabrous and a deep green. Find it a really sunny corner away from the winds, then it will live up to its true perennial habit and not deteriorate too much in refinement of flavour and aroma.

maritima 8–20in

SEA WORMWOOD

A woody-based plant, found wild in Britain in the wild salt marshes, but the cultivated forms have downier and woollier leaves. The aroma is more pronounced than in many other artemisias, a mixture of anise and seaweed, perhaps. Small reddish flowers appear late in the summer, without any ray florets. Tolerant of, if not preferring, poor soils or path edges, it is a plant only to seek for collections.

pontica 12–20in

OLD WARRIOR, ROMAN WORMWOOD

A rhizomatous plant of upright habit, once introduced it will march on like the old soldier after whom it must have been named, over all surrounding

Artemisia abrotanum

territory. The foliage is beautifully soft and green to silver green, quite delightful after rain and strongly fragrant rather than aromatic, and sweetly refreshing. A good ground-cover plant without any doubt.

schmidtiana 8in

Densely tufted growth from a woody base, with silver white downy leaves, makes a rather distinctive plant. It seems to dislike the dampness more than most other artemisias, and sometimes does not survive winters for this reason. The foliage is highly aromatic but not one of the sweetest in fragrance. Altogether better in the form *A. s.* 'Nana'.

tridentata up to 6½ft

SAGE BRUSH

The little three-toothed wedge-shaped leaves crowded in clusters give this species an unusual appearance, but it is a memorable plant because the aroma is the sweetest and the most outstanding of all artemisias. After rain it scents the garden. Somewhat spreading in habit, the leaves are a not very exciting grey, but give it a sunny place beneath a window or by a terrace for sheer garden enjoyment.

BALSAMITA (*Compositae*)

Closely allied to Tanacetum, and although originally from the Orient, now naturalized in parts of southern Europe. The strong balsamic fragrance made it a favourite strewing herb, especially *B. major*, and Gararde said 'It groweth everywhere in gardens'. Today it has to be sought out in collections; this is a pity because both the following perennial plants are among the most fragrant of aromatic plants.

major (Often catalogued as *Tanacetum balsamita*) 2–3ft

COSTMARY, ALECOST, HERB SAINT MARY

Foliage is long, ovate, picot-edged, irregularly veined, pale green and glaucous; when pressed it is richly balsamic in fragrance, sweet and penetrating. Insignificant flowers, button-like and rayless, appear often reluctantly in July and August, and if the plant is in the shade, fail to appear. Fertile warm soils suit it best.

vulgaris 2–4ft

CAMPHOR PLANT

Although the simplest of plants, visually, its fragrance of leaf is exciting, richly and refreshingly redolent of camphor, and in drying it sweetens even more. The foliage is very like that of *B. major* but much greyer and more glaucous, and the flowers are small white daisies, with sparce ray florets. It requires full sunshine, a sheltered spot but where there is some moisture-retentive material at the roots, and it seems unable to tolerate neighbours about its shoulders!

CALAMINTHA *grandiflora* (*Labiatae*) 9–18in

CALAMINT

The soft green hairy foliage of calamint qualifies for inclusion in a collection of fragrant plants. It is highly aromatic when rubbed, varying from a pleasant minty aroma to something rather more pungent. Fragrance is enhanced by planting it in sunny positions, though the plant itself seems to enjoy equally being in partial shade. Any soil is acceptable to it provided it is not too moist. The flowers are pink in early summer, rising above the dainty mint-like growth, and will seed in most seasons. The plant is perennial.

FOENICULUM *vulgare* (*Umbelliferae*) 5–6ft

FENNEL

A plant usually grown in the herb or kitchen garden, but of great value in the decorative border for its filmy foliage making a delicate shower of thread-like leaves, and looking superb when spangled with raindrops. Sometimes richly brown-black when young and at the young tips, the foliage is strongly aromatic of anise. The flowers are typical of the family, yellow in high summer and not very pronounced, followed by strongly aromatic seed which showers down if not collected. True green and bronze (or black) forms are offered, sought by flower arrangers, and the Florence Fennel, *F. dulce* is the vegetable grown for its sweet and faintly aromatic swollen stem base. All like sunshine and a well-drained soil.

HELICHRYSUM (*Compositae*) (E)

Rather doubtfully hardy sub-shrubs, some providing attractive silver posy-like light foliage which is warmly aromatic. Given full sun, shelter from winds and good drainage they are reasonably hardy and those with aromatic foliage are natives of southern Europe.

plicatum 2–3ft

A dwarf, somewhat temperamental sub-shrub with long thin silver leaves. Their downiness is attractive but the aroma less interesting than that of *H. serotinum*, and rather stale after a moment of inhaling. But it makes a lovely ball of silver growth if it can be persuaded to stay long enough. It bears drab yellow flowers in July but these can well be sacrificed and the whole plant clipped back to refurbish itself with silver spikes in the late summer. Successful in containers where it can be kept away from draughts.

serotinum 3ft

CURRY PLANT

Dense-growing shrub-like perennial with a

persistent shrubby base, often cut right back in the winter by frost and damp. The needle-like metallic silver-grey leaves and wholly unattractive dirty-yellow bobble flowers in late June and July are all redolent of a scent suggestive of curry being cooked. Strictly a plant for the herb garden where its 'cooking smells' aroma seems appropriate, but on the other hand, useful in the decorative border for its burst of silver foliage which sparkles like tinsel when wet. The scent is carried a considerable distance when the sun shines, the warmth extracting it from the plant.

MELISSA *officinalis* (*Labiatae*) 2½ft

LEMON BALM, BALM

The Latin name *Melissa* is from the Greek for 'bee' and this attractive aromatic perennial has long been used to contain bees within a hive particularly when they were restless. The aroma is refreshing and strongly enriched with lemon. The plant can be used to good decorative effect in the flower borders, especially in its variegated form 'Variegata' and the more handsome 'Aurea', as it assumes a good rounded bush shape to the clump. The flowers are aromatic in the same way but are insignificant, deep in the axils of the oval rugose bright-green leaves, and are a washed-out mauve in July and August. Any well-drained soil in sunshine suits it but it dislikes windy corners and heavy soils.

MENTHA (*Labiatae*)

MINT

Many mint species and hybrids, both wild and cultivated, tend to cause confusion, which is complicated even further by the array of English names. But they have in common, the four-sided stem and paired leaves of labiatae, and to a greater or lesser degree are aromatic in all parts of the plant, some of them strongly fragrant. Their crawling underground stems need to be restrained unless the plants are required as ground cover. They will grow in all moderately fertile soils provided with some moisture-retentive material, although several like quite damp conditions, notably the water mint, *M. aquatica*. The flowers, in whorled spikes in summer, usually blue or mauve, are of secondary importance to the foliage. Pressure with the hand is sufficient to release the aroma in all the mints; there is no need for crushing.

aquatica 10in–3ft

WATER MINT

A vigorous invasive waterside plant, smelling strongly of peppermint, rather harsh.

× *gentilis* (*M. arvensis* × *M. spicata*) 1–3ft

GINGER MINT, SCOTCH MINT

Usually grown in its form 'Variegata' with lettuce-green shining foliage, the mid-rib and some veins picked out in yellow. Aromatic of dull spearmint, but spicier and more gingery when pressed. The type has darker bronzed leaves.

longifolia (*M. sylvestris*) 1½–4ft

HORSE MINT, LONG LEAVED MINT

Narrower leaves than most other species, downy beneath, and the stems usually greyish. A poor garden plant, musty or pungently minty in aroma.

× *piperita* (*M. aquatica* × *M. spicata*) 1½–3ft

PEPPERMINT

The source of the world's supply of peppermint oil and, as to be expected, strongly aromatic of peppermint. The stemless leaves are rather heart shaped, often swirling in some forms. M. × *p. citrata* is fragrant of orange or lemon, the most refreshing of all the mints in aroma; it is known variously as Eau de Cologne Mint, Orange Mint or Lemon Mint and is the Bergamot Mint of most herb catalogues. Curiously, it has the reputation of enhancing the fragrance of any plant near which it is cultivated. *M.* × *p. officinalis* is White Peppermint, so called because the stems are a jade green and the plant quite slender, quite distinct from the black stems of × *p. piperita*, the tougher Black Peppermint with darker foliage.

pulegium 3–8in

PENNYROYAL, PUDDING GRASS

A good mat-forming plant, used to make mint paths or mixed with grasses, a mint-scented lawn. Not to the forefront for sweet aroma, it has a more pungent pepperminty scent than most.

requienii 3–10in

CREME DE MENTHE MINT, CORSICAN MINT, SPANISH MINT

A tiny-leaved creeping plant that forms a pepperminted scented patch.

spicata (Syn. *M. viridis*) 1–3ft

SPEARMINT, GARDEN MINT

Leaves rather more sharply toothed than in most species and with the cleanest and most refreshing spearmint aroma.

suaveolens (formerly *M. rotundifolia*) 1½–2ft

APPLE MINT, EGYPTIAN MINT

As its old name implies, rather rounded of leaf, fragrant of mint and apples, or russet apples, and far more often cultivated in the form 'Variegata'. Here the pale green leaves are splashed with white or cream, or have decorative broad white margins, and sometimes sprays of totally albino style. The form is far more fruity in both smell and flavour.

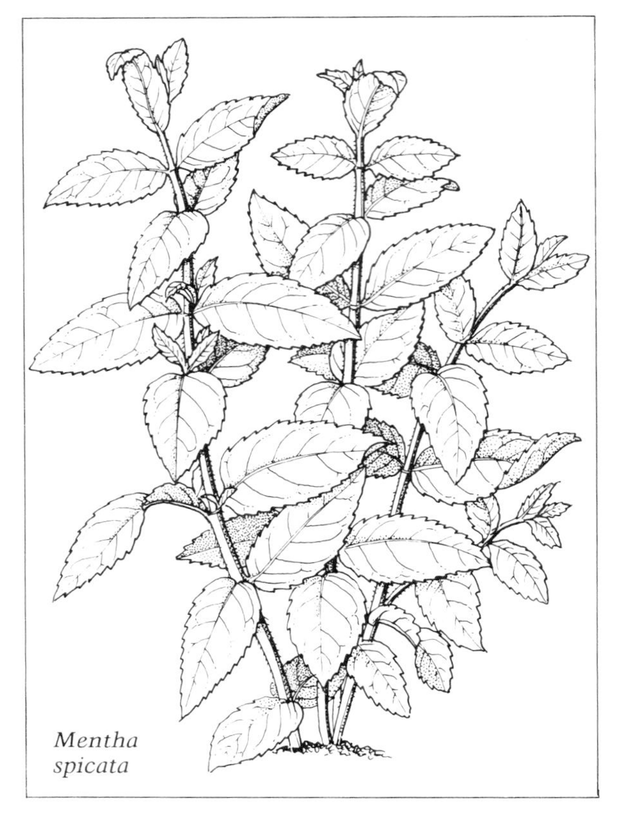
Mentha spicata

× villosa (*M. spicata × M. suaveolens*) 3¼–6½ft
BOWLES'S MINT, FRENCH MINT
The tallest-growing mint, with soft downy broad leaves which are much nested with veins; it is stemless and fresh with mint scent. Connoisseurs consider it to be superior for culinary use. Best for culinary purposes in the form *alopercuroides*, with a fruit mint aroma and flavour.

MYRRHIS *odorata* (*Umbelliferae*) 3–4ft
SWEET CICELY
Essentially a perennial for the herb garden, although the foliage is elaborately decorative and the stems die a beautiful burnished red, so that it may be used in the decorative border. The leaves are mid-green and delicately downy and lacy with characteristic flacks of creamy white. Tiny white flowers during May and June are followed by large seeds, sweet when they are green, then turning to black. The aroma comes from the foliage and is sweet like liquorice, but simultaneously suggests anise.

ORIGANUM (*Labiatae*)
MARJORAM
A group of perennials or sub-shrubs, three of which are commonly grown as herbs. Light sandy soil where the drainage is good and they can relax in the sun is best for all of them.

majorana (Syn. *Marjorana hortensis*) 1ft
KNOTTED MARJORAM, SWEET MARJORAM, GARDEN MARJORAM
A somewhat doubtfully hardy sub-shrub usually grown as an annual. Slender of growth, the plant bears flowers in little hop-like heads or blobs (or 'knots') white or dusty pink. They bloom in late summer and are fragrant. The greyish soft foliage is aromatic, and used as a flavouring, and is a sweeter version of the fragrance of thyme. The stems are rather brittle.

onites (Syn. *Marjorana onites*) 1ft
POT MARJORAM, FRENCH MARJORAM
Similar to *O. marjorana* but with rounder leaves and flower heads less globular in shape, it is hardier and sometimes erroneously called Winter Marjoram. Highly aromatic, more bitter in taste, it is a sprawling woody plant which appreciates plenty of room and a sheltered site, sending little puffs of growth upwards bearing white terminal heads.

vulgare 1½–2½ft
WILD MARJORAM, OREGANO
Clump forming and altogether pinker than the other species. Flower buds, bracts and some flowers are pinkish purple, flowers otherwise white or pale pink. Again, loving a sheltered site in well-drained soil where it can flop about. A good golden-leaved form is *M. v.* 'Aureum', the foliage marvellously golden and closely clustered when young, with a petal-like quality. A first-rate ground cover or edging plant. Fresh leaves will reappear if growth is cropped back. Flowers are of secondary importance on this plant; they are in heads of pink. There is a neater-growing form, *M. v.* 'Compactum', with very aromatic foliage and dwarf somewhat shrubby habit, bearing lilac-mauve flowers in late summer.

PIMPINELLA *anism* (*Umbelliferae*) 2ft
ANISE, GREEN ANISE
Grown in the herb garden in a light soil and sunny spot for its aromatic seeds, strongly redolent with the sharp sweetness of anise, this is a dainty white-flowered annual plant with fern-like leaves of bright green, earning it its vernacular name of Green Anise. The flowers are carried on many-rayed umbels in June and seed is ripe for collecting in September.

SATUREIA (*Labiatae*) (sometimes SATUREJA)
The savories of the herb garden are plants which so often go unrecognized. Winter Savory is especially useful as an edging or as a container plant.

hortensis 6–12in
SUMMER SAVORY

A little grown herb, mainly because the pungency of the leaves in flavour is too fierce for most palates, and it would probably not be considered truly aromatic. Grown as a half-hardy annual, it is slender and upright, bearing small washed-out lilac flowers and pale green leaves. The whole plant is rather soft and lax.

montana (Semi-E) 6–12in
WINTER SAVORY

A small hummock plant of sub-shrub habit remaining almost evergreen, certainly in southern counties. The growth is dark green, almost spiky, and the flowers lilac/white, fragrant in midsummer and best in the form 'Caerulea' where they are purple-blue in late summer. The leaves are pungent, and peppery used as a flavouring herb with much discretion.

repandra 4in
A mat-forming little plant with tiny dark green leaves, hugging the ground, and spangled with a profusion of small white flowers in June and July. The foliage is again pungent when bruised.

rupestris (Syn. (*Micromeria thymifolia*) 8–20in
Woody-based, erect-growing perennial with tiny glaucous elliptical leaves which are aromatic, rather more refreshingly so than in others of the genus, and less peppery. The small flowers in summer are purple and white, but of no great interest.

THYMUS (*Labiatae*) (E)
The thymes are a difficult genus to identify as they bear strong family resemblances. They enjoy a sunny well-drained spot and a light not-too-acid soil. They are good for planting on banks, in raised beds or troughs, or about the paving of terraces and patios. Tolerant of under-treading and clipping back, they only ask to be sheltered from bitter winds. There is a general tendency for some of the varieties to become bare in places, but when growing luxuriantly, they offer excellent ground cover and look delightful in little pools of pink flowers across a terrace. Some, noteably *T. erectus* and *T. fragrantissimum*, make unusual indoor pot plants.

azoricus 3in
Compact cushion-like growth with fine leaves set rather closely, like tufted pine needles. Fragrant of pine needles or to some people, orange peel, the flowers are pale washed-out purple, and there is a white-flowered form.

× *citriodorus* 9in
LEMON THYME

Rich green tiny leaves cover this sprawling plant, and its creamy white variegated form 'Silver Queen' is delightfully attractive, but, alas, not very hardy. (Not to be confused with *T. vulgaris* 'Silver Posie', *q. v.*) The leaf variegation in 'Silver Queen' is variable and the fresh shoot tips are pink. It reverts to the dark green of the form sometimes. One obvious distinguishing characteistic is the lemon scent of the leaves. *T.* × *citriodorus* and its forms are really best in the warmer places, but a plant kept under a cloche in winter will always produce propagating material. The tiny mauve flowers smother the plant in June and July.

erectus (Syn. *capnosus*)
An excellent little plant for growing in a trough or raised bed, resembling a miniature Irish yew in form. The foliage is tiny, grey-green, strongly fragrant of camphor and the tiny white flower heads appear all over the plant in June and July.

fragrantissimum
The leaves are wee and spatulate, and both upright-growing and more lax forms exist; in fact it seems to be a very variable plant. The balsam or orange scent on crushing is quite distinctive and, an interesting aroma to include in *pot pourri*. The little flowers are typical pink-lavender in June and July.

herba barona 2in
CARAWAY THYME

A loose mat of growth is formed as the stems creep about rooting as they go to gain a foothold. Aromatic minute hairy leaves emit a caraway scent and identify the plant as the one formerly used to rub over the baron of beef to impart flavour. The scent has been likened, also, to polish and Christmas trees, proving once again that perfumes mean all things to all people! The little heads of flowers are a deep pink in June and July. Not really reliably hardy and certainly not so in colder districts, it suffers the ravages of winter damp because of its down foliage, which sometimes looks as though a spider has enmeshed it in a filmy web. Grown in a pan in the alpine house, it is attractively maintained.

odoratissimus 6in
Greyish green foliage, tiny and mid-green, fragrant and fruity, but varying markedly according to the situation in which the plant is grown. The mauve flowers are earlier than most thymes, opening in May, and the habit is very floppy or prostrate.

serpyllum (of gardens Syn. *T. drucei*) 2in
WILD THYME, ENGLISH THYME

A native plant in Britain, creeping and carpet-rooting, which seems to have confusing catalogue names especially for some of its forms. The leaves are very tiny and hairy and a crawling single plant may run around over as much as 18in of territory. Flowers are lilac pink in midsummer and they and the leaves are fragrant of the true thyme scent. Within this 'true' scent there is a considerable range detectable, and some forms of *serpyllum* are quite distinguishable as lemon-scented or fruity. 'Coccinea', with bronze-green foliage and purple spotted flowers in July, is the least fragrant, but 'Lemon Curd' is richly and refreshingly lemon-scented; 'Pink Chintz', silvery and hairy of foliage, is fruity; 'Annie Hall' has smooth leaves and pale peachy pink flowers and a slight fruity fragrance. 'Nosegay' with small narrow leaves heavily scented of thyme has pretty mauve flowers. The form *T. s. minus* is one of the smallest-growing of all aromatic plants, with pink flowers and minute leaves comparable only to those of *Mentha requieni* in size, and difficult to distinguish from it by fragrance.

vulgaris 10in

A good hummock-forming plant with tiny dark green fragrant leaves, but usually cultivated in one of its coloured-leaved forms. *T. v.* 'Aureus' is the golden-leaved thyme, dense-growing and very decorative, the colour persisting well into the winter. The tiny flowers are rose-purple in midsummer and the whole plant is fragrant of balsam. 'Variegatus' has green and white leaves, pale lilac flowers in midsummer, and is similarly fragrant. 'Silver Posie' has silver variegations on the leaves and pale pink flowers in midsummer and a true thyme scent, which distinguishes it from *T. citriodorus* 'Silver Queen' which, whatever the foliage colour variegation, is aromatic of lemon. The culinary thyme.

TREES

Trees are the primary long-lived features of any garden, and once established lend an air of permanence and character. Since the 19th century when many introductions were made, in particular from North America, China and Japan, and because of the hybridizing that has ensued, gardeners today have an extensive selection of small and medium-sized trees. Any number of them bear scented flowers, to a greater or lesser degree, or have aromatic foliage, and are eminently suitable for planting in the small or medium-sized suburban garden.

When choosing trees to plant, their ultimate height and the space required upon maturity are vital considerations, and some serious thought has to be given to their suitability to the garden. Exposure, altitude and lack of light will all inhibit growth and shape, and the quality of soil controls and speed with which they become established. More than any other feature in the garden the trees ought to be considered and reconsidered, for once established they are more difficult to control or eradicate than any other kind of plant.

Many of them provide more than one season of interest, such as by decorative winter bark, brightly coloured leaves or fruits in autumn, in addition to their fragrant flowers. Some are only slightly scented in flower or leaf, and in addition to those described in the following pages there are also:

Atherosperma moschatum, with creamy flowers is highly fragrant and followed by muskily scented nuts in good summers. *Cercidophyllum japonicum* is grown mainly for the carnival dress it assumes in the autumn, and at the same time the burnt sugar scent of the carnival's toffee apples! The wood of the tender and rare Chinese *Cinnamonum glanduliferum*, provides the camphor of commerce and the leaves, when crushed, give off a clean crisp camphorous scent. The walnut *Juglans regia* has bright green sweetly scented leaves, and resinous silvered bark when young, and some of the willows, noteably *Salix pentandra* bear aromatic foliage. This one is known as the Bay-Leaved Willow because the foliage is aromatic of bay leaves, especially as it unfolds in spring, a pleasing scent which it retains on drying, making it a useful addition to *pot pourri*. Another delightfully fragrant willow is the Almond (Leaved) Willow, *S. triandra*, where the male catkins are strongly almond-scented in spring, pervading the surrounding air.

Of primary interest for aromatic foliage are the conifers, many of which now have good garden forms, and are interesting by virtue of variation in foliage colour, but which space does not allow us to describe in detail in this catalogue, Dwarf forms or 'miniature conifers' have gained in popularity, resulting in miniature and semi-dwarf plants, no longer trees, but useful for planting in heather gardens, rock gardens or trough gardens, or even for use in the cold greenhouse as specimens. These all retain their aromatic foliage.

A stroll in a pinetum after rain or on a warm sunny day brings almost a confusion of resinous scents – camphorous, turpentine-like, fruity, pungent – and it is only by rubbing or fondling the foliage that the individual scents are released. Our native juniper (*Juniperus communis*) is apple scented and remains so on drying. The Monterey Cypress (*Cupressus macrocarpa*), so popularly grown as a hedge, is lemon-scented and now superseded by the bigeneric hybrid Leyland Cypress (× *Cupressocyparis leylandii*) for screening and hedging, and reputed to be the fastest growing conifer in the British Isles . . . but alas, lacking the crisp fresh lemon fragrance of its parent, and producing a far less rewarding, woody aromatic smell. The other parent is the strongly turpentine-scented Nootka Cypress (*Chamaecyparis nootkatensis*) which carries the strong scent in all its forms.

Of the other cypresses, consider the Lawson's Cypress (*Chamaecyparis lawsoniana*), with forms ranging from large conical trees to columnar trees, in varying shades of green, grey or yellow, and from hedge plants to dwarf shrubs. Usually the aroma is resinous and it is supposed to remind some people of parsley. One of Robert Fortune's introductions in the 19th century was the Sawara Cypress (*Chamaecyparis pisifera*) which now has numerous cultivars, all with a bitter resinous smell to a greater or lesser degree. The Hinoki Cypress (*Chamaecyparis obtusa*), seen most frequently as some of the smallest known conifers, dubbed 'Tennisball Cypresses', carries its strong sweetly aromatic scent best in the larger forms. 'Crippsii' resembles encalyptus in scent, clear and sharply aromatic.

The Douglas Fir (*Pseudotsuga menziesii*), also called the Oregan Douglas Fir, is on maturity a stately conifer, perhaps emitting the strongest fruity rich resinous aroma of all conifers; but the glaucous forms fail to carry the scent, only giving it up when crushed, and then inferior and turpentine-like.

The thujas, or Arbor-Vitae, all have very pleasantly aromatic foliage. The Western Cedar (*Thuja plicata*) with rusty red-brown bark, is especially remarkable for its pineapple-like fragrance and the Japanese Arbor-Bitae (*Thuja standishii*) another of Fortune's introductions, resembles lemon verbena when rubbed. Alan Mitchell gives a far more realistic impression of the thuja's scents in *A Field Guide to the Trees of Britain and Northern Europe*, when he describes the scent of *T. standishii* as that of 'cheap sweets, lemony'.

Which of us would not recognize the smell of a Christmas Tree (*Picea abies*) immediately? When first brought indoors its spicy-musky scent is strongest because of the rise in temperature. The Colorado Spruce (*Picea pungens*), including its more frequently encountered glaucous cultivars, has a powerfully pungent aroma; the White Spruce (*Picea glauca*) emits a foetid odour when bruised, but this seems to be one of those scents which some people find more pleasing than others, some even saying it reminds them of molasses.

The native Scots Pine (*Pinus sylvestris*) sometimes still called Scots Fir, impregnates the surrounding air with the resinous smell of the exudation from its bark. Formerly cones were collected and used for their air-deodorizing quality. Most pines emit a clean resinous or camphorous smell and many cones are quite tacky because of the resin. The lovely long hanging ones of the Weymouth Pine (*Pinus strobus*) are often decorated with blobs of exuded, strongly aromatic resin.

In addition to those plants described in detail in the following pages, *Buxus sempervivens* (Common Box), and *Gleditschia triacanthos* (Honey Locust) may be tried, as may also *Malus* spp. (Flowering Crab), and *Pawlonia tomentosa.*

AESCULUS (*Hippocastanaceae*) (D)

These are perhaps the most flamboyant ornamental trees commonly grown in Britain. The Common Horse Chestnut (*A. hippocastanum*) introduced in the 17th century from Albania, needs no description. The enormous 'candles' of flower are worked over by bees for the only slightly fragrant nectar at the base of the flower, but one or two other species are more highly scented, in May. All are unselective of soil, provided it is deep enough. They are loveliest when grown as specimens where their round-headed form can develop uninhibited.

californica 40ft

The compound palmate leaves, typical of the genus, uphold the 'candles' in May. The inflorescence is white often tinged pink, and dense; this is the most fragrant species of the genus. The perfume is heavily sweet like that of the hyacinth.

× *carnea* (*A. hippocastanum* × *A. pavia*) 20–23ft

RED HORSE CHESTNUT

Frequently planted in association with the Common Horse Chestnut, but flowers marginally later and it is a tree of duller appearance and not as well formed. Often quite short-lived, it is really only grown for its red flowers. They continue to bloom into June and are deep rose-pink, blotched with yellow and crimson, and secrete a fragrant sticky nectar.

CLADASTRIS *lutea* (*Leguminosae*) (D) up to 33ft

YELLOW WOOD

A highly ornamental tree, little seen, and then probably as a large bush, generally similar to a robinia, with ash-like foliage. Both flower panicles and pinnate leaves are pendulous, the bark dark grey and, unlike the robinia, smooth. The white flowers in June and July appear only on established plants and are deliciously scented. I can never forget coming across this tree in the evening when the fragrance trailed across the garden. The foliage assumes a bright yellow in autumn. The tree has a strong preference for light soils, and accepts some shade.

CRATAEGUS (*Rosaceae*) (D)

HAWTHORN

A large genus of small tough trees, usually thorned and decked with frothy blossom in late May and early June. Few are sweetly scented; many are described variously as fishy, stale, or mouldy. Totally unselective of site, they are tolerant of town conditions, windy seaside gardens, breezy hills and even quite dark corners. They never fail to produce flowers and haws to follow. The leaves are lobed and sparsely toothed. A first-rate hedging plant, though if it is clipped, the flowers may be sacrificed.

crus-galli 22ft
COCKSPUR THORN

A small wide-spreading tree with long thorns on the shoots. The leaves are deeply lobed, dark green, glabrous beneath changing to a good scarlet-orange in the early autumn. Haws also are the same scarlet-orange and both these and the leaves persist, making it distinct among hawthorns, and another good tree for autumn colour. Its rather horizontal form begs to be put against a darker background to set it off. The flowers are cream, tinged with red in May and early June, and the fragrance is heavy but free from the fishy odour.

× *lavallei* (Syn. × *carrierei*) 18–20ft
Frequent as a street tree, with few thorns and dark shining leaves with a pink mid-rib; these are paler beneath and often fall late. The fruits are orange in mid-autumn and persist, making it a good little tree for late autumn colour. The creamy white and pleasantly fragrant flowers are devoid of the fishy undertones usually associated with hawthorn.

oxycantha (Syn. *oxycanthoides*) (*leavigata*) 19½ft
Frequently seen in town parks, especially in its double bright-red-flowering form 'Paul's Scarlet', it is happy on heavy soils and in shade. The lobes are less pronounced than in many hawthorns, flowers cream, except in the red-flowered forms when they are a deep scarlet red without any orange tones. In all of them the scent is sweet and fairly light and undoubtedly superior to that of the hedgerow hawthorn *C. monogyna*.

DRIMYS (*Winteraceae*) (E)
In a few favoured gardens large enough and sheltered enough to grow drimys as a specimen tree, it forms a most elegant towering plant of pyramidal shape. It is more generally grown with wall protection when some good humus-rich moisture-retentive material can be incorporated into the border.

lanceolata (Syn. *aromatica*) up to 16½ft
MOUNTAIN PEPPER

A small tree or large dense shrub with shining pale green or pinkish foliage, somewhat glaucous beneath. The June flowers are dioecious, held in clusters, cream stars backed by long tubes and waxy. Both bark and flowers are scented.

winteri up to 46ft but much less normally
WINTER'S BARK

This is grown as a large upright wall shrub generally in sheltered gardens in south-west England. I first saw it at Powerscourt, Eire, and subsequently failed to recognize the wall-grown plants elsewhere, for their lack of shape. The long narrow leaves are a good bright green with lighter prominent mid-rib, glaucous beneath, and more so in the somewhat hardier forms 'Latifolia' and 'Glauca'. Noble South American plants bearing rich waxy starry flowers, with a long tube behind in June, and richly fragrant in both bark and flower. Its English name, Winter's Bark, does not allude to a winter attractiveness, but to the fragrant bark that was brought home from the Magellan Straits in 1578 by a Captain Winter, in one of Drake's ships. The plant itself was not introduced into cultivation in this country until about 1827.

EUCALYPTUS (*Myrtaceae*) (E)
Where protection from prevailing winds can be provided some eucalypts are hardy in many areas of Britain, and certainly as far north as a line from the Cotswolds to Norfolk, and in the western coastal areas of northern England and Scotland. They grow quickly and are shallow-rooted, so need to be staked to avoid a certain gawkiness of form. Astonishingly beautiful pale bark and silver grey glaucous leaves demand to be planted against a dark backdrop where they can act as an eye-catcher. Tender species are attractive cultivated under glass as decorative pot plants. There is an old theory that in species of eucalyptus the quality of leaf scent is associated with certain patterns in the veining of the leaf.

citriodora 30ft height restricted as required
LEMON-SCENTED GUM

Grown under glass as a foliage pot plant for its lemon scented foliage, this is a tender plant with greyish-pink bark and long narrow leaves. The white flowers are fragrant in September and October, but it is really the leaf glands containing oil of citronella that provide the interest.

coccifera up to 26ft
FUNNEL-FRUITED GUM

A slow-growing tree, rarely seen, with attractive snaking habit and bark of grey, cream and brown. The young foliage is glaucous, later darkening and is very strongly aromatic and sharp. Flowers purple in October and November, only enjoyed when the plant is cultivated under glass and growth restricted to about a metre.

ficifolia restricted to 3¼ft

CRIMSON-FLOWERED EUCALUPTUS

Very tender, but cultivated under glass for its orange-scarlet fluffy flowers and broad long aromatic leaves. Often sold in florists' shops, but it makes a striking plant of lax habit when grown in the frost-free conservatory.

globosus up to 130ft restricted to 4ft

TASMANIAN BLUE GUM

Only for the very mildest localities, as a fairly quick growing tree of considerable elegance, it is cultivated as a dot plant in summer bedding schemes. Its branches spray when used in this way, and the blue sickle-shaped leaves resemble mobiles. The foliage is balsamic in fragrance, not as sharp as some other species, and is that cultivated for the extraction of oil of eucalyptus.

gunnii up to 100ft

CIDER GUM

One of the hardiest, and grown in secluded gardens in northern districts, and maintained at shrub-like proportions by frequent cutting back. The foliage then tends to remain rounded rather than adopting the pronounced sickle-shape. White fluffy scented flowers appear in July, the foliage is freshly aromatic; and the attractive peeling pinkish-orange bark leaves dove-grey beneath. In northern and eastern areas, the variety *whittingehamensis*, narrower in leaf, is more likely to be successful.

EUCHRYPHIA (*Eucryphiaceae*) (E and D)

These are ornamental trees that thrive best in a neutral-to-acid soil that does not dry out too rapidly, and in a position where there is some shade, especially at the roots. Suited to sheltered sites, they do not flower until established, although when cultivated in pots for patio or garden-room decoration they will flower when young.

glutinosa (Syn. *pinnatifolia*) (Semi-E or D) up to 19ft

A Chilean species tolerant of harder conditions than others, and well worth trying in the north, when good shelter can be provided. Unlike other species it is lime-tolerant when the soil is enriched with humus. The leaves are a lustrous bright green, the creamy flowers carried singly or in pairs in July and August. Resembling a single rose in form with rose-red anthers, they are delicately perfumed. The foliage adds to the autumn scene with good rich colours.

lucida (Syn. *billardieri*) (E) up to 30ft

A Tasmanian small tree, attaining less height in this country, and of slender elegant habit. The leaves are a deep lustrous green, pale beneath, and the cream flowers solitary and pendulous, beautifully fragrant in June and July. Usually seen as a large shrub which pervades the surrounding air with its hawthorn-like fragrance.

milliganii (Syn. *lucida milliganii*) (E) 10ft

Considered by some authorities to be but a dwarf form of *E. lucida*, the small shining dark green leaves and sticky flower buds are really quite distinctive. The cup-shaped flowers, creamy white and strongly fragrant of hawthorn, are produced freely even on fairly young plants in July and August. It is slow growing and compact of habit but looks well when cultivated as a pot plant for porch or patio decoration.

× *nymansensis 'Nymansay'* (E) up to 50ft

A lusty tree of great beauty, lime-tolerant and bearing an abundance of sweetly scented cup-shaped flowers in August and September. It was a selected seedling of a number raised in 1915 at Nymans, Sussex, hybrids of *E. glutinosa* × *E. cordifolia*. Another clone of the same parentage is *E. nymansensis* 'Mount Usher', the flowers of which are often double, but still carry the sweet fragrance.

FRAXINUS *ornus* (Oleaceae) (D) up to 60ft

MANNA ASH, FLOWERING ASH

Usually seen as a small tree in Britain, the manna ash belongs to the Oleaceae, which include so many sweetly scented plants, and is *the* ash to include in fragrant collections. It is rather dainty in appearance with a grey bark, and deep olive-green foliage with blunt-ended velvety grey-brown buds, unlike the common ash. In late May and early June the strongly fragrant flowers, almost sickly sweet and smelling of honey, are borne in dense terminal panicles. Just before flowering the buds are a brilliant green, opening to creamy white, and in common with the genus produce 'keys' as fruit, first green then brown. A fine specimen is planted on the lower terrace at Mapperton, Dorset, so that from the higher walk it is possible to inhale the scent in passing. A dried sugary exudation from the stem is the manna, or manna sugar formerly in the British Pharmacopoeia.

HALESIA (*Styracaceae*) (D)

SILVER BELL TREE

Except in exposed gardens and on chalky soil, the snowdrop tree offers a delightful white-flowered interest in early summer, when the flowers are suspended below the branches. For effect, it needs to be planted against a darker background.

carolina 15ft

SNOWDROP TREE

A large shrub sometimes attaining the habit of a small tree, it is also catalogued as *H. tetraptera*. Of somewhat spreading habit and with toothed leaves which break after flowering, the blossoms are delicately perfumed in May and are followed by interesting four-winged seeds.

monticola 15–20ft

More robust than *carolina* in size and form, *monticola* is more densely flowered and somewhat stronger in perfume. It makes a first-class specimen tree. Attractive in the form 'Rosea', with very pale pink flowers, sweetly fragrant.

LABURNUM (*Leguminosae*) (D)

GOLDEN RAIN

An astonishingly decorative small tree, enjoying suburban conditions, tolerant of light shade and quite satisfied with shallow or limey soils. Best planted for effect against a dark conifer or purple-leaved tree. The whole plant is poisonous, the seeds particularly so.

anagyroides (Syn. *vulgare*) 26ft

Very commonly planted in all parts of Britain and decked with pendulous racemes of butter-yellow flowers in late May and early June. Sweetly fragrant but less so than other species, unfortunately almost always transcended by the heady scent of the lilacs, which flower at the same time. *Laburnum anagyroides semperflorens* (catalogued as *L. a.* 'Autumnale') sometimes flowers again late in summer and autumn. All forms are rapid of early growth, but rather short-lived, and therefore a popular choice for the new garden.

alpinum 12ft

SCOTCH LABURNUM

Less commonly planted than *L. anagyroides*, with long slender pendulous racemes and well-spaced flowers blooming up to a month later. The fragrance is pronounced and there used to be a form *L. a. fragrans* which, as such, appears to have fallen out of cultivation.

× *watereri* (*L. alpina* × *L. anagyroides*) 20ft

The flower resembles *L. alpina*, opening only by mid-June, with long racemes, quite strongly perfumed. An abundance of flower drips from the tree; the dense racemes, all perfumed, are not generally followed by seed pods. It is now being more widely planted than *L. anagyroides*, and is safer where there are children because of the absence of seed. A particularly floriferous form is 'Vossii' with long drifting racemes of scented flowers, and a spreading form with somewhat pendulous branches is 'Alford's Weeping'.

Laburnum × watereri

LAURUS (*Lauraceae*) (E)

BAY TREE

Small trees from the Mediterranean regions, with aromatic leaves, bay trees are generally suited to moist soils in the milder areas. Enormous specimens of *Laurus nobilis* flourish behind the orangery at Margram Park, South Glamorgan, South Wales.

azorica 10ft

CANARY ISLAND LAUREL

Really suitable only for the mildest maritime areas of south-west England, and rarely planted, it forms a arge open shrub or small tree with good clean broadly elliptical leaves, which become narrower as he plant ages. They are richly aromatic. The twigs re downy, and both wood and bark are aromatic lso. There is a good plant in the Abbotsbury Gardens, Dorset.

nobilis up to 50ft

WEET BAY, BAY, POET'S LAUREL, BAY LAUREL

Rarely seen at its full height, it is quite frequently planted in the warmer areas and very commonly cultivated as a tub plant to decorate entrances, balonies and courtyards in towns. It lends itself to lipping, and thus retains its usefulness for cultiation in this form. Somewhat leathery elliptical eaves have a finely crinkled margin which should be ommended to the layman for identification as it losely resembles the Cherry Laurel, *Prunus usitanica*, which is poisonous. (A further identiying feature is that when the leaves are crushed in water, those of *Prunus lusitanica* will emit a bitter lmond or ratafia odour, while those of *L. nobilis* will not.) The bay of the kitchen, the leaves snap eadily giving off the easily recognized agreeable aroma. It flowers in April with fluffy cream nisexual and scented flowers which are sometimes ollowed by black berries. Again, wood and bark are romatic also. In coastal areas it is sometimes used s a hedging plant.

LIGUSTRUM (*Oleaceae*) (E or semi-E)

Quick-growing shrubs from the Far East, which make good round-headed plants with a neat outline. The upstanding panicles of flowers late in the summer add a fragrance to the shortening days that erhaps only the viburnums can rival. They are unselective of soil, but thrive best in an open position, ven as specimens, where the shape may be appreciated.

japonicum (E) 6½–13ft

APANESE PRIVET

Dense growing, introduced by Siebold along with several other fragrant evergreens, and bearing dark lustrous leaves, ovate and not unlike those of amellia, this is invaluable as a shelter or screening lant. Creamy white flowers are borne in important panicles late summer to autumn and are heavily fragrant, followed by black shining berries. *Ligustrum japonicum* 'Rotundifolium' is slower-growing with more rounded and much darker leaves, but the same heavily scented flowers. (see also Shrubs, page 000).

lucidum (Semi-E) 10–30ft

CHINESE OR WAX LEAF PRIVET

L. lucidum is usually seen as a shrub or small tree, but forms a good hemispherical head and is sometimes seen in city parks as a larger tree, or as a street tree more frequently in southern Europe. The leaves are broad lustrous green, the bark smooth, often streaked buff and fluted when grown to tree proportions. But the delight lies in the late-arriving branched loose panicles of flower. Buds appear to hesitate until August or September, then burst into sweetly and strongly scented creamy flowers which sometimes go on until Christmas. *Ligustrum lucidum* 'Excelsum Superbum' has leaves margined and speckled creamy yellow; those *L. l.* 'Tricolor' are tinged with pink when young, and are smaller with a definite border of white. Both forms carry the fragrant flowers of the type, in autumn.

MAGNOLIA (*Magnoliaceae*) D and E

Aromatic of bark, foliage and flower, several of the large race of magnolias are quite commonly grown. Tolerant of town conditions and really heavy 'unmanageable' clay soils, many flower early in the spring before the leaves appear; others bloom in summer. They are popular in newly laid-out gardens, because they have the habit of flowering when very young. Some are rarely cultivated, such as the tender evergreen *M. nitida*, seen only in south-west England, and which is reputed to have orange-aromatic seeds. Also fragrant are *M. fraseri*, faintly scented, *M. dawsoniana* with pale rose-pink flowers, and *M. salicifolia*, the Willow-Leaved Magnolia the flowers of which are of a fruity fragrance, and the leaves when bruised fragrant also.

denudata (D) 30ft

YULAN, LILY TREE

The fragrant white cup-shaped flowers with broad fleshy petals open early in the spring. It makes a small spreading tree, and is especially attractive in its cultivar 'Purple Eye' which, as the name suggests, has purple marking deep at the heart of the fragrant bloom.

grandiflora (E) 33ft

LAUREL MAGNOLIA, BULL BAY

Perhaps seen most frequently as a luxuriant wall shrub, this makes a magnificent round-headed tree with large glossy elliptical leaves, when grown in a free-standing position. Choose a sunny sheltered site, where space permits, if it is to be grown in this way. The large waxy flowers are cream in colour and bloom throughout the summer and early autumn. Of special note are the cultivars 'Exmouth' with very fragrant lemon-scented flowers, and 'Goliath' with fragrant and very large flowers with undulating petals.

sinensis (D) 12ft

In bloom during late May and June, the remarkably attractive goblet-shaped flowers, pure white with a crimson cone within, hanging like lanterns below the branches, emit a heavy sweet lemon fragrance. A large spreading shrub, with large rather bright green leaves.

× *soulangiana* (D) 10–30ft

Tolerant of city conditions, and handsomely planted as a street tree in Edgbaston, Birmingham where it looks really splendid. Tolerant too of heavy clay soil, × *soulangeana* and its cultivars are commonly grown, and all have the rewarding habit of flowering when young. Gently fragrant white flowers tinted purple at the base appear in early April. There are several good cultivars: 'Alba Superba', flowering earlier than the type; 'Alexandrina'; 'Amabilis'; and 'Rustic Rubra'.

stellata (D) 10ft

A spreading shrub, and another with the bonus of flowering when young, it is attractive during the winter for its felted buds which open into slightly fragrant flowers with flaring white strap-shaped petals, giving the whole plant a very decorative air. The flowers appear in March and April before the leaves, and its most outstanding form is 'Water Lily'.

× *thompsoniana* (*M. tripetala* × *M. virginiana*) (D) 10ft

A large wide-spreading shrub, blooming mainly in July, but intermittently during the summer months. The strongly scented flowers appear even on young plants.

virginiana (semi-E) 6–15ft

SWAMP BAY

One of the first magnolias along with *M. grandiflora* ever to be grown in England and now of old cultivation, the glossy green leaves are large and somewhat turquoise beneath. Flowers are globular, creamy white and delightfully fragrant from June and September.

× *watsonii* (D) 8–26ft

Although not often encountered, and requiring a lime-free soil, × *watsonii* has perhaps the most refreshingly fragrant flowers of all the magnolias. It seems generally to be considered lacking in constitution, but really has a place in the fragrant garden if it can be encouraged to establishe itself. It flowers in June, when quite young; the blooms ar creamy white with deep rose anthers.

wilsonii (D) 6–15ft

A large wide-spreading shrub for a shaded shrub border. The exquisite white flowers with crimson central cone, unlike those of most magnolias, hang from the branches in June, and are sweetly scented

PHILLYREA (*Oleaceae*) (E)

A small genus of handsome evergreens widely planted in the past as a garden tree and as a hedge plant and for topiary work. Seemingly, they are neglected today, and not seen very often. They thrive in any fertile soil that is properly drained and prefer a position in which they get their share of the sunshine.

angustifolia 5–10ft

Compact of growth with dark, thick rather glabrous leaves and small cream-green flowers in cluster among them. The flowers carry a delicate swee perfume rather reminiscent of osmanthus, in late May, and are followed by black fruits. Tolerant o clipping, it can be used in stark formal settings, o even as a hedge, but then the branches of scente flowers are forfeited.

latifolia 16½–30ft

A small tree, strongly resembling a smaller versio of the holm oak and useful in the same kind o positions. Small glossy green leaves are its main at traction; the rather insignificant flowers are cream white in early summer, but give a very swee perfume.

POPULUS (*Salicaceae*) (D)

The catkin-bearing balsam poplars can be planted i all areas, the large-growing ones useful as a quickl attained light shelter belt. Autumn colour is good i them all, often contrasting well with the whit lower surface of the leaves. Their chief delight is th lingering way in which the buds open in May, emit ting a powerful fragrance of balsam, detectable man yards away.

balsamifera (Syn. *B. tacamahaca*) to 80f

BALSAM POPLAR, EASTERN BALSAM POPLAR

As the large sticky buds open in the spring, a stron balsamic aroma is emitted from the unfoldin leaves. This is a strong-growing tree from the easter regions of the North American continent with goo clean tough foliage, a rather oily yellowish whit beneath, as with all balsam poplars. A tree really fo an extensive garden because of its ultimate heigh and its habit of suckering to produce a veritable poc of growth beneath it. Best on a rich moist soil.

× candicans (*P. balsamifera* × *P. trichocarpa*) 66ft
ONTARIO POPLAR
Again, the broad green leaves are whitish yellow beneath and strongly balsam-scented when unfolding. Its form 'Aurora' is the only variegated-leaved poplar, the large green leaves heavily blotched cream and sometimes pink, and the foliage remains very pale throughout the summer and to a certain extent is scented also. An increasingly widely planted form, highly ornamental (occasionally listed as *P.* × *gileadensis* 'Aurora').

simonii 33ft
Earlier to flush than the other balsam poplars, it is a pretty tree from China. It has red-brown twigs and the same creamy under-surface to the diamond-shaped leaves. It is good as a hedge plant or dividing screen in the form 'Fastigiata'.

szecnuanica 100ft
Leaves large in proportion to the growth with a pronounced crimson mid-rib, and again the glistening creamy lower surface to the leaves. Even larger foliage in the form 'Tibetica'.

trichocarpa 100ft
BLACK COTTONWOOD
Slightly more upswept in form, with attractive clean peeling bark when young, the same balsamic scent from the buds and young foliage is carried for some distance on the air. Quick-growing, suggesting use as a good screening tree, and again with the pale undersides to the leaves and a tendency to sucker for some distance around the bole.

PTELEA *trifoliata* (*Rutaceae*) (D) 10–25ft
HOP TREE
A plant from Mexico, where it earned the name of Stinking Ashwood, for its aromatic leaves, either liked or hated. Perhaps redolent of hops, the trifoliate leaves, in which the central one is three times the length of the lateral ones, are pricked with oil glands, which need to be bruised to give off their aroma. The flowers are highly fragrant, small and yellowish in June, followed by persistent winged fruit rather like those of elm. In the form 'Aurea' the leaves are butter-yellow when young, later turning to a pale green. A tree for a deep moisture-retentive soil, enjoying some shade, and growing well in Cumbria in the herb garden at Acorn Bank, near Penrith.

PTEROSTYRAX hispida (*Styraceae*) (D) 15ft
A native of China and Japan, hardy and unselective of soil, except that it displays an aversion to shallow chalks, this small tree is not seen very often. There is a lovely specimen growing in the white garden at Cranborne Manor, Dorset, where in June and early July the pendulous racemes of creamy flowers hang below the leaves. Each flower resembles a tiny tassel, and the leaves are rounded or oval, toothed and pale beneath. Curious ribbed bobbin-like fruits follow. The flowers are sweetly scented, especially following rain, with a truly 'flowery' fragrance.

ROBINIA (*Leguminosae*) (D)
Fast-growing, rather decorative trees and shrubs with pinnate leaves and pendulous racemes of pea-like flowers. Hardy and tolerant of town conditions, making a good street tree, they seem happy on most fertile soils, except the very heavy ones. Damp and windy sites ought to be avoided. Not often planted in the north of England. The barks are elaborately fissured, making the trees worthy of specimen planting.

pseudoacacia 60–90ft
FALSE ACACIA, ACACIA TREE, BLACK LOCUST
Native of the eastern regions of North America, and quite commonly seen in southern England planted on sandy soils, the white flowers hang in dangling racemes shaking fragrance onto the air. They are followed by pea-like pods which often persist into the winter. The bark is particularly attractive and the leaves dark green on purplish stalks. There is a fastigiate form 'Fastigiata' and a lovely golden-leaved form 'Frisia' affording good autumn colour, when it totally assumes a slightly orange shade in foliage.

STEWARTIA (*Theaceae*) (D)
Where they are established the stewartias can make arresting small trees, when in flower. The enticing fragrance envelopes them in sweetness, and once encountered in a damp peaty woodland garden, they will not be forgotten. The individual flowers are fleeting, but a long succession is sustained so that there are usually fallen blossoms about their feet. Good autumn colour follows – such a pity that they are only for the milder counties.

malacodendron 10ft
Rare in cultivation, although available, this is the species that earned the genus its name from Catsby when it flowered first in his garden at Fulham in May 1742. John Stuart, Earl of Bute, was being commemorated, and the plant had arrived from Virginia. The large white flowers are borne in considerable profusion in May and have deep purple stamens and indigo anthers. A rich heavy perfume pervades the branches when the plant is in flower.

serrata 30ft
Remarkable for its autumnal effect, the summer foliage of deep green contrasts well with the profuse

white flowers, shaded deep crimson at the throat. A strong rich perfume is emitted when they bloom in June.

sinensis 30ft

Perhaps the most popular stewartia seen in cultivation and notable for its rich autumn colour and very attractive flaking bark. As if this display were not sufficiently effusive, the white flowers are carried in great numbers in June, and are heavily perfumed, and cup-shaped, less starry than those of the foregoing species.

TILIA (*Tiliaceae*) (D)

LIME TREE, LINDEN

Widely planted as town and street trees, though *Tilia × europaea*, the Common Lime Tree, frequently attains too large a size for the situation, resulting in ugly mutilation. Eminently suitable for large garden or park planting where it can develop into an elegant and graceful tree, sometimes it is planted for pleaching, when the scented flowers are sacrificed. The Common Lime is always easily recognized by its asymmetrical leaves and habit of suckering prolifically. It is too large for general garden planting; some of the smaller forms are preferable.

× euchlora (*T. cordata × T. dasystyla*) 60ft

CAUCASIAN LIME

A mushroom-shaped head grows above a good silver-grey bole, with glossy 'lime green' foliage when young, the underside noteably paler. It is planted as a street tree in Cambridge. The honey-scented flowers dangle from the finger-shaped bracts in June and July, and are said to have a narcotic effect on bees.

oliveri 66ft

OLIVER'S LIME

An infrequently planted tree, from China, but very elegant with smooth pale fresh green foliage almost metallic silver beneath. The flowers are honey scented in July, shaking their perfume on to the breeze, as with all lime trees, and dangling from a particularly large green bract.

petiolaris 100ft

WEEPING SILVER LIME, SILVER PENDENT LIME

A large round-headed tree, the branches sweeping downwards very gracefully. The leaves are dark green, silvery tomentose beneath and rather more strongly toothed than many limes. Flowers bloom in July and are heavily honey-scented and, again, narcotic to bees.

FLOWERING PLANTS

The flower garden provides the calendar effect, as far as colour is concerned, especially because generous planting is required. A single plant rarely makes an effective display; bold splashes or areas of colour are far better. Consequently most of the plants included here are for summer garden effect, though there are winter-flowering herbaceous perennials, such as the bergenias. The summer flowering season can be prolonged a little, by careful selection, but for true border effect it is always better to settle for the high summer display. An ever-blooming border or island bed is an impossibility.

The range of fragrant flowering perennials is not very extensive, but it is of these plants that William Robinson said, 'A man who makes a garden should have a heart for plants that have the gift of sweetness as well as beauty of form.'

Other plants to include here would be *Acorus calamus* for its fragrant roots and foliage scented of tangerine, *Crambe cordifolia* for its huge flowering spike that in the twilight can take on the effect of a frosty Christmas tree across the garden. Then there are iberis, hemerocallis, onosma, some of the salvias, *Romneya coulteri* and saponaria, whose fragrance deepens as it fades.

ALYSSUM *Maritimum* (*Cruciferae*) 3in

When grown as a half-hardy annual, it is probably the most universal edging plant for bedding schemes, but useful also to naturalize in gravel about courtyards and parking areas. It seeds itself in the milder periods and localities, filling corners, old brickwork and all sorts of spots in which it could not otherwise be persuaded to grow! It forms tiny blobs of growth smothered in small white, typically cruciform flowers all summer, with the refreshingly summer smell of new mown hay. Garden forms are 'Little Dorrit', an old favourite, and white-flowered; coloured flowered kinds are available but they have forfeited their perfume.

BERGENIA (*Saxifragaceae*)

ELEPHANT EAR, PIG SQUEAK

Perennials hailing from the cold mountainous regions of Asia, the bergenias provide winter and early spring interest in the gardens of Britain. Grow them in a spot where they will be sheltered from strong cold winds to encourage early flowering, and avoid the drip of trees, although they are shade-tolerant. It seems that winter success has its beginnings in some summer sunshine, and good moisture-retentive soil.

cordifolia 1½ft

A Siberian plant, with tough rounded large leaves crinkled and somewhat puckered, not unlike those of the water lily. Thick stems bear short spikes of pale to deep rose-pink flowers in panicles. They are very sweetly scented, and more so on being taken indoors. *Bergenia cordifolia purpurea* has its leaves flushed a metallic bronze-purple, particularly in winter, and makes useful winter colour at ground level, and an attractive foil for the pink flowers.

crassifolia 1ft

A fleshy leaved plant from Siberia, with a thick tough rootstock, thick stems and branching panicles of flowers. The shape of the leaves is somewhat variable on the same plant, from cordate to round, and of a shining bright green. Flowers are rose purple, and sweetly scented in winter.

× *schmidtii (B. ciliata × B. crassifolia)* 1ft

Again the leaves vary a little in shape on the same plant, stems are thick, with rose-pink flowers in a branched panicle. Often grown as *B. crassifolia*, and spanning the same flowering period, often blooming first in the last autumn and going on until March, varying with the season.

× *smithii (B. cordifolia × B. purpurascens)* 1–1½ft

Again, winter-flowering, and resembling *B. cordifolia*, with marked burnishing of the leaves and dark margins often rosy red. Flowers are held in rather one-sided branched panicles, displaying a range of colour in the cultivars. *Bergenia s.* 'Pugsley's Purple', fuchsia purple; *B. s.* 'Margery Fish', glowing pink; *B. s.* 'Bressingham Bountiful', cyclamen pink, are all slightly fragrant, more so on being taken indoors.

CENTAUREA *moschata (Syn. C. odorata) (Compositae)* 2ft

SWEET SULTAN

A rich musk-like, almost oriental, perfume is lodged with this single annual species of an otherwise large and scentless genus. The flowers resemble large cornflower heads in varying shades of mauve, pink, yellow and white and are in bloom from a spring sowing *in situ*, in July and go on until October.

CHEIRANTHUS (*Cruciferae*)

WALLFLOWER

There are few plants that adapt so readily to almost any situation, tolerant, for the season at least, of the most inhospitable conditions, though obviously showing their appreciation of good cultivation.

cheiri 1½–2ft

The type is single-flowered but cultivation has produced numerous forms embracing a whole arc of flower colour from yellow to deep red and back to pink, lilac and white, with several mixtures. A delightful range of pastel-flowered kinds is available, slightly more compact in habit and with them all the double-flowered ones are more exquisitely scented than the single flowers. The richness of scent is a feature of the spring garden, when it is often carried on the breeze, so profusely is it produced. *Cheiranthus cheiri* 'Harpur Crewe' is a very old fully double-flowered form, the flowers yellow, borne in small rounded spires, and very fragrant. The named cultivars are usually grown as biennials for spring bedding schemes, window boxes, tubs and pots, but in many localities they survive as perennials, when they grow to their full height, of perhaps 2–2½ft.

mutabilis 2–3ft

A plant whose flowers give a piebald effect as they mature, and which comes from Grand Canary and Madeira. Erroneously described as a synonym of *C. semperflorens*, the flowers are pale yellow at first, opening to buff-brown and ageing to purple, so that all stages of the transformation are revealed on the same flower head – or certainly on the same plant. The leaves are narrow, mid-green and form a basal clump of foliage. A plant for a mild sunny border edge in the more favoured counties, and for April–May effect.

semperflorens 2–3ft

A tender sub-shrub for a very sheltered site or for growing under glass in a cold house or garden room, when it will make a floriferous plant. Strongly scented flowers on domed flower spikes are lilac and white and are produced at all times of the year., but if the plant is shorn, it responds with renewed vigour a few weeks later. *Cheiranthus s.* 'Constant Cheer' is a hybrid with *Erysimum × allionii* and has dusky purple-red flowers.

CONVALLARIA *majalis (Liliaceae)* 6in

LILY-OF-THE-VALLEY

One of the loveliest of our native perennial flowers, indigenous to almost all regions of Europe, where it thrives in shaded woodland. Introduce it into the garden in low-lying shaded spots, north-facing banks or beneath trees and shrubs where it can enjoy diffused light. It is happy in any good loam though in nature it shows a predilection for calcareous soil. The main attraction is abundant scent from the dangling white bells throughout May and June. Each flower is green in bud and turns to hang its head as it opens. Leaves are broad linear in pairs, upright all season. By August or September bright vermillion fruits ripen, perhaps only several to each stem. The perfume, strong and very sweet, remains for the life of the flower, even when picked and taken indoors or tucked into a bridal bouquet. Cultivated in pots, lily-of-the-valley can be slightly forced, or grown indoors. Specially retarded crowns are available.

DIANTHUS (*Caryophyllaceae*)

CARNATION, PINK

A large and diverse genus that is among the oldest of scented plants in cultivation, always with grass-like glaucous leaves (except in a very few instances) of tufted habit, and jointed stems, also often glaucous. Only a cursory survey of the genus is possible here because the plants are legion, and the interrelationships complicated. The predominant factor has always remained the deep sweet fragrance with stronger, or more subtle, clove overtones. Broadly, there are three main groups, carnations, pinks and dianthus species proper. Many, the carnations and pinks in particlar, are heavily fragrant with a unique spiced clove-like perfume that has been described innumerable times in the past by generations of writers.

To the Greeks the carnation was the Flower of Jove, and it was used in forming garlands or coronets, hence 'coronation' and the corruption 'carnation'. For centuries grown and described as gillyflowers, not, as erroneously supposed, a corruption of 'July flower' but from the Arabic *quaranful* – a clove, descriptive of the scent of the flower. The name was perpetuated in the Greek *karyophillon*, and the Latin *caryophyllus*. So, we find a universal name perpetuated around the very scent of the flower. The spiciness rests also in the flavour of the flower head; the Tudors mulled wine by steeping blooms in it and hence the old name of Sops in Wine. Gerarde wrote: 'The conserve made of floures of the Clove Gilliflower and sugar, is exceeding cordiall, and wonderfully above measure doth comfort the heart, being eaten now and then.'

The name 'gillyflower' seems to carry considerable old-world sentiment, always referring to sweetly scented flowers. There were Clove Gillyflowers (carnations and pinks), Stock Gillyflowers (Matthiola), Wall Gillyflowers (*Cheiranthus*) and Queen Gillyflowers (*Hesperis matrionalis*).

The majority of the species of dianthus are native to the Balkans and Middle East, North Africa, and the Iberian Peninsular, and three are native to Britain. Happiest on chalky soils, they range from border plants to rock garden inhabitants and many, dodgy of cultivation, are best when grown in pots under glass.

alpinus 3in

ALPINE PINK

The glaucous growth of the rest of the genus gives way in this little plant to glossy dark green leaves, hailing from the Eastern Alps of Yugoslavia and Austria. Flat single pale-rose-pink flowers spread their petals. A pale eye is intensified by a ring of purple spots. Most alpine species are devoid of scent, wasted on mountain winds, but this flower has a sweet fragrance.

barbatus 9in–2ft

SWEET WILLIAM

Broad flattened heads posied by a green barb or beard are the distinguishing features of this species, setting it apart from the remainder of the tribe. Late in the 16th century, it enjoyed the name of London Tufties, on account of this green ruff. Usually cultivated as a biennial in colder areas, it is a short-lived perennial elsewhere, that sets seed readily. But when the flower stalks are removed immediately the blooms fade the plants will thicken up and live longer.

The older ones were compact of stature, and they were among the first plants to be cultivated decoratively in English gardens, Gerarde says: '[They] are not used either in meat or medicine, but are esteemd for their beauty to deck up gardens, the bosoms of the beautiful, garlands and crowns for pleasures.'

In general, the auricula-eyed forms are most heavily scented, but all have a sweeter, more velvety and less clove-toned perfume than their relatives, the carnations and pinks. Modern cultivars include double- and semi-double-flowered forms in a colour selection from wine purple to pink and white. Some are giants with mopheads of combined colours, often white with a painted bull's eye or auricula fashion colour laid on. The annual sorts, (treated as half-hardy annuals) are often self-coloured, but all have the rich fragrance, especially after rain. All flower in June and July.

Immediately after World War I, Montague Allwood made crosses between *D. barbatus* and *D.* × *allwoodii*; the resulting progeny was the now well-known Sweet Wivelsfield strain. Perhaps the best is still 'Red Bedder', a double scarlet-flowered form, blooming from June to October and strongly scented like the Sweet William (see also *D. superbus*, below).

caryophyllus 1–1½ft

CARNATION

Space forbids the telling of the whole story of the carnation. The species itself is a southern European from Spain to the Balkans and was clearly described in 300 BC. Much development has been carried out, starting mainly in the 19th century in the United States of America, and although briefly its popularity flagged in Britain in the middle of that century, an enormous amount of work has been accomplished during the last 70 years. It tends to be a connoisseur's flower, grown lovingly by specialists, and if ever there was an elite race of modern-day florists, it is the dedicated amateurs who fill their greenhouses with the superbly fragrant perpetual-flowered carnations, and those that persevere with the widely varying, but often short-lived, border carnations.

The species itself is characterized by smooth slender leaves and spicily scented flowers with notched petals, blooming mainly in July and August.

Dianthus caryophyllus

Many border carnations shy away from winter dampness, though, certainly in the south, their foliage makes bold turquoise-grey tufts of growth in the winter garden, and are therefore often cultivated in pots in the conservatory or cold greenhouse. Their clove perfume is strong and spicy. On the other hand, the Perpetual Flowering Carnation, or Tree Carnation, often less scented, demands some form of heat under glass to maintain a succession of flowers in the winter months. These are the carnations of the florists, available all the year around. (Of these each enthusiast will have his favourite for perfume; not all are richly endowed, but 'Clayton's White', 'Edward Allwood' (rose pink), 'Fragrant Ann' (white) and 'Royal Crimson' are among the strongest scented.)

Border carnations notable for their scent are: 'Fenbow's Nutmeg Clove', a truly old-world plant resurrected in recent years and brought back into cultivation for its strong nutmeg scent; 'King of the Cloves', crimson, spicy; 'Oakfield Clove', an old variety of glowing red and particularly richly clove scented; 'Scarlet Fragrance', bright red, and both sweet and spicy at one and the same time; 'Yellow Clove', with lemon yellow blooms, a rare colour in this genus, to combine with scent. Personal selections can be made from the numberless varieties offered. All have clove perfume to a marked degree.

There is a strain intermediate between these two types, known as cottage carnations, and they are seemingly an improvement upon the garden qualities of border carnations. Their flowering period is extended to September and their less wavering, shorter stems are more garden-worthy.

gratianopolitanus (Syn. D. caisius) 4–8in

CHEDDAR PINK

A British native, confined to the limestone cliffs of Chedder Gorge, Somerset, but available in the cultivated form. Tufts of grey foliage and fringed rose-pink sweetly fragrant flowers are attractive in June and July. The double-flowered forms are superior and more fragrant. Cultivars to try are: 'Prichard's Variety', rose pink; 'F. C. Stern', rose red; 'Isolde', white flushed pink, and double; and 'Little Jock', pink, semi-double.

plumarius 9in

PINK

It is believed that the various garden pinks have been derived from a series of crosses from *D. plumarius* which eventually gave rise to the race known as *D.* × *allwoodii*, which in turn led to the glorious colour and form range now available as 'pinks'.

Their number is legion, their faces painted or pale, they often bloom all season or keep peeping out. They are hardy everywhere, and above all delightfully scented. Is it any wonder that they are among the most popular plants for the summer scented garden?

The classification comes first from the way in which the colour is displayed on the petals: selfs, bi-colors, laced or fancy. Beyond that, classification depends upon parentage, but broadly there are several popularly grown groups.

Garden Pinks These are mainly 19th century in origin, with large flowers, often loosely held in a falsely inflated and totally inadequate calyx, so that it often splits. They flower in June only. Of these, the universally known and heavily scented 'Mrs Sinkins' is an example. Raised in the 1870s in the garden of a workhouse, by the Master of the Slough Poor Law Institution and named in honour of his wife, the white-flowered 'Mrs Sinkins' has been perpetuated in the coat-of-arms of that town. 'Dusky', 'Ice Queen', 'White Ladies', 'Inchmery' (which does not split its calyx) 'Earl of Essex', 'Sam Barlow' – little seen now but with an intense clove perfume, and 'Paddington' raised in the nursery of Thomas Hogg and very richly scented, are all examples of this type of pink.

Allwoodii Pinks These have been raised during and since the 1920s from crosses including the highly fragrant garden pink, 'Old Fringed'. The results are slightly more squat plants, hardy, and flowering several times in the season. Such pinks as the fragrant 'Monty', which is rose pink with a chocolate-brown eye, and a string of others all bearing Christian names, which before the World War II represented suspect familiarity! 'Doris', soft pink, 'Isobel', cherry-red, 'Vera', pale pink with a red eye, 'Ian', rich crimson, 'Alice', white with a red eye, and 'Winston', with outstanding clove perfume and bright crimson flowers.

London Pinks The flowers of this group, raised in the 1950s by F. R. McQuown, with × *allwoodii* and Garden Pinks in their parentage, have laced flowers, that is, with a loop of colour, or an edging right round the petal, of the same colour as the eye. Generally the perfume is good, richly clove, the stems just a little longer than most other pinks – and the names are prefixed 'London' as a rule: 'London Superb', semi-double with a pale pink ground laced in purple; and 'London Poppet', white ground laced in ruby red, are two good ones.

Such laced pinks generally display an old-world fascination, and there are others, some raised by the Allwoods and some probably surviving from the fanciers of Lancashire and Scotland during the last century, all of which carry the deep spicy clove fragrance.

Hybrid Alpine Pinks The name may seem confusing, but arises because among their parents, grandparents, uncles and aunties *D. alpinus* finds a place. Various crosses and recrosses in this group have all resulted in fragrant blooms, because scent was no hit-and-miss affair. When both parents carry fragrance the hybrid is bound to do so, and as the four or five species used in raising this race of pinks are all fragrant, the progeny provides some interesting results. The tiny 'Miss Sinkins', a miniature of her namesake, has a delicious perfume and the same fringed white petals. 'Nyewood Cream' is similar with deep cream flowers exquisitely fragrant, and 'Elizabeth', a smudgy pink with brown eye, spends all its days scenting the air and is a delightful plant for a trough garden near a patio. Another dusky pink of this group is 'Grace Mather', also useful in the trough garden for its strong scent. The clove perfume has been retained in 'Mars', a red gem with foliage somewhat more silvery than that of the others, and crimson flowers.

superbus 1ft

FRINGED PINK, SWEET JOHN

At home in the lower slopes of the mountainous regions of Southern Europe and of Asia, this is a rather lax plant lacking the pert little tufts of growth common to so many other dianthus. The flowers are pale lavender with a green eye, and a sweet fragrance less rich and spicy than one expects from a dianthus. Grown in a sheltered spot it may well flower on until the shortest days of the year – or it can be cultivated in a pot for conservatory scent during the autumn and winter. Parkinson gave it the same Sweet John, and Allwoods crossed it with Sweet Wivelsfield, to produce the popular *D.* 'Loveliness'. This retains the late-flowering characteristic, the green eye, but displays a colour range from deep red through lavenders to white. As if to prove how happy the family is to interbreed 'Loveliness' itself was crossed with its parent, 'Sweet Wivelsfield', to produce *D.* 'Sweetness', with powerful scent and an even wider range of colour.

DICTAMNUS *albus (D. fraxinella)* *(Rutaceae)* 1½–3ft

BURNING BUSH

A perennial clump-forming plant with woody rootstock, and plenteous lanceolate leaves which are glandular and aromatic of citron especially in hot weather. A volatile oil is exhaled which is reputed to be perceptible after dark, and which is inflammable. When rubbed the foliage scent is balsamic. A profusion of stout stems is produced with white flamboyant flowers, the petals like a fan with protruding anthers at the base. There is a dull purple-pink form *purpureus* with darker feathering on the petals. Tolerant of partial shade, it is at its best in full sunshine in a good fertile loam.

ERYSIMUM (*Cruciferae*)

Strongly resembling the wallflower, (*Cheiranthus*), with which they are much confused, these plants are generally daintier of growth. Foliage is clean and linear as in the wall-flower, and some species bear the same honeyed fragrance of flowers; others, not often grown, are sulphurous.

alpinum (Syn. *Cheiranthus alpinus* of gardens) 4–6in

A hummock-forming habit, the outer growth flowing over the ground to form a mat of mid-green leaves. Flowers grow in small globular heads of lemon yellow in late spring and sometimes continue spasmodically into the summer. *Erysimum alpinum* 'Moonlight' has clear light yellow flowers. Both are intensely fragrant with a sweet cinnamon perfume.

linifolium 6–18in

From the Iberian Peninsular, a grey-leaved woody-based plant, sometimes a short-lived perennial in southern gardens and forming a good stout sub-shrub pricked all over with flower heads of deep lilac-mauve. It blooms continuously from spring to late summer, but if shorn in mid-summer provides good flowers for cutting throughout the autumn. Perfumed richly, like the wallflower and at best in the form 'E. A. Bowles' ('Bowles' Purple'). The foliage in both is grey, rough and linear, and in the form 'Variegata' roughly marked with cream; a less attractive plant except for collections.

pumilum 8in

A rigid plant, notable among erysimums for its strong green prolific foliage, closely tufted about the stem. Mushroom-shaped heads of deep acid-yellow flowers in June and early July are held very upright. Perfume is quite unmistakeably that of hawthorn without any of the mustiness or fishy overtones, and is richly fragrant. Flowering seems to continue to August and September especially where there is midday shade.

FILIPENDULA *ulmaria* (Syn. *Spiraea ulmaria*) (*Rosaceae*) 3ft

MEADOWSWEET

The frothy blossoms of the perennial meadowsweet will smudge the edges of a pool or boggy area from mid- to late summer. The aroma is rather heavy and sickly, or of almond, and the leaves are fragrant also. The leaflets are sharply toothed, with the leaves golden in the form *F. u.* 'Aurea', and striped and blotched in *F. u.* 'Variegata'. The rhizomatous rootstock revels in dampish soil and is the feature distiguishing it from the wild plant *F. vulgaris*, of thin dry limestones, with which it ought not to be confused.

HESPERIS *matronalis* (*Cruciferae*) 3–4ft

SWEET ROCKET, DAME'S VIOLET

A popular biennial cottage-garden plant that will seed itself and produce lilac purple, or white flowers, typicaly cruciform in May. A single upright stem is well clothed with rather hispid leaves, the flowerhead at the top. During the day time its violet fragrance needs to be sought, but in the evening it strengthens, enriched with clove overtones. Double-flowered forms of both the lilac and the white flowers are to be found.

HOSTA *plantaginea* (Syn. *H. subcordata*) (*Liliaceae*) 2–2½ft

A splendid perennial for moist humus-rich soil in either dappled shade or sunlight, hailing from China and Japan. The heart-shaped leaves, so strongly resembling those of a large plantain, bright green and firmly veined, are fairly upstanding. Flowers sweetly fragrant, pure white and flute-like on opening, tubular and cigar-shaped in bud in July and lasting to September intermittently, vary with the position. The variety *grandiflora* has larger blooms. This is a lovely plant for the white garden, and for foliage effect, especially if the caterpillars can be kept at bay!

HYSSOPUS (*Labiatae*) (E or Semi-E)

HYSSOP

These small low-growing sub-shrubs have aromatic leaves which when rubbed, give off a warm scent.

aristatus 6in

A tiny plant of prostrate habit, with small dark green leaves, and plenty of white flowers in summer.

officinalis 2ft

The hyssop of the herb garden, intolerant of damp sites and shade or windy corners, flourishes best in good summers. It lends itself to clipping, but the flowers are then sacrificed. The flowers are blue and there are also white- and pink-flowered forms; they all attract bees and butterflies. Both flowers and leaves retain their scent on drying and can be added to *pot pourri*.

INULA (*Compositae*)

ELECAMPANE

The perennial species described here are all clump-forming and tend to run about unless confined. Some are handsome plants useful in the sunny border where moisture-retentive material lies about the roots. They are tolerant of semi-shade and moist conditions, when they tend to grow taller. All of them are sweetly fragrant and wholesome; the roots especially are aromatic when dried.

conyza 8–12in

PLOUGHMAN'S SPIKENARD, CINNAMON ROOT

A native biennial plant, little cultivated, but worth including in the herb collection for the interest of its ancient cultivation. Slightly odoriferous, but not unpleasantly so, giving it one of its local names, Cinnamon Root. The stems are often metallic purple, the flowers shaggy-petalled, small, rather dingy yellow or dusty purple bobbles, the ray florets usually wanting; they bloom in July.

helenium 3–4ft

ELECAMPANE

Arresting, large and shaggy, bright-yellow daisies in June and July on tough stems, with a clump of soft pale-green large leaves, make a bold block of colour in the flower border. This is strictly a perennial border plant. The leaves are bitter to taste and aromatic when pressed, the roots rich in resins, oils and starches (inulin), all of which resemble banana in aroma when fresh and become sweeter on drying, generally likened to the scent of violets.

hookeri 2ft

A Himalayan perennial species suffused with a sweet violet-like aroma. The flowers are greener and a paler yellow than those of other species. Eminently valuable for late flowering in September and October, these large, slightly recurved daisies have the same spiky ray florets as other species, giving a shaggy appearance.

IRIS (*rhizomatous* – see also Bulbs, page 88)

arenaria 3in

Totally intolerant of lime, this little rock-garden gem is apt to flower itself to death, but is most attractive when grown in a pan in the alpine house. It is yellow with a golden orange beard and fragrant of violets.

florentina 2½ft

FLORENTINE IRIS, ORRIS, FLOWER DE LUCE

The bluish-white flowers, almost grey, lend a very delicate air to this European species, anciently cultivated as the source of orris root. The fragrance is centred in the roots which when fresh have an earthy smell, but on drying the scent of violets gradually develops. It is said to continue to intensify for two years after lifting and certainly remains even after pulverizing, hence its use as a perfume fixer (as orris) up to the 19th century. It grows easily in sun or partial shade and seems to enjoy both light soils and the moister corners just as well. Its ease of cultivation has earned it the name of Poor Man's Orchid.

germanica 3ft

Iris germanica itself has stiff fans of pale green sword-like leaves, rather glaucous, fading in a horribly untidy fashion. The flowers bloom in May and June and are large, deep blue or purplish blue, with a yellow beard. The falls are paler than the standards and the flowers are fragrant of orange blossom.

The bearded iris hybrids are a complex group of cultivars, derived from several bearded species, but *Iris germanica* has obviously contributed its scent. They are truly rainbow flowers, proud of habit and display such an extensive range of colour and colour combinations that selection is a matter of personal choice. Some latitude needs always to be allowed for their colour which can vary from garden to garden, season to season and soil to soil.

Tangerines, buffs, yellows, apricots, black, maroon, lavenders, blues and pinks are all represented, bi-colours and striped, feathered and stippled, with beards of yellow, tangerine and brown. Marvellous flamboyant flowers have been raised in America, Australia, and Holland as well as in England (with a valuable contribution from amateurs in this country) and almost all of them are richly scented, some even pouring their perfume for some yards around them.

This is not the place to eulogize on the colour of the bearded irises, but by hybridizing, first with the early flowering *Iris pumila* to provide a race of dwarf bearded iris, and then back with taller ones, a range of flowering plants has now been made available that spans not only the spectrum but the flowering weeks from April to July, and heights of 1–4ft.

All of them are pert elegant plants, sweetly and richly fragrant, fading to something less sweet and rather more fruity.

graminea 20–36in

A bearded iris, native of Central Europe and not of any particular garden value because of its tufts of grass-like foliage, amongst which flowers nestle. However, its reddish purple blooms in late May provide attractive cut flowers and are richly scented of ripe greengages.

pallida 18in

The flower stems are taller than the leaves in this Eastern Mediterranean plant, although most garden designers probably know the plant for its clump of glaucous leaves, broadly banded with cream in *I. p. dalmatica variegata*, which remain in good condition for a considerable period. The flowers are pale lavender and sweetly scented in June and July and are somewhat larger in *I. p. dalmatica*. Silvery spathes remain behind the flower adding a glisten to the bloom. They are fragrant of orange blossom and elder.

unguicularis (Syn. *I. stylosa*) 2ft

WINTER IRIS

An Algerian species which adores the parched soil at

the base of a wall, preferably when mortar rubble has been incorporated, and the plant can be starved. The flowers tend to hide away among the stiff sword-shaped leaves, and range in colour from pale lavender to quite a rich violet, and sometimes white. They begin to flower in November continuing throughout the winter. Always most prolific in flower following hot summers. A delectable gentle fragrance attends the blooms, but it is most noticeable when they are used as cut flowers.

MONARDA *didyma* (*Labiatae*) 2–3ft

BERGAMOT, BEE BALM, OSWEGO TEA

A quick-growing, clump-forming herbaceous perennial, robust and useful for full sunshine or semi-shade. Its main requirement is a generous amount of moisture-retaining material about its roots. It can be maintained also in damp grassy places. The whole plant is strongly impregnated with a delightful fragrance; even after the summer growth has died away, the roots remain aromatic. The nettle-like leaves are very strongly aromatic and pleasant and the flowers emit a compelling fragrance.

Monarda didyma itself has scarlet flowers strongly hooked in shape with prominent styles; the flowers are arranged like a carousel atop the stems. Cultivars with various-coloured flowers all bloom at the same time from June to September and all are fragrant. 'Cambridge Scarlet', crimson; 'Croftway Pink', soft pink; 'Mahogany', chestnut red and 'Snow White', white. The most popularly grown is 'Cambridge Scarlet'.

NEPETA (*Labiatae*)

Perhaps not as frequently cultivated as it was some thirty years ago, given a sunny position and well-drained loam the nepetas are effective over a long period. Even when past their best, they are still quite fragrant.

cataria 2½ft

CATNEP

An indigenous plant of the hedgerows in Britain and the whole of Europe, accurately described as a perennial, it most frequently behaves far more like a biennial, dying off after flowering. Strongly scented of mint and pennyroyal, and attractive to domestic cats, this was the plant that provided catnep tea before the introduction of China tea as a beverage. The little leaves are heart-shaped, grey-green and closely covered with soft hairs, adding a hoary appearance to the entire plant. The white flowers, which on close inspection are seen to bear reddish spots, are somewhat insignificant when in flower in May and June. There is a lemon-scented form, *N. cataria citriodora*; which is in the herb garden at the Royal Horticultural Society's garden at Wisley, Surrey.

Monarda didyma

faassenii (*Nepeta mussini* of gardens) 2ft

Its decorative hummocks of growth soften the border edge, pathway boundary or fall from the top of a dry wall to add considerably to garden decoration when it is in flower from late May until July. The leaves are a soft dark green, deeply toothed and veined, greyer beneath, and smell of mint sauce when crushed. The

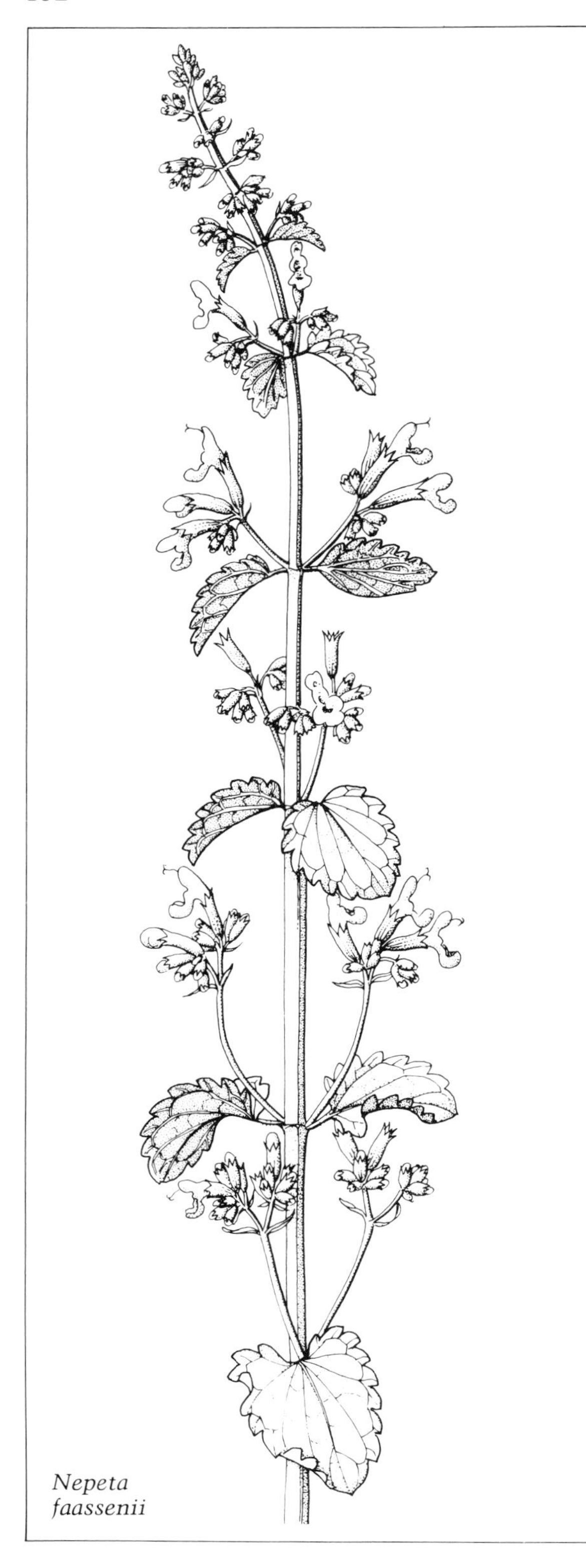
Nepeta faassenii

deep blue flowers are carried in soft spikes and are so numerous that the foliage effect is lost when in flower. They are fragrant also of mint, with rather sweeter overtones. They fade slowly, and retain their scent after cutting. Both flowers and foliage can be incorporated into *pot pourri* preferably just before the flowers reach full maturity, for this is the point at which the essential oils are particularly fulsome and sweet-smelling. (The species *mussini* is a poor plant and probably only seen in botanic gardens, but the plant so called is probably a garden hybrid. It does not set seed and originated in the garden of a Dutch grower named Faassen; so its correct name is *N. faassenii*.) There is a fine tall-growing garden hybrid, 'Six Hills Giant', which is a more erect form of *faassenii* with the same extended flowering period.

nervosa 1½ft

A bushy little plant with dark green leaves with a similar aroma to the other species, and clear blue flowers on a short spike from July through the late summer into September.

× *Souvenir d'André Chaudron* (Also catalogued as × *Blue Beauty*) 2ft

A handsome strong-growing hybrid, over which authorities disagree; it may be *N. grandiflora* or *N. superba* according to which catalogue is consulted! But both describe its more robust habit. Clear lavender-blue flowers, mauve in bud, resembling those of salvia, are in bloom from early June to September, Foliage is dark green, lanceolate and strongly aromatic when crushed of a fruity camphorous mint. It tends to run about like a mint.

NICOTIANA (*Solanaceae*)

TOBACCO PLANT

Most nicotianas are grown as half-hardy annuals, in well-drained humus-rich soil and given full sunshine. All seem to appreciate shelter from prevailing winds and are good plants to grow near a patio, perhaps even in tubs, for they are mostly evening scented, the flowers opening fully in the twilight. All bear flowers like five-pointed stars with long narrow throats behind.

alata 3ft

FLOWERING TOBACCO

The whole plant is hispid and gluey to the touch, but the white flowers fragrant at dusk are suffused with green and are in bloom in late summer and autumn. 'Dwarf White Bedder' holds its flowers open all day, although the fragrance is in some ways lacking. *Nicotiana alata* 'Grandiflora' (Syn. *N. affinis*) has larger flowers tinged with yellow on the outside and fragrant at dusk. Seedsmen now offer good cultivars, excellent for bedding or planting in the flower border where a colour preference is considered. They are good for containers and pot work, and because they remain open all day can also be used for flower arranging. They are all distinctly fragrant, the fragrance stronger in the evening. Recommended ones are 'Tinkerbell', 'Crimson Bedder', 'Lime Green', and 'Evening Fragrance'. The last-named is in fact fragrant throughout the day to a lesser degree, and the flowers come in a variety of colours, from purple through the pinks to lavender.

suaveolens 2ft

A pretty dwarf species from Australia with sweetly scented white flowers, and especially useful for pot work under glass.

Nicotiana alata

OENOTHERA (*Onagraceae*)

EVENING PRIMROSE

The evening primroses require a sandy well-drained soil and given full sunlight or a very lightly shaded spot will be perfectly happy. The rich fragrance of the biennial or monocarpic kinds is not as marked in the perennials, although for garden-worthiness the latter are preferred. The common name suggests that these flowers open only in the evening and this is so of most of the biennials, the flowers then fading to be replaced by a long succession of blooms from day to day. But the perennial sorts overcome this fleetingness of flower and one or two are fragrant also. Modern biennials are now available, the flowers of which remain open all day, and the seedsmen recommend that they be treated as half-hardy annuals – noteably *O. trichocalyx* with grey foliage and large white, very sweetly scented flowers.

One or two are naturalized in many areas; *O. biennis* in northern and western England and Scotland where it ornaments railway sidings, dunes and waste ground, and *O. odorata* in south-western England. But the cultivated forms are superior.

biennis 1½–3ft

A biennial plant with a fleshy edible rootstock, used in France as a spring salad, forming a rosette of leaves, later topped by a tall lax stem bearing deep bright-yellow flowers from high summer to autumn. The true plant opens its sweetly fragrant flowers between 6 and 7 pm to attract evening-flying moths.

caespitosa 1ft

TUFTED EVENING PRIMROSE

An almost prostrate perennial species, this therefore needs to be planted at the front of the border or where it may straggle a path. The blooms are almost stemless and white, deepening to rose-pink with age, fragrant with a rather fresh magnolia-like scent from May to August. It is best in the slightly taller form, *exima*, which can only be described as a more alert plant, and which is the one now usually grown.

odorata (which the botanists call *stricta*) up to 3ft

An upright perennial of branching habit with undulating leaves and sweetly scented primrose-yellow flowers in April and through to June, blooming at night. The flowers mature to red. A paler-flowered form is *sulphurea*. Both are short-lived, but seed themselves quite freely, and are intensely sweetly fragrant and worthy of inclusion for that reason alone.

PEROVSKIA *atriplicifolia* (*Labiatae*) 3–4ft

RUSSIAN SAGE

A shrubby perennial from Afghanistan that is usually planted in herbaceous borders, because of its immensely decorative quality; late flowering. It appreciates full sun and good drainage best, and will tolerate all but the heaviest of soils. Some protection is needed from wind in exposed areas.

The entire plant is downy, with silver-grey foliage and stems that are erect and woody at the base. Silver-blue flowers are carried in August and September. The plant is aromatic, when bruised, in all its parts, pungent and warmly aromatic like the sage. The cultivars 'Blue Spire' and 'Blue Haze' are both grown, the latter with the less decorative leaf shape. By cutting back almost to ground level in spring, the new soft white felted growth gives a good early summer effect, an added bonus for a scented late-flowering plant. *Perovskia abrotanoides* is also grown, and sometimes confused with the cultivars of *atriplicifolia*. From Russia, it is a slighter plant, but pungent in all its parts, and otherwise quite similar, flowering at the same time.

PHLOX (*Polemoniaceae*)

The scented species of phlox are clump-forming perennials and many garden varieties with gaily coloured flowers have been introduced. They like a fertile soil with moisture-retentive humus material incorporated, and partial shade. If the laterals are removed throughout the summer, the plants will flower over a longer period, and, as the opening and fresh flower has a distinctly fresh sweet scent that deteriorates as the blooms fade, it is best if a continuity of blooms can be maintained. The scent is strong and its sweetness is open to dispute, for it has a sickliness about it on fading, and is not to everyone's taste.

Phlox paniculata

maculata 2–3ft

WILD SWEET WILLIAM

A vigorous perennial with purplish, spotted stems, except in the white-flowered forms. Terminal heads of violet, purple flowers continue to bloom from July to September, all sweetly fragrant especially when fresh. *P. m.* 'Alpha', a good clear pink, and *P. m.* 'Omega', white flowers with a flush of violet, are recommended forms.

paniculata (*P. decussata*) 3–5ft

BORDER PHLOX

A clump-forming floriferous plant for the herbaceous border where it provides bold blocks of colour from July to September. Stiff stems carry upright panicles or domed flower heads in an extensive range of colour. Again, catalogues need to be consulted for a personal selection, as characteristic flowers are available to complement almost any colour scheme. They repay good cultivation and need a good fertile moisture-retentive soil. They are at their best perhaps on a greensand where rainfall is high and the drainage good.

PRIMULA (*Primulaceae*)

An extensive genus, comprising some most colourful and highly scented flowers. The oval, deeply veined leaves form a characteristic basal rosette, and the plants are clump-forming, enjoying a variety of positions usually in some shade. Most are hardy, a few, notably the scented *P. malacoides*, require greenhouse protection.

florindae (*Sikkimensis Section*) up to 3ft

GIANT COWSLIP

One of the largest plants in the genus, from South Eastern Tibet, a plant that delights in damp soils. The flowers in June and July are cowslip-scented, great yellow shining bells of sulphur yellow powdered with meal.

helodoxa (*Candelabra Section*) 2ft

GLORY OF THE MARSH

The bright rich butter-yellow flowers in June and July are sweetly fragrant and are held in tiers upon straight stems, above the basal rosette of leaves. It loves a rich moist soil and is tolerant of shade. At its best in boggy areas that get sunshine for part of the day at least.

nutans (*Soldanelloideae Section*) 1½ft

A difficult species to grow, and one which hovers under some doubt as to its identity. A neutral soil, well drained at the surface with a dressing of stones, on a north-facing slope has been recommended. The fragrance of the dangling lavender-blue bells in July is rich and sweet.

prionites (*Sikkimensis Section*) 1ft

A slighter *P. sikkimensis* in general appearance with the same saw-edged leaves and flowers of mahogany red, like dangling bells, grey inside. It is sweetly scented and flowers in May and June, flourishes in boggy, rich, moist soil and likes dappled shade.

× *pubescens* (*P. auricula* × *P. rubra*) (*Auricula Section*) 10–15in

A hybrid of garden origin, now, together with its forms, offering a large group of cultivars with characteristics of both parents in various combinations. Some are very sweetly scented and the flowers are usually in shades of crimson or purple with a white eye. The whole group likes a good limy loam sharply drained with surface chippings.

sikkimensis (*Sikkimensis Section*) 1ft

Large wrinkled saw-toothed leaves, bright green in colour, cluster round the base of the stout stem which carries good-sized funnel-shaped pendant flowers. They bloom in June and are sweetly scented like cowslips. They are a deep pale yellow and are frosted with meal within. It seeds itself and flourishes in damp soils. *Primula s. hopeana* has creamy white flowers and is a more slender plant, but carries the gentle fragrance.

sinoplantaginea (*Nivales Section*) 6–8in

A small plant with a flower of unusual purple with a grey eye. The pale flowers, almost yellow, form a rosette or ruff behind it and are farinose beneath. The flower is slightly fragrant, honey-like in May and June and needs to be protected from sunshine. Choose a position that is moisture-retentive in summer, but not water-logged in winter.

vialli (Syn. *P. littoniana*) (*Muscarioides Section*) 16–24in

Long bright-green hairy leaves form an upstanding shuttlecock as a base for tall stems topped with flower spikes, more resembling a polygonum than a primula. The flowers are tiny, strongly fragrant bells of blue-violet with scarlet calyces, held in dense poker-like spires in June and July. They are remarkably arresting before the flowers open, when scarlet calyces form the pointed heads.

veris (*Vernales Section*) 6–15in

COWSLIP

The pendulous bells of the cowslip, deep yellow, flaring slightly from a tight bell-shaped calyx, need little description. A red spot at the base of each petal distinguishes it from all other primulas. The fragrance is fresh and sweet and unlike other flower scents. More markedly than in any other primula, it fades once the flower has been pollinated. Neutral to chalk soil suits it best and it really thrives best in grass. Variable forms arise, as it hybridizes fairly freely, so flower colour and size vary from gold to blood red but always with some fragrance; it is often known by the vernacular name of oxlip (see also *P.* × *tommasinii*).

vulgaris (*Vernales Section*) 6in

PRIMROSE

The primrose has wrinkled long oval leaves, usually soft and downy beneath, with flower stems often short and tucked well down among the leaves – often growing as the bud opens. The flowers are pale yellow with a slightly darker eye and fragrant – said to be the true smell of the countryside in spring. Flowering starts in the shortest days of the winter in favourable areas, and continues until May. Rich loam is best, but not waterlogged conditions, and they like companionship, so flourish best among ferns and the early flowering bulbs, the sort of situation they select for themselves in the wild. Specialists' plants are the scented double primroses and there are old, rather rare, hose-in-hose forms, rarely encountered except in collections.

RESEDA (*Resedaceae*)

MIGNONETTE, LITTLE DARLING

A perennial treated as an annual, with spires of tiny flowers often heavily fragrant. Modern plants suffer from loss of much of the scent through cultivation, and they are not grown, as they were in Victorian times for room and window box decoration and delight. They are now grown in odd sunny corners, where the soil is light and firm, attractive to bees, and useful in scented flower arrangements or in *pot pourri*.

alba 1ft

UPRIGHT MIGNONETTE

Numerous thin spikes of small white flowers in June have a really sweet almond scent, the strongest of any of the species. Leaves are deeply divided, mid-green and mainly basal. This is a plant from Western Asia and Iran, and sometimes naturalized in southern areas of Britain, where it usually behaves as a biennial, and in gardens, perhaps as a very short-lived perennial. Worth tracking down for its fragrance.

odorata 1ft

SWEET MIGNONETTE

Grown as an annual, with short spires or club-like heads of uninspiring yellowish brown flowers, the petals in fact yellowish white and the brown colouring present in the numerous protruding reddish-brown stamens. The scent is heavily sweet of musk in late June and July. Seedsmen now offer 'large' sweet-scented flowered kinds, which are useful mainly for cultivation in pots in the garden room or as patio or porch decoration where the fragrance may be enjoyed.

SALVIA (*Laviatae*)

SAGE

Of this enormous genus of annuals, perennials and shrubby plants, both hardy and tender, many have aromatic foliage to a greater or lesser degree. Many are bitterly pungent. Few plants are more striking in the late summer decorative garden with their decorative persistent bracts and colourful clayces, but these are not necessarily the ones to grow for fragrance. Most of the shrubby ones, with the exception of *Salvia officinalis* and its forms, are doubtfully hardy except in very favoured localities and warm dry seasons, but are attractive cool greenhouse plants. Some of the pleasanter-smelling species are suggested here. The smell of the seeding spikes on most plants is quite different from that of the plant itself, usually more refreshing and sharply lemon-like.

lavandulifolia 1ft

A sub-shrub or woody perennial, that much appreciates being clipped hard back in spring. The leaves are narrow, deeply veined and dark grey-green in colour and soft of texture. Aromatic with a typical sage scent at first, but subsequently more highly scented and resembling lavender. The terminal flowers are violet-blue at the end of May and in June. It has a tendency to spread.

officinalis 1½–4ft

SAGE, GARDEN SAGE, KITCHEN SAGE.

Garden sage usually assumes a bush-like habit, but in its various forms it little more than a woody perennial. Usually relegated to the vegetable plot, it is a lax-growing plant with wrinkled pungent grey leaves. At home in calcareous soils, requiring good drainage, any patience exercised in establishing a sage bush for culinary use will be rewarded, because the pungency varies from one plant to another, as does the aroma. They can vary in any given border, and it is possible to find that the idiosyncrasies of one plant are better suited to the soil, than those of another – a strange fact, but true, and worth consideration in the search for a culinary leaf devoid of bitterness. The narrow-leaved forms are always more pungent than the broad-leaved ones, and broad-leaved, non-flowering ones, best of all. For decorative use (and the leaves no less useful in the kitchen), the Purple Sage, *S. o. purpurascens*, with soft plume-purple foliage especially in the young shoots, is a delight. There are two or three variegated kinds, where the foliage is splashed carmine and cream, called the Painted Sage, and a good form with golden markings dominating the leaf in *S. o.* 'Aurea'. The variegation differs in interest from one plant to the next and from one season to another.

rutilans (Syn. *S. elegans*) 2ft

PINEAPPLE SAGE

A half-hardy perennial of shrubby habit when established, but when seen cultivated out-of-doors, little more than the season's growth from rooted cuttings – except in favoured areas. As a cool greenhouse plant where it can be given sufficient light to encourage it through the winter, its basal growth thickens. The leaves are a deep purple green, soft, pointed oval and absolutely deliciously scented of pineapple when rubbed. Red flowers in tiny panicles appear in late summer, sometimes.

sclarea up to 4ft

MUSCATEL SAGE, CLARY SAGE

This is usually classed as a biennial because it gives all its strength to produce flowers, and seems defeated after-wards. It has wrinkled leaves, woolly when young, and a dramatic flower spike with variously coloured bracts. The form 'Turkestanica' with more woolly leaves is perhaps the finest from July to September. The entire plant is aromatic of grapes and is known commercially as the source of muscatel oil or clary oil, much employed as a perfume fixative.

verbenace 1–2ft

Little grown, it is of immense interest for its aromatic properties. The 'oculus christi' of the herbals, it has pale lavender-coloured flowers with large calyces, blooming from June to August. It has wrinkled, lightly lobed leaves, woolly in the spring basal rosette, and the mucilage produced from the seeds when put under the eyelid will clear foreign bodies from the eye.

SMILACINA (*Liliaceae*)

FALSA SPIKENARD

A North American herbaceous perennial with rather gnarled rootstock that requires good moist, rich soil, and some shade. Variable for planting in light woodland conditions or for the perimeter of shrub borders, once established they form good clumps.

racemosa 3ft

Useful for its early flowering, it adds height to the planting, with which it associates so well, of Lily-of-the-valley, primulas and anemones. White flowers in May are carried on terminal feather sprays above quite stately stems and smell slightly sweet. The leaves are linear and a larger version of those of the lily-of-the-valley.

stellata 1½ft
STAR FLOWERED LILY-OF-THE-VALLEY
Smaller in habit with stem-clasping linear leaves and a dense raceme of starry white flowers in May. The fragrance is quite substantial and more powerful than in *racemosa*. The English name, which is a complete misnomer, records the fact that when these plants were first introduced they were classified as *Convallaria*. The rootstocks tend to spread, but this is always an attribute in woodland plants.

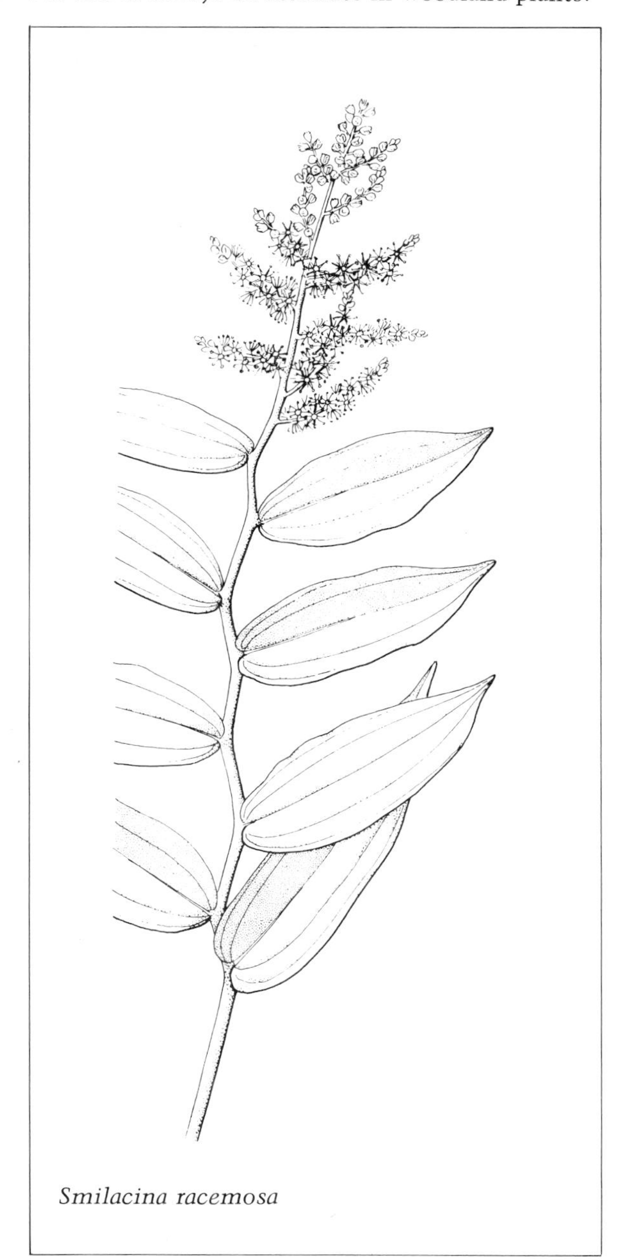
Smilacina racemosa

TANACETUM *vulgare* (*Compositae*) 2–3½ft
TANSY
Native to Britain and Europe in general, it is a tough plant of waste land and roadsides. It was cultivated more as a pot-herb in the past than it is today. Relentlessly invasive, it will stalk across the garden by its creeping stolons and needs to be restricted constantly.

The foliage is bright dark green, very deeply pinnate, indented and feathery, and strongly and sweetly aromatic. It is, in fact, dotted with glands which give it a somewhat tough oily texture, and in botanic gardens slightly varying forms can be seen, which afford an interesting comparison. I am increasingly convinced that some of the plants sold as tansy by nurseries are not *vulgare*, and may be *Achillea magna* or even one of the chrysanthemums. Where the form *T. vulgare* 'Crispin' is available it should be grown, for it is superior in scent, sweeter and less rough.

The close relationship between tansy, chrysanthemum and achillea, most of which have aromatic foliage to a lesser degree, leads to some confusion, and there are obviously several forms of some of each plant. Mace, for instance, is *Achillea decolorans*, with cream daisy flowers, but one sees it in a white-flowered form also. It is when comparing one herb garden with another, and then searching the natural order beds at a botanic garden, such as Oxford Botanic Garden or the Royal Botanic Garden at Kew, that the close resemblances of this group of plants becomes so apparent; because of the use of vernacular names for herbs more than for any other kind of plant in the past, everything has come to be grown as 'tansy'.

TROPAEOLUM majus (*Tropaeolaceae*)
NASTURTIUM
The nasturtiums of gardens have curious long-spurred, funnel-shaped flowers with flamboyant reflexed petals, sometimes heavily marked with darker or paler colours. Modern hybrids are in an extensive colour range from cream to deepest mahogany red. It is the double forms, of Golden Gleam Hybrids which are very pleasingly scented. Foliage is round and balanced like a spinning plate on the central stem and is, unfortunately, very attractive to blackfly. It is pungent with a peppery aroma and, like the peppery seed, it edible. The imperturbability of the plant renders it invaluable for town gardens, window boxes, poor soils and children's gardens. Both trailing and compact forms are offered by seedsmen, all sweetly scented when derived from the Gleam Hybrids.

VERBENA (*Verbenaceae*)
It comes as a surprise to find that only one or two species of this large genus are scented, and yet the

perfume 'verbena' is apparently commonly known. They prefer a rich well-drained soil in a sunny position, but are tolerant of some shade.

corymbosa 3ft

Hardy, in all but very exposed situations, a handsome leafy plant with dense terminal bunches of numerous blue-mauve flowers. The individual flowers are small and funnel-shaped and intensely fragrant, heavy and reminiscent of heliotrope when in bloom from July to September.

tridens (E) 20in–3¼ft

A rather gawky plant from southern Patagonia, whose small mature leaves appear to be dead and spiky, it does not come through winters very well in our climate. Not much of a recommendation! But, it is worthy of inclusion in collections for its intensely fragrant flowers, heavily scented of vanilla and spreading its perfume about it.

Bibliography

Beckett K. (Ed) *Greenfingers A–Z* (1978)

Bloom, Alan *Hardy Perennials* (1962)

Brownlow, Margaret *Herbs and the Fragrant Garden* (1957)

Day, Ian *Perfumery with Herbs* (1979)

Fletcher H. L. V. *The Fragrant Garden* (1965)

Genders, Roy *Scented Flora of the World* (1977)

Gorer, Richard *The Flower Garden in England* (1975)

Grieve, Mrs M *A Modern Herbal* (1931)

Hampton, F. A. *The Scent of Flowers and Leaves* (1925)

Hillier & Sons *Catalogue and Manual of Trees and Shrubs*

McDonald, Donald *Sweet Scented Flowers and Fragrant Leaves* (1895)

Mitchell, Alan *A Guide to the Trees of Britain and Europe* (1974)

Perry, Frances *Collins Guide to Border Plants* (1957)

Preston, F. G. *The Greenhouse* (1964 edition)

Royal Horticultural Society *Dictionary of Garden Plants* (1952)

Rohde, Eleanour Sinclair *The Scented Garden* (1931)

Salisbury E. S. *The Living Garden* (1936)

Sanecki K. N. *The Complete Book of Herbs* (1973)

Synge, Patrick *Collins Guide to Bulbs* (1961)

Thomas, Graham Stuart *Shrub Roses of Today* (1974 edition)
Old Shrub Roses (1978 edition)

Walker, Elizabeth *Pot Pourri* (1978)

Wilder, Louise Beebe *The Fragrant Garden* (1974 edition)

Index

Figures in brackets indicate an illustration, and those in **bold** are the main references